Daylight Must Come

Also by Alan Burgess
NO RISKS — NO ROMANCE
THE SMALL WOMAN
(*Filmed as 'The Inn of
the Sixth Happiness*')
SEVEN MEN AT DAYBREAK
THE LOVELY SERGEANT
THE WORD FOR LOVE

Daylight Must Come

The Story of Dr Helen Roseveare

by Alan Burgess

London
MICHAEL JOSEPH

N3— 213444
ROS   8\88

First published in Great Britain by MICHAEL JOSEPH LTD
52 Bedford Square, London, WC1B 3EF
1975

ISBN 0 7181 0999 6

Set and printed in Great Britain by
Tonbridge Printers Ltd, Peach Hall Works, Tonbridge, Kent
in Plantin eleven on twelve point on paper supplied by
P. F. Bingham Ltd, and bound by James Burn
at Esher, Surrey

Illustrations

Foreword

My most sincere thanks are due first of all to Dr Helen Roseveare for allowing me access to her letters, diaries, and other material and for putting me in touch with Norman Grubb in the U.S.A. whose invaluable loan of Helen's correspondence with him began as far back as 1953.

I am also deeply indebted to Helen for those splendid weeks in the Congo when she introduced me so patiently and explicitly to the locations and people pertinent to this story, and for the long days we spent together while she talked about her experiences, hopes, beliefs and philosophies.

I am also very grateful to Jack and Jessie Scholes, Frank and Mrs Cripps, Florence Stebbing, Daisy Kingdon, Agnes and Margery, Amy, both Elaines, Pat, Gladys, John, Brian, W.E.C. in general, and many others for their absorbing reminiscences recounted against the hot sunlight or starlit darkness of that most original and dramatic background: the tropical rain forest of Equatorial Congo; thanks also to Stuart Rising the young mercenary soldier for the graphic details of the quite incredibly heroic rescue foray of 54 Commando.

Finally my sincere thanks to Dr Carl Becker and his staff at Nyankunde, not forgetting Bud and Marie MacDougal whose hospitality and kindness during that period I shall always remember with gratitude and affection.

Place-names create a small problem: Congo is now Zaire; Léopoldville – Kinshasa; Stanleyville – Kisangani; and Paulis – Isiro; but I have used the old names, as they were at the time of this story.

AB

Part One

I

The truck door slammed. The driver, placid, docile, and as far as they knew, disinterested in their future, pumped the accelerator pedal to produce a series of staccato roars. The crowd of Congolese cheered derisively as grating into gear they laboured slowly away from the dilapidated store which acted as rebel headquarters in the tiny tropical rain forest village of Ibambi.

It was Saturday, mid-morning, November 28th, 1964. They might have been off for a day out, the annual picnic, a visit to market; a casual spectator could never have guessed from the noise, the excitement, the jeering laughter, the purpose of the journey. But Helen and all the others, trapped by this ferocious Congo uprising, were well aware where they were going.

With total conviction she was certain that they were on their way to execution, that death was inevitable and only a few hours away; the time in fact, it took them to drive to the settlement of Wamba some fifty miles to the east. And it was a death certain to be hideously cruel.

The fear which consumed her was numbing. So many others had been tortured and killed, and it was obvious that their end had merely been fortuitously delayed, and thereby made more terrifying. Indeed, she wondered why her captors were wasting so much time taking them to Wamba at all when they could have executed them immediately. But perhaps they thought that the sight of seven Christian missionaries on their way to slaughter would provide a thought-provoking and cautionary spectacle for the public generally. Certainly it would endorse the fact that the new Simba regime was implacable in its vengeance.

From her perch high up on the truck she looked down at her colleagues. Seven little missionaries in sun helmets, khaki shirts and shorts, or print dresses and open-work sandals, the suitcases neatly packed, the Bibles to hand, the noses sunburned, the years of endeavour, hymns, sermons and pious exhortations soon to be finally concluded on the blood-stained grass at Wamba. So silly. So absolutely ridiculous. A long Congo road to Calvary marked not by carrying a cross but by sitting on a bunch of bananas.

Yet despite her fear, Helen could still recognise with one uninhibited part of her mind how ludicrous their situation was. Who but the Congolese could cart off prisoners to execution in such a manner? Who else would think of piling them up on the back of an old truck and use the same vehicle to transport suitcases, boxes and bales, chickens, goats, bicycles, stalks of green plantains and a dozen Africans hitching a lift to various villages along the route? Even the French aristocrats jolting in their tumbrils towards that eighteenth-century guillotine must have retained a shred of dignity. For Helen and her friends there was no dignity at all.

Doctor Helen Roseveare, Cambridge graduate, thirty-nine years old, skinny from a disinterest in food and a total commitment to work, wore a loose crumpled print dress which maintained coolness, comfort and modesty, and avoided any known fashion trend by approximately ten decades. Her hair was trimmed short and the grey-green eyes behind the glasses were attractive and eager. As family and friends had readily confided over the years, of the four Roseveare daughters, she was not 'the pretty one'; she was the one with 'the brains'. Helen had never been very excited by having 'the brains', but she was quite reconciled to hearing about her own shortcomings, always prepared to own up to them, and even, occasionally, to admit to some she did not possess. Helen thrived on a lively sense of humility.

She was aware that she was diligent but headstrong, and that for the past eleven years she'd been driven by a sense of urgent purpose. It was a characteristic which in a country functioning by 'moons', 'seasons', 'births', 'deaths' and 'harvests', rather than hours or minutes, drove everybody to the edge of distraction. She couldn't help it. It was the way that God had made her. On a utilitarian level she thought of herself as a serious, dedicated employee in the service of God; she gave Him her entire love, belief and loyalty and was therefore His complete responsibility. Endorsing that philosophy she had accepted the present situation as inevitable, written her last letters, concealed her diary hoping that it would eventually reach her mother, and in her prayers tried to impress upon her Maker that her impending arrival was near. However, at the very back of her mind it is just possible that two mental fingers were firmly crossed in case a miracle did happen, for she did not – most certainly did not – think that this was much of a way to end her life.

Stuck up on a black-japonned steel trunk, its sharp edges sticking into her legs, she could see that the faces of all her friends – Amy and Elaine, Brian Cripps, dark-haired, cheerful and twenty one, Stebby, veteran nurse-midwife, and Jack and Jessie Scholes, who led the mission at Ibambi, both in their sixties and greying – were tight and drawn and she guessed her own must look the same, for fear prohibited conversation. And even though quite recently Amy had declared, 'Helen, you'll still be chattering when they lead you out in front of the firing squad', she dared not exchange even a whispered remark.

As the truck rumbled up the red clay road past the twin rows of ramshackle wooden houses which identified this village in the middle of Congo's tropical rain forest, her lips shaped the words, 'Goodbye, Ibambi.'

In this district she had worked for eleven years building her own hospital, delivering babies, labouring over the sick, grieving for the dying, and for the past four years – since the Belgians granted independence to the new Congo state and the country quickly emptied of most of its professional classes – for much of the time she had been the only doctor for hundreds of miles around. 'And a fat lot of good that is going to do me now!' she thought.

They crawled up through the avenue of trees, the fierce Congo sunlight probing the dark green of the branches. The bright blossoms of geraniums, bougainvillea and marigold bloomed wild and unattended in patches of garden, against wooden fences and wherever they could find roothold.

Colour, reflected Helen, was synonymous with Congo: deep blue sky, vivid green grass, red earth . . . reds as rich as the blood which had spilled so liberally in these last few weeks. Blues, greens, oranges, purples, heliotropes, colours as strident and harsh as the passions released in this bewildering Simba rebellion which had so recently swept across Congo.

On her first arrival eleven years before, in 1953, she had been inclined to compare these Congo landscapes with the pastel rain-washed scenery of the English countryside. Compared but not missed. Not regretted even, for she had deliberately abandoned her past. Congo was home. Those tides running in through the morning mists over the hard-packed sand of Cornish beaches, those scarlet buses moving with dinosaurian calm through London's traffic were the nostalgic memories of childhood and adolescence. This Congo village from which she was being taken for execution was 'home.'

Ironic perhaps that these black people with skins dark and smooth as purple grapes – who after a few weeks she hadn't even seen as 'black' – who had been her friends, neighbours, colleagues, and pupils, were soon to be her executioners. But on reflection she knew that this also was only a half truth. All decent people were stunned by this sudden Simba uprising. The People's Army of Liberation they called themselves, but so far all they had done was torture, slaughter, and destroy in a particularly bestial manner.

The lorry reached the top of the hill, the driver changing up into second as they passed the cotton factory. One of the three Simba guards, dangling his legs over the tailboard turned to brandish a hand-grenade in her direction. 'If the mercenaries come we'll kill them,' he shouted exultantly.

Half naked, wearing khaki shorts, his body decorated with sprigs of green and bits of animal fur, in a different situation he might have looked ridiculous, but harsh and bitter experience had proven that the Simbas were dangerous and vicious. From the very first moment a few weeks ago when the first group had driven up to the hospital at Nebobongo she had been conscious of their definite aura of evil, that they were barbaric and terrifying because of their intimidating power over life and death.

The Simba now mimed the action of wrenching out the grenade's firing pin with his teeth and tossing it into the cloud of red dust billowing behind them. 'That'll be the end of the mercenaries,' he yelled, imitating the noise of the explosion, 'Boom! Boom!'

Helen had never seen a mercenary. Indeed she was not quite sure what the word really meant. She had heard over the BBC that a force of white volunteers had been raised to help the National Congolese Army fight the Simbas; but such people were as far removed from her normal life as lunar astronauts.

More to the point, however, she was a little surprised that with the insatiable curiosity of all Congolese, the Simba hadn't already pulled the firing pin of his grenade just to see 'if it worked.'

At this particular moment it seemed to Helen that all was madness. Her world, and its day-to-day sequence of events, had slipped out of focus into nightmare unreality. Even motherly Jessie Scholes, wife of the mission leader, a champion of conservative prudence and common sense, was at that moment hatching a plot which to Helen reeked of peculiar lunacy.

Under the blanket draped across her knees was a large flag. A Union Jack! In the unlikely – indeed near miraculous – eventuality of one of these legendary columns of jeep-borne mercenaries closing in behind them, she intended to leap to her feet and wave it boldly to attract their attention thus proving that they were British and in desperate need of rescue.

Having experienced the pathological fury of the Simbas when opposed, Helen knew that if they discovered the flag they would react with predictable and lethal rage. In the first place they would not know whose flag it was; in the second they would believe it was either the flag of the U.S.A. or of some other equally hostile organisation; and in their anger they would almost certainly execute them all on the spot. At that moment all Belgians because of their recent colonial ownership, all Catholics because they were an official part of that regime, and all Americans who were said to be helping the Belgians, were the hated enemies.

Helen however, did not argue or even protest to Jessie. Civilised thought and rationality had flown into the jungle weeks ago. Indeed, she looked with a new interest and respect at the innocent Jessie clutching her Union Jack under the blanket with the same dedication as the Simba brandishing his hand-grenade.

The contiguity of death, it seemed, made conspirators of them all.

The truck swerved round a corner; the hot blue sky framed between dark segments of forest wheeled across Helen's vision; centrifugal forces heaved chickens, goats and people to one side, the animals bleating or clucking disconsolately, the Africans squealing with glee.

From any hill-top, she knew from long experience, they would look like a small black bug dragging a trail of scarlet foam in its wake along a light-brown pencil line. Similar pencil lines drawn wire-straight across a vast, dark green landscape represented dirt roads stretching for hundreds of miles and joining practically nothing.

Flying in eastwards for a thousand miles from Léopoldville a vast, empty green landscape was all you saw. You stared down on a surface so tightly forested that it resembled the texture of an endless cauliflower or the exposed membrane of some gigantic brain, stripped from its skull, stained green, mottled brown and veined with the shining streaks of black and turbulent rivers. It was a wilderness of tropical rain forest sometimes opening to reveal a huge swamp of bright, iridescent colour like a freshly-spilled pool from a lime green paint pot.

The first mutinies and troubles at the declaration of Congo's independence in 1960 had not disturbed the Protestant missionaries at Ibambi overmuch. Indeed, even when the Simba rebellion broke out late in 1964 they had been allowed to continue their work and were told, 'It is nothing to do with you. This is a People's Liberation Army dedicated to over-throwing the corrupt regime in Léopoldville. Carry on with your work, you will not be harmed.'

But a week before their arrest, on that Saturday of November 21st, 1964, all seven of them had gathered round the radio and with grave concern listened to the bland English voice reading with firm assurance and total unawareness the news item which spelt out a death sentence for hundreds of white civilians in north eastern Congo.

'It is reported,' the voice said, 'that a thousand Belgian parachutists have arrived at Ascension Island, flown in by American transport planes. They are waiting there for permission from the Congo Government in Léopoldville to drop on the town of Stanleyville and rescue the many hundreds of white civilians held hostage by the Simba rebels.'

Helen had stared disbelievingly at Jack Scholes. So fatuous a revelation was beyond comprehension. She could barely stutter out her protest. 'Don't they understand that the rebels listen to the radio too? Why tell them what's going to happen? Why tell them?'

Jack had looked round at the stunned faces of the others, aware of the importance of maintaining morale but unable to conceal his own anxiety. 'I don't understand it,' he said. 'I really don't understand it at all.'

'They must be mad,' continued Helen angrily. 'Why give away the plan? Do they have to tell the whole world they're mounting a rescue operation which is supposed to be a surprise? Don't they realise we're all front line hostages?'

The voice (and there were dozens of such radio voices beamed from all over Africa) continued:

'A rebel statement claims that all white civilians have been moved out of Stanleyville. Other reports from Nairobi, where talks about the safety of white civilians trapped in the north-eastern provinces are still continuing, claim that negotiators are horrified by this move on the part of Belgian and American authorities. They declare it sets Africa back, with a violent slap in the face, four years, to the worst moment in Congo's history.'

They sat dumbfounded in Jack Scholes's living room. There was little anyone wanted to say; or could say; or could think of to say. There was nothing they could do. Stanleyville was a two-day journey to the south-west over a terrible road. At Ibambi they were hundreds of miles behind the front lines, if there were any such things as lines at all in these countless thousands of square miles of rain forest. They were locked in Simba territory with the Belgians about to mount a well-advertised rescue attempt which would result inevitably in angry rebel retaliation against hundreds of white civilians.

On Tuesday the radio told them that Stanleyville was surrounded by the National Congolese Army. A little later they heard that the paratroopers had dropped, and that they had rescued a hundred hostages and were waiting to fly them out.

'The Belgian and American authorities have agreed,' droned on the endless radio voice 'with Tshombe's Central Government in Léopoldville that the paratroopers have only been used as a humanitarian gesture. They will withdraw as soon as all 'desiring to leave' have been removed.'

Later in the day came the real and horrifying news. As soon as the parachutists closed in scores of white men, women and children had been herded out of their Stanleyville hotel and massacred by vengeful machine-gun and rifle fire from the angry Simbas.

Within hours the announcers in tones of well-bred gloom were reading scripts which added to Helen's anger: 'Very little hope can now be held out for white missionaries or civilians in the north-eastern territories still in rebel hands.'

It was this new broadcast which angered her more than anything else. The radio networks had scandalously broken security about the Belgian and American parachute operation thus precipitating the massacres. Now they had the impertinence to anticipate the death of herself and her friends; opinions which could only serve to alarm her mother and family back in England, and everybody else's relatives all over the world.

The lorry coasted down a long slope, its engine spluttering, and they stopped in the shade of some trees. It had been obvious to Helen for some time now that if you only put two or three pints of petrol into an engine the size of theirs you would speedily run out of power. It did not seem obvious, however, to the three Simba guards, the dozen African villagers hitching a lift, or even to the driver himself.

Not that it mattered. Why should she fume over the length of a journey likely to be her last?

All she needed now was patience while they fiddled with the engine adding another few pints of petrol, and as they laboured away again she stared up at the blue sky and at the great ironwoods and mahoganies thrusting upwards towards a high tent top of leaves.

The engine was already spluttering again as they passed Mbandi. The sun in its afternoon loop across the sky was now very hot. The shade beneath the thick-leaved banana plants at the roadside gathered in small dark pools around the roots;

farther back, beyond the spiky, bright green grass which fringed the twisting red road, the temperature in the deep shade of the big trees was that of a medium oven.

Of the other women on the lorry Amy Grant was a secretary, Florence Stebbing and Elaine de Rusett qualified nurse midwives. Elaine, self-possessed and cheerful, with a dry laconic sense of humour, was Australian. Like Amy and Stebby she enjoyed working in Congo; it gave point and purpose to their Christianity and their commitment was total. The astute Aussie had also noticed the strange behaviour of the driver.

The youngest member of the Protestant group destined for execution was Brian Cripps. Both his mother and father were zealous mission workers at Ibambi and both were away in England on leave at this time. Frank Cripps senior was in charge of the printing works at Ibambi, and affably demonstrated to visitors the complexity of his machines, explaining how the typeset word of the New Testament printed in Swahili had helped the spread of Christianity to this remote part of Africa.

Helen understood how Brian, now facing an agonising death, must feel. He was the only young man in the party. 'Things' were expected of him. What legacy of 'good behaviour' would he leave behind? Or would he crack under the stress?

Hourly since the mass killings at Stanleyville four days earlier on Tuesday November 24th they had expected attack or at least arrest. For safety's sake a month previously on November 1st Jack Scholes had ordered Helen, Stebby and Elaine to leave the mission hospital at Nebobongo seven miles away and join them at the main mission centre at Ibambi. Reluctantly Helen had complied for even though in John Mangadima she had a worthy African deputy, she experienced a worrying premonition that she might never again see the hospital she had helped to create.

On the crucial Saturday morning of November 28th it was against their own instincts and common-sense that they allowed the senior African members of the mission to dictate the sequence of their actions. When the inevitable moment of Simba reprisal arrived, and news that lorries were rumbling out from Ibambi village two miles away reached them, the African evangelists insisted that all seven white missionaries must hide in Jack Scholes' study. Hidden behind locked doors, the shutters closed, the

Africans would deceive the Simbas with the news that the missionaries had fled and that the house was deserted.

Hindsight proved that the plan was far too naïve to stand even the remotest chance of success. Crouching in silent tension in Jack's office they heard the front door smashed open, the heavy footsteps approaching, the doorknob rattled, the panels banged with a violent fist, the protesting voices of the mission Africans vainly trying to head them off. Jack and Brian braced their shoulders against the door as the Simbas shouted threats. The woodwork bulged and it was Jack who realised that this stupid resistance was tantamount to suicide. He motioned Brian to stand back and unlocked the door. But it was Brian who stepped boldly forward into their path ready to take the first blow or bullet should it come.

Since that moment a few hours earlier Helen had only, with difficulty, prevented herself from saying, 'Don't do it, Brian. Don't be rash just to prove your manhood.'

But she knew if she did say this he would simply look at her with his dark serious eyes, a smile would appear and he would make some light-hearted remark to dismiss the matter.

The calmest member of the party perched on the back of the lorry was undoubtedly Jessie Scholes. Jessie and Helen had many things in common. The first and most obvious was a total and uncompromising belief in God. Jessie, with her blunt Lancastrian honesty – the echoes of the northern shires still hob-nailing through her speech – was constantly puzzled that people could not or did not seem able to, grasp the simple, essential, and eternal truth that if you *believed* – really believed – then nothing could ever really harm you again. You might grieve, yes. You might suffer pain, yes; be hungry, miserable, experience all the frailties and despairs inherent in the human condition, yes. But life led irrevocably to death. Life was, for the individual, a transitory moment in eternity, a quick journey you undertook protected and guided by God to a far more joyous and eternal kingdom, and believing this Jessie's philosophy was both comforting and formidable.

Jolting therefore towards execution, her hair already rimed with the red dust swirling about them, Jessie Scholes was undiminished and unafraid.

To Helen's continuing irritation the truck driver was making an ever increasing number of stops and all manner of idiotic detours. He halted at every roadside shack where drinks were sold, made interminable journeys up endless tracks to deserted or near-deserted cotton plantations ostensibly to look for whites, when everyone knew there was not a white within miles; he stalled his engine with incredible and complete incompetence, decided that mechanical repairs had to be performed every five miles or so and then stood in absorbed contemplation looking down under the open bonnet for what seemed like hours.

He was not a Simba at all, Helen knew that, merely a hanger-on. All right, he was probably afraid, as they were all afraid. He knew, as they all knew, that if you were not *with* them then you must be against them, and that assumption invited a quick and cruel death.

Indeed, the farther they moved away from Ibambi, the more threatening became the mobs which surrounded the truck at every roadblock. At the last one before the Nepoko River, the mob gathered round shaking their fists, yelling their demand to be given the prisoners to torture, kill and eat. Helen, they indicated, they would flay alive, and such was the state of her mind that she spent the next few minutes trying to work out how you could possibly skin a person from head to toe. It was here also that one of the Simba guards decided to have his fun with Jack Scholes.

He reached up and flipped off Jack's sun helmet. Jack said nothing, merely turning round to pick it up, and replace it. The guard knocked it off again. And as if this was the signal for violence one of the Africans in the crowd thrust a spear forward so that the point pricked Jack's throat.

Baiting him the guard mockingly held aloft the sun helmet. 'We don't have hats. Why do you have hats? It's because you think you're better than us, don't you?'

The guard tossed the topee back into Jack's lap. 'Now it's your turn to take off your hats to us.'

Helen found it hard to control her anger. That they should treat this brave and honourable man in such a manner was sickening. Jack Scholes had taught Africans to find love where once there was only evil and superstition. He had given direction and purpose to hundreds of people where none existed before. He had abandoned his own home and friends and lived on a few tins of bully beef and a handful of vegetables; he had laboured at Ibambi giving all he had to give, and now they piled him into the back of an old truck and stuck a spear at his throat and led him off to death like an animal. They should be ashamed ... ashamed!

But she did not shout or protest, for another compartment of her mind had acknowledged the bitter truth inherent in that triumphant cry, 'Now it's your turn to take your hats off to us!'

The whites had had the power and often misused it. The missionaries had had the power and tried not to misuse it. The missionaries had not schemed for power, they did not even want it; they had inherited it because of their white skins and superior skills.

Helen had tacitly accepted these facts because she had not known what to do about them. She lived as modestly as she could; gave away any money she had; tried to pull down all the barriers between herself and the Africans. But she had to have a car, drugs and instruments, even though she knew that to thousands of Africans they represented unattainable wealth. She had to teach, and teaching by its very nature presupposed a degree of superiority.

But in that moment Helen realised with startling clarity how deep those African resentments had cut. Now it was too late to do anything about them. A journey to the gallows is an unpropitious starting-point for atonement.

The threat to Jack's life ended as quickly as it began. With a rough joke the guard knocked the spear point away. The driver got back into his cab, and restarted the engine. 'Come to Wamba tomorrow,' the Simba promised as they moved off. 'You can see all of them executed, a free show for all!'

They drove on towards Obongoni, and when they reached the cross-roads Helen realised that once again the dreary driver had made a wrong turn, and that it would be dark by the time they crossed the ferry and got to Wamba.

It rained heavily before they reached the Nepoko River soaking them all, but as they crawled down the incline the black clouds rolled back and the sun balanced itself precisely on the crown of the road behind them. The beauty of the river crossing always fascinated Helen. Now, even in their situation, the sight of the deep, fast-flowing river, its polished black surface reflecting the lurid sunset and the sweep of trees on the opposite bank lightened her heart.

The Simbas yelled for the boatmen to bring across the pontoon. Everyone was ordered off the truck. Helen took a few steps along the bank to stretch her legs and without the pounding roar of the engine breathed in the peace and stillness. The short interval between day and night meant that suddenly it was cool; the deepening shadows brought tranquillity; voices were softer, the bark of a dog in the distant village, the ripple of water, even the laughter of the ferrymen coming towards them was muted and restrained.

The truck drove on to the pontoon and they were ordered back into their places again. When they reached the opposite bank, the sense of peace and serenity still persisted as darkness closed in and a thin mist seeped across the road. But at Didi Oil Refinery six miles from Wamba the crowd gathered at the road block was infinitely more menacing and evil than any of the others. Helen had a feeling that this crowd had already – and probably literally – tasted blood.

As soon as the mob realised there were European prisoners aboard they pressed in, mainly old men brutish and angry, threatening with clubs, spears and knives. There was no laughter this time, only waves of vicious hatred flowing up at them. They hammered on the side of the truck rocking it from side to side. 'Mateka!' they screamed, 'Mateka!' 'Dead flesh! Give them to us! We'll rape them, mutilate them, eat them!'

Helen sat paralysed. She knew that Amy and Elaine's lack of the Bangala language prevented them from understanding most of the obscene threats, but they could not miss the crude gestures of castration for the men and equivalent atrocities for the women.

For a few terrible moments it looked as if the guards had lost control, and there is little doubt that only the authority of the senior Simba guard prevented their journey ending fatally at Didi. Holding his rifle ready he shouted, 'You can't have them. We're responsible for them. They're Simba prisoners. Come to Wamba tomorrow, they'll be publicly executed. You can see it all then. We shall flay the woman alive. You can do what you like with the remains.'

[23]

The scene was unbelievably nightmarish; the sheer physical intensity of feeling shocked Helen more deeply than she had ever been shocked before. The dark, glaring faces and bloodshot eyes hated *her! Her* personally! Before this moment she had had no conception that such strength and ferocity of group-animosity existed. They hated *her!*

It was an assault upon her brain and spirit which sickened her soul. As the truck edged away from the angry crowd on its final lap to Wamba she sat shaken, trembling from the experience. She came from a world where verbal anger and aggression, the sharp retort, the argument, the slanging match, the hard-fought debate were natural corollaries – the keen edges, if you like – to reason and rationality.

But that mob, left in the darkness behind them, represented the personification of evil. Those people had returned to the jungle. They represented the primeval terror, the simian bestiality, the barbaric fear that walks in the night.

Jung had observed that man is the origin of all impending evil. Sheltered inside a mass hysteria, man absolves himself from all responsibility. This was a mass hysteria. Jung had added that the pattern of God as well as the devil also exists inside every-man. But it was difficult to accept that credo after the experience they had just endured. It needed time for Helen's mind to re-establish the belief that those people were God's creatures at all. Now she understood completely why so many of the hundreds of simple Africans had fled into the forest. What she did not know, was that it would be many years before some of them – having suffered dreadfully – would emerge again.

None of the Protestant missionaries really understood why their world had blown up like a landmine in their faces; why blackened and bewildered they stood in the debris trying to disbelieve the evidence of their own eyes. But terrible maggots of doubt fed on their imaginations and certainly upon Helen's.

Perhaps it was all a mirage: the love and gentleness, the belief of their converts, the continuity provided by the pastoral and spiritual peace in their isolated mission station with its printing shop, its small bungalows set in quiet acres of grass and shady trees. But now the doubt persisted. Was it any more real than those pastel-coloured illustrations in holy textbooks manufactured by Christians to comfort their own souls?

Perhaps the ugly distorted faces of the men who had threatened to flay her alive and eat her – and she knew such dreadful deaths had been inflicted on many during the last few weeks – were the real faces of Africa?

She sat high up on her black box, her arms clutched tightly across her body, in great despair. To die before one's time in a world which was sane and secure was hard enough. To die when her personal universe had disintegrated was bewildering, and to die in terror made a mockery of life itself. No matter what words tumbled out of her mouth she could not stifle her fear. Cerebrally she decided she could resign herself to the approach of death, but somewhere inside her vulnerable female body a pulse of terror as regular as her own heart plagued her, and although she appealed to God to excuse this ridiculous female manifestation there seemed nothing she could do to lessen it.

Wamba is an attractive town of wide, red-earth streets. The pretty bungalows hide behind low white railings and flowering hedges. Everywhere there are bushes and trees, green lawns, flower beds, trellises dripping purple or cyclamen-coloured bougainvillea. The shops sit under wooden colonnades. There is an air of rural colonial peace about the little town.

Like the British and French colonists the Belgians built it thousands of miles from home, long before jet aircraft made travel an absurdity, to remind them of their own far-away, summer countryside.

Now it was shuttered and dark and no one moved on the streets. They stopped outside a large bungalow set well back from the roadside and one of the guards went up the path to fetch the commandant. A few moments later, followed by a young lieutenant in khaki uniform, he strolled down towards them apparently disinterested.

The lieutenant took over. 'Your passports,' he demanded. They were handed across, Helen conscious that hers was out of date and contained no Congo visas. It didn't seem to matter.

'Your nationality is British?'

'Yes.'

'What is your occupation?'

'We are Protestant missionaries.'

The passports were snapped shut and handed back. The commander and the lieutenant talked together for a few moments.

They seemed bored or perhaps it was uncertainty. But Helen plainly and incontrovertibly heard that last order in French.

'Drive the women to the convent. Take the men to the priest's dormitory. They will be shot tomorrow.'

II

As they drove round to the huge Roman Catholic mission station, a series of handsome red-brick buildings scattered in a wide area of lawn, Helen did not dare to look at Jessie Scholes, or consider that Brian would meet his martyrdom after all.

The main building was dark and silent. At its front door the five women were ordered down. Jack and Brian helped them with their suitcases. They had only a few seconds to say goodbye. They clung together. There were tears in Helen's eyes. She wanted to say, 'God bless you!' but couldn't get the words out. It seemed unfair to her at that moment that no intimate language existed with which to confide her real and agonised feelings. That Jack and Brian would be killed in the morning was too dreadful a burden for her either to contemplate or accept. She thought that Jessie Scholes was behaving magnificently. Only much later did she discover that neither Mrs Scholes nor any of the others had heard or understood the commandant's final order given in rapid French.

One of the guards climbed the steps and pressed the bell. They heard its penetrating buzz deep within the building. There was a long delay, then the lock was turned and the door half opened. A face framed in the grey head-dress of a nun peered round. She seemed quite small in stature but she barred the way. She spoke in French.

'What do you want?'

As Helen's French was best she answered. 'We're the Protestant missionaries from Ibambi. They've brought us here.'

Immediately the door was opened wide and Helen saw that the Mother Superior wore the simple grey robe and head-dress of the Belgian teaching order of the Community of the Infant Jesus. She smiled at them. 'Please come in. You are very welcome.'

As they filed through carrying their blankets, boxes and suitcases Helen thought what a strange invasion it must have seemed: five women, sweaty, dirty, their hair tangled, their faces pale and strained.

There were several more guards inside who crowded around them. Other nuns – there seemed to be a great number – sat on benches facing an inner courtyard. With heads bent they appeared cowed and desperate. Few even glanced up to look at them, and Helen guessed it was fear rather than inhospitality which prescribed their behaviour. The heavy door was closed. They heard the truck with all its terrible memories grind away into the darkness. The sense of relief was so overwhelming that they were almost in tears and the Mother Superior, sensing their distress, was gentle and comforting.

'Now would you like to sleep with us in our large communal dormitory, or would you sooner have a smaller room to yourself?'

Helen translated, and Amy, Elaine, Stebby and Jessie Scholes looked at each other in bewilderment. Lately they had only been *given* orders. Now they had to make a decision and it seemed an enormous problem to solve. Eventually Mrs Scholes made the choice. 'We'd sooner stick together. A small room to ourselves, perhaps?'

The Mother Superior smiled understandingly. 'Of course, now if you'll come with me.' But before they could move off a guard intervened. He was pugnacious and offensive, and over his shoulder he carried that prime symbol of authority these days: a rifle. He indicated their baggage.

'This will have to be searched.'

They froze. Their eyes flicked from each other to the luggage, the sudden quick memory of what the blanket draped over Mrs Scholes's suitcase concealed, terrifying them all. To the guards that strange, unknown flag would mean only one thing: they were enemies. And enemies must be executed.

Helen began to argue. 'But we've been examined already. Four times we've been examined.'

The guard glared at her angrily. 'The luggage must be searched.'

'But it's been searched already.' She was too tired, too exhausted, too frightened to sound convincing. The Mother Superior, seeing their hesitation and sensing danger, stepped in to rescue them.

'You can search it tomorrow then,' she said placatingly. 'They will still be here.'

Her reasonableness and quick action brushed past his indecision. 'Now if you come this way.' She atarted off along the veranda and picking up their luggage they trailed after her, the guard following, surly and suspicious, but not experienced enough to intervene.

Half way along, the Mother Superior stopped at a door. She opened it and walked through into a small room turning rapidly on her heel to speak quickly in an undertone to Helen before the guard had time to get closer.

'Be careful. Don't undress at night. You'll be watched. Be careful.'

Immediately Helen felt the fear flood back. Terror was reinstated. The immediate danger confirmed. The convent was not a refuge. It was a prison.

She turned to see the others crowding in after her. They realised that the Mother Superior had said something important and instinctively they knew it was a warning and there was fear again in all their eyes.

It was Jessie who now lifted their spirits a little by pointing out that the strange and apparently inexplicable behaviour of the truck driver had probably saved their lives.

He was not a Christian in their terms. A casual appraisal would reveal him as an ordinary mortal with the usual male appetite for women and strong drink, his character undoubtedly fashioned by an inclination to sleep in the sun rather than do a heavy day's work.

Nevertheless, it seemed that while wishing to pursue his own uncomplicated life he concealed a determination to play no part in ending theirs; there was evidence in fact that he admired them. He had witnessed the blood lust in Wamba; he knew that it had reached a crescendo of mob hysteria with executions and tortures treated as daily spectacles. He knew that if he brought them to Wamba, in daylight, before the hour of the strictly enforced curfew they would inevitably be killed, snatched down from the lorry – as had almost happened at Didi – and no Simba authority would have been able to protect them; it would probably connive at having them torn apart in this fashion.

So . . . the long diversions, the Buddha-like contemplation of his engine, the slow conversations, the sips of petrol he added to the tank, all were the stratagems he adopted at considerable risk to himself.

For his part in their survival no one would ever give the little driver a medal. It was certain that neither Helen nor any of her friends would ever feel like buying him a drink. But reflecting on this news afterwards she wished she could have thanked him. And shaken his hand. And murmured her apologies for her impatience.

The Mother Superior was in her early fifties, small, and straight-backed, and she moved with an air of quiet assurance and dignity. Framed by the grey surround of her head-dress her face was clear and unblemished, her mouth firm, the eyes candid and often amused in even the most desperate situations. But they were eyes which gave orders, accepted responsibility and expected obedience. Like the other sisters in her order she had left her friends and relatives in Belgium many years before and dedicated her life to Congo. For those Catholic sisters there had been no 'home-leave', no eventual retirement to a small town on the South Coast; they had worked until they died and then had been buried under the warm tropical soil.

Now, by a bitter turn of political history, these good, saintly, and essentially simple women had been declared enemies of the People's Liberation Army. They were repaid by rape, torture, imprisonment, and often by a death so hideous that the sight of a nun stripped naked, hanging upside down between stakes and cleaved down the middle like an animal carcass, sent many tough, cynical professional mercenaries into a wild orgy of reprisal killing.

In the past few weeks the Mother Superior had been forced to watch many bestial executions. They were intended to humiliate and shock her. They did both. But they did not intimidate her. The Simbas might kill her. That was probable. They might rape her. But at her age – with so many of her younger charges already violated and still available, and with nightly excursions to the African novices' quarters next door – this was unlikely.

But whatever pain or humiliation they inflicted upon her she would not be silenced nor intimidated. She would speak up; she would seek to protect those in her charge.

Oh, yes, she'd been attacked. On that first occasion the angry Simbas, furious at being baulked for even a few seconds while the door was being unlocked, charged in and might have killed her. But Sister Marie Frances, a giant peasant woman whose height, breadth and strength came from Flemish farming stock and whose work for God was done in the kitchen and the laundry, had anticipated violence and been close at hand. Her Breugel face contorted with determination, she had bashed her way into the brawling mob of soldiers, grabbed her Mother Superior like a doll, gathered her to her breast and pushed through to the wall. Jamming the Mother Superior beneath her, she had arched her own body into a protective shield until the vicious blows with rifle butts and rubber truncheons smashed her down into a kneeling position. Almost unconscious but unyielding she had protected her Mother Superior until the violence and fury ended.

Helen had heard of the incident even before Mother Superior inquired gently if she would mind examining Sister Marie Frances. Helen had dressed the bruised, lacerated back, legs and body, injuries sufficient to kill some women and certainly put most in bed for a month. But not Sister Marie Frances. Her broad beam of victory and bland assurance of perfect health told Helen of a most extraordinary and courageous woman.

This first attack did not for one moment dissuade the Mother Superior from fulfilling what on the face of things seemed a humble and common-place task but which was, in reality, a most hazardous operation: opening the front door when the bell rang.

The sound of the electric bell was usually followed by a fist hammering on the panels. And everyone's reactions to the sound were instinctive: it curled a spring of terror in their stomachs, dried their throats, made them pause in mid-stride or mid-sentence, their eyes and minds seeking for a place to run, to hide.

Every woman in the convent and there were seventy of them, realised that her life hung on a spider strand. Practically all of them had witnessed or endured the most terrible experiences, and knew that the sound of that doorbell might presage the end of dignity or of life itself, a brutal beating up, selection for rape, a firing squad!

When the bell rang it was always the Mother Superior who answered it. No one else. If she was away in a distant part of the convent she would be fetched. That act was symbolic of how much morale in the convent depended upon her. It was the Mother Superior who in the matter of the hidden flag, on that very first night, came to their rescue.

After a subdued supper in the refectory Helen took her aside and told what Jessie Scholes was hiding.

When she suggested they might burn it the Mother Superior led her to the kitchen and indicated the guard. 'You see. Far too risky. If he caught you destroying such a thing . . .' she shook her head at the enormity of the offence. 'Couldn't you cut it up?'

Helen remembered she had a pair of nail scissors. So did Jessie. 'I suppose we could unpick one of our pillows and stuff the bits inside,' she said thoughtfully.

They settled on this method even though it turned out to be a laborious decision.

All of them took it in turns, a sentry posted at the door to warn of the approach of a guard, to snip the Union Jack into confetti fragments and stuff them amongst the down in an unpicked pillow case. It was wasted effort; next morning the guard forgot his threat to search the luggage. It was a typical example of instant authoritative rebel reaction, like the commandant's threat that Jack and Brian were to be shot. Undoubtedly he went back to his bed and forgot all about it. Certainly the Mother Superior who was in touch with the priests and male civilians held prisoners in another part of the compound, assured Helen that they were both quite safe and as yet, in no danger of execution.

It was the Mother Superior who sought Helen out during those first few days and took her to the quiet seclusion of the chapel.

'I need your help,' she said.

'Of course,' replied Helen.

'Mrs Scholes tells me that you are a doctor.'

'Yes.'

'You have heard that many of the sisters have suffered terribly last week?'

'Yes.' The rumours were everywhere. No one really wanted to go into detail.

'It was quite dreadful. It all began when the Belgian parachutists attacked Stanleyville.'

Helen nodded. The true and tragic dimensions of that well-publicized and ill-fated expedition would probably take months to reveal.

'The commandant in Wamba is a decent man,' continued the Mother Superior, 'But the Simba colonel in charge of the troops here is a fiend. When the news reached him he ordered his men to drive out to all the convents within fifty miles of Wamba, arrest the sisters and bring them into the hotel in Wamba.'

Helen looked at her solemnly as she told her story in a flat impassive voice.

'Two of the younger girls, Sister Dominique, an Italian, and Sister Clothilde, who is Belgian, suffered dreadfully. The young Italian, Sister Dominique, even after many men, was taken to the colonel to be used for his purposes.'

Outside Congo the word rape could still be treated as a comic starting point initiating a whole folk lore of jokes. In Congo no one was amused. The warm upholstery of civilised laughter had been frayed to tatty ribbons against abrasive reality.

It had become a shock word, incendiary and intimidating, violent in implication as the explosion of a mortar shell and in practically every white society in Equatorial Africa it triggered off immediate panic stricken reactions: 'petrol in the car?', 'best escape route?', 'plane schedules?'

Helen heard the Mother Superior pause and sigh – a long, lonely exhalation of breath.

'She is young. Very pretty. This colonel wants her as his property – as his wife so he says.' Her eyes came up to meet Helen's.

'Will you speak to her?' Helen was surprised.

'Speak to her?'

'You are a doctor.'

'You mean she has been injured physically?' The Mother Superior paused. 'No.'

'But what can I say to her?' Helen asked in bewilderment.

Indeed, she was a doctor, but at such a moment it seemed to Helen that consolation of the soul was the first treatment needed by Sister Dominique.

The Mother Superior guessed what was in Helen's mind. She said sadly, 'I have tried to reach out to her spiritually. I cannot get through to the poor child.'

'But I'm not of the same faith.'

'Does that matter?'

Helen drew in her breath. Her experience of consoling girls after rape was non-existent. This girl was a Catholic nun from a vastly different background and philosophy; her faith and all that surrounded it were so different.

The Mother Superior said quietly, 'If I had not failed myself I would not turn to you.' She hesitated and then she made the appeal which left Helen no alternative. 'I think she is on the edge of madness. I fear she turns towards insanity because she cannot attain death.'

Helen also realised that her reluctance must appear discourteous. 'Of course I'll talk to her, Mother Superior. It's just that I don't think I'll know what to say . . .'

'You are a doctor, you are also a missionary . . .'

Helen considered the practical aspects. 'Won't it be difficult . . . the guards? If we're seen talking? Where can I meet her?' No matter where you were, you had to be careful. Very occasionally the guards were cheerful, even helpful, but usually they were brutal and domineering, and to be seen chattering or whispering brought instant retaliation: a brutal blow from a rifle butt and the possibility of serious injury.

'I shall arrange for you to meet her in the laundry. You could both be working there. We can post a lookout.'

'It will take some time. We'll have to know each other. I'll need her confidence.'

'We will arrange several meetings.' The Mother Superior hesitated. 'Besides . . .'

'Yes? '

'This colonel is a very wicked man. And this girl is quite beautiful . . .'

'You mean he'll come for her again?'

The Mother Superior nodded, and Helen sensed that she carried many burdens.

'There is so much tragedy and we must do what we can to help,' she said and then added, 'I will instruct Sister Dominique to come and see you at once.'

The laundry was large and, with no one washing there at that moment, cool. Helen looked round at the concrete tubs which in their time had frayed a thousand pairs of hands and scoured ten times as many surplices. She ran her finger along the top of one of them and sighed. She did not relish this impending talk with Sister Dominique. Her own emotions were confused and tumultuous; how therefore could she make sense or console anyone else? She looked up at the sunlight slanting down through the high windows and sighed again. Only one thing seemed to be on her side: she knew that it was often comparatively simple to point out a path for others even when you found the path difficult for yourself.

There was a movement at the door and Helen turned to see the young woman standing there.

'Sister Dominique?' she asked gently.

The girl nodded, came closer and now Helen could understand the Mother Superior's concern. Sister Dominique wore the long white robe – small red buttons dotted down the front – and a simple white head-dress of her Italian order. She was tall, her face oval, her features classical, and her beauty was self-evident. Helen did not really know how to begin the conversation and from the first it was obvious she was not going to get much help from Sister Dominique.

'The Mother Superior asked me to talk to you,' she said lamely.

The girl nodded again. She looked straight ahead twisting and untwisting the tiny handkerchief clenched in her fingers, and Helen wondered how she was ever going to get the girl to unbend. Yet she should have known that to pour out your grief, to confess your sin, to talk to someone of your deepest need is a therapeutic remedy as old as the human condition, understood by priest, physician and psychiatrist alike. And very often a stranger is the best recipient of such confidences.

She decided she must be blunt. 'You must tell me what happened,' she said plainly. 'We are all in this together and I am a doctor.' She saw the girl's eyes fill with tears

[35]

and Helen at once relenting put her arm round her shoulders.

'It's all right,' she murmured consolingly. 'Tell me something about yourself. You're Italian and I'm English. You believe in God as I do. How did you enter the Church?'

Slowly, hesitantly, Sister Dominique began to tell her story. She came from the north of Italy, from a poor but prolific family; the custom of one son for the Church and one daughter for the convent set a precedent which went back through many generations. She had embraced the faith gladly. She had found joy in Africa; she taught and played with the children. In many ways Helen realised later she was no more than a child herself. She was 'a bride of Christ'. She had forsaken the sensual earthly pleasures, abandoned the purpose for which nature had created her, the procreation of children, and given herself entirely to God. And now, in her mind she had betrayed that trust. She had been forcibly grabbed, her robes torn away, paraded naked, ridiculed, her flesh molested. All she had lived for had been destroyed – and here there was no doubt that the Mother Superior was right – her senses were taking refuge from hideous reality by fumbling towards the absolute release of insanity.

She said in a despairing voice: 'There is no point in me living any more. I have no purity left.'

Helen could not listen to such nonsense. 'That is simply not true,' she replied.

Sister Dominique was insistent. 'It is true. You know it is true. I have betrayed my trust. I have no purity!'

Helen said forcefully: 'If you belong to Christ, if you know of Christ living in you, no one can touch your *inner* purity. Don't you understand that?'

The girl was crying now, still whispering 'I have no purity – no purity.'

'No living man can touch or destroy or harm that real purity *inside* you. Believe me.'

Helen sighed and thought how ironical it was that in a Western society where virginity was often no more than a sad joke, where the whole world in the safety of their warm sitting rooms watched the television beatings, shootings and murders, with no power to halt them and little will to intervene, she should be sitting here trying to explain to a broken-hearted girl that her plight was not all that desperate, and that her salvation rested simply in the hands of the God in whom she believed.

'You have not lost your purity,' repeated Helen severely. 'If anything you have *gained* purity in the eyes of God.'

To Sister Dominique this was so outrageous a statement that she had to stop crying to consider it. 'I do not understand.'

'Do you understand then, that the world in which the Virgin Mary lived must have been quite certain she had lost *her* purity?'

The dark tear-filled eyes turning towards her were suddenly hostile.

'That is not true.'

'Of course it is true. They would jeer at her and call her adulteress.'

The eyes were still disbelieving.

'Joseph was not the father of Jesus Christ. Your religion tells you it was a virgin birth. Joseph knew that. But his neighbours would never believe such an absurd story. They would sneer behind her back, rumour that she was an adulteress. Yet you know that God said she was blessed amongst women...'

The eyes were now puzzled and Helen went on:

'Jesus Christ suffered for us. Now you have suffered for others.'

Again there was confusion in the girl's eyes as Helen reiterated the point. 'You suffered. Many of you suffered. But the Mother Superior tells me that you and a Belgian sister suffered most because you were the youngest and most desirable. So you saved others from the same shame. God will not judge you harshly because you saved others from the same fate, will He?'

Helen knew by the touch of the girl's shoulder against her own that she had made some progress. She was not convinced, but she was ready to consider the thought.

'It was Tuesday, in the night,' she said. 'They came for us in a lorry. They were like savages. They shoved us aboard as if we were cattle. Then they drove us to a hotel in the centre of Wamba. They were all drunk. They jeered at us and struck us. Then they began to tear off our robes. They threw our crucifixes down into the dirt and trampled on them. We were naked. They drove us out into the street so everybody could jeer at us ... spit at us ... '

'Go on,' said Helen quietly.

'Seven of us, the younger ones, in front of everybody...' This was really too much for her to recount.

'Go on,'

'They forced us. Afterwards, after many times by the soldiers, they took me to this colonel. He is little and black and wicked. He too...'

There was now no stopping the outpouring of grief and outrage. 'He is such a wicked man. He has murdered the bishop and now he lives in his house. They took all the priests and laid them down naked in a path and then they danced over their bodies screaming with joy.' Her hands were at her mouth, the memory vivid and destructive. 'They killed them all; they slaughtered them, they made us watch.'

'I know,' said Helen gently. 'I know.'

The remembered agony of the hideous cruelties inflicted on the priests who had believed as she did in the goodness of God and the certainty of salvation was almost more than Sister Dominique could bear. She covered her eyes with her hands.

'Now do you understand why I say there is no point in living any more, that I have no purity left?'

'I understand what you say but I know you're wrong,' Helen replied.

'But you don't understand. You can't understand. Unless it has happened to you how can you – ?'

'But it has,' intervened Helen gently. 'It has happened to me.'

The girl's head lifted slowly. The large eyes widened with disbelief, and then clouded with pity. Strange really, Helen thought. No longer was she a funny English doctor-lady in spectacles, offering motherly advice of no practical value. Now she understood. Now she was a comrade.

'You,' whispered Sister Dominique. 'You also?'

III

Helen regarded the young nun with solemn eyes. If confession was good for the soul of Sister Dominique perhaps it might also benefit Helen.

'Yes,' she replied. 'To me also. More than a month ago now, when the Simbas really began to cause trouble. '

That terrible night of Thursday October 29th had started in her house in the hospital compound at Nebobongo. And Helen could never have anticipated that by the end of it she would be left hurt and bewildered, her clothing torn, her face smashed, forced by brutal experience into an arena where both her philosophy and her faith were in jeopardy.

'I heard the banging and shouting at the front door somewhere between 1 and 2.30 a.m.' she said, and paused to remember.

The noise woke her from a sleep which those nights was never far from the edge of wakefulness. She sat up fumbling for her dressing gown, mentally noting where her slippers lay. The dryness was in her throat again, the queasy sickness stirring in her stomach.

The hurricane lamp by her bedside filled the room with a soft glow; you kept your light burning all night in times like these. The noise at the front door grew more violent. She could hear the screeching drunken orders. 'Open up for the Armée Populaire. Open up or we smash down the door.'

'It's just a house inspection,' she told herself in the calm voice she affected to rationalise her fears. 'Just a house inspection, just a normal house inspection. Now don't panic. It's happened before. It will happen again.'

But the other inner voice, the one she didn't want to hear, was insisting querulously. 'A house inspection at this time of night? A house inspection after midnight? Don't be absurd.'

'All right,' she shouted. 'I'm coming.'

Elaine de Rusett and Florence Stebbing slept in a cottage too far away to hear the disturbance, as did John Mangadima, but in the living room Hugh and Francis, the two young male student nurses, appointed as official bodyguards, were watching the bulging door apprehensively. They had strict orders not to open any door until Helen arrived.

Helen turned the key and they roared in; six of them, drunk, coarse, and angry at being kept waiting. They were army. She knew that at once. Not 'jeunesse,' or the young hangers-on, the ones who shouted and waved sticks and spears and got in on the act; this lot were hard-core army and as such dangerous and ruthless.

Only one wore what you could call a complete uniform. He was a youngish lieutenant, well-built and truculent, his authority enforced by a gun-belt, cartridges and a revolver in a thick black holster which hung at his hip. He turned on her.

'Where's your husband? Where's he hiding?'

The attack put Helen immediately on the defensive. 'I haven't got a husband.'

'Don't lie to us. Fetch him. Where is he?'

Helen shook her head. 'I haven't got a husband. I'm a missionary. This is a hospital and school.'

They all cursed at once, they seemed incensed at this lack of a husband.

'He's somewhere here. We'll search the house and find him.'

Their filthy language, the jostling and near physical attack upon her numbed Helen. She didn't know what to say. She was frightened and confused. Search the house? All right, search the house. If this was a house search or a house inspection, what was the difference? She had no husband; she had nothing to hide. Let them get on with it. They'd survived house searches before. So the soldiers stamped and blundered around, and it was now clear that the search was going to be cruder and more violent than anything that had taken place before.

'What's in here? What are you hiding? Where are the keys?'

They knocked things over, they smashed glasses; abusively they broke up her home.

As before they were just looking for tape recorders, record players, radio sets, typewriters all to be 'liberated' in the sacrosanct name of the revolution.

In the first room they made her unlock the huge cupboard where she kept many of the glass utensils used for school and hospital teaching, and they jeered like malignant hooligans as they smashed them on the floor and against the walls.

She began to protest but stopped, realising it was useless. They stole the money set out on the table for buying plantains; they stole her watch, uniforms and berets for the students, and the primary school children; they stole the gramophone and records, anything they fancied they filched, piling them up in a heap in the living room.

It took them what for Helen was a long, tiring destructive hour. Then they ordered the two students Francis and Hugh to carry the loot out to the lorry.

'Now,' thought Helen in relief 'at last they're going. Thank God they're going. It's all over. We're safe. We can go back to bed. We can sleep.'

The two soldiers and the two students were carrying stuff down the path when she heard the lieutenant call her from the narrow corridor which led to the bathroom and her bedroom.

No real fear came to her, simply a feeling of irritation, of 'Oh Lord, what's he found that he wants now?' She went to see what was up. The inspection was over. There was nothing else really left for them to steal. 'Why didn't the beastly man join his friends on the lorry and go away?'

It was dark in the corridor but she still carried the hurricane lamp. He was standing in the darkness. He indicated the bedroom. His voice was harsh.

'Go in there and get undressed,' he said.

Whether this fear, this threat, had lurked at the back of her mind and the edge of her thoughts from the moment the banging on the door woke her up, she would never – even in the future – be able to resolve.

But her reaction was immediate and spontaneous.

'No!' she cried, turned on her heel and ran. She scuttled along the corridor, through the living room and out on to the veranda almost bumping into Hugh who was just coming back to the house for a second load of booty.

'Go, Hugh, go!' she shouted, realising at that second how idiotic she was to be flying through the night in bare feet, thin dressing gown and flimsy nightgown, still carrying a hurricane lantern to mark her flight. She threw the lamp at him and raced round the back of the house like an animal seeking the shelter of darkness. A terrible fear had suddenly engulfed her; and hearing the shouts of rage and pursuit starting behind her, there was a sort of wild madness about her confusion.

Suddenly the blackness was impenetrable. Branches slapped across her face. It had poured with rain only an hour or two before and her feet skidded in the mud. She had never run away from anything or anybody in her life before; she didn't know how to run away; she had no experience of escape, and already nagging at the back of her mind was the dreadful thought that now *she* had precipitated violence. Now, if they didn't catch her, they would take it out on the Africans. All this flashed through her brain and her reason kept protesting weakly: 'Why hadn't they gone? They'd stolen all there was to steal. They'd got all they wanted. Why hadn't they gone? They should have gone. It was all so unfair.'

She could hear them yelling and screeching all round her. Obviously they thought her plan was to race past the hospital some seventy yards away and hide in the bush beyond. To forestall this they had spread out in a half circle at an even greater radius and were now moving back towards the house to flush her out.

She didn't consciously choose a place to hide; instinctively rather she threw herself down under a small hedge which in daylight would hardly have concealed a cat let alone a human being.

She could see their torches cutting bright swathes through the darkness as they crashed nearer, swearing and threatening.

Amongst the leaves and mud she scrabbled the dressing gown down around her feet trying to conceal her white skin, curling herself into a ball, holding her head in her hands, her terror blind, primeval, paralysing; she'd never dreamt that such a primitive agony of fear could exist.

Of course it was useless. Within seconds she was transfixed in the cross-beam of six powerful torches, shown cowering in the mud entangled in the thin stems of the hedge like a small terrified animal.

She never knew who jerked her to her feet, only that he was huge and brutal. His breath stank of drink, she could smell his sweat. Then the lieutenant banged into her, blazingly angry, furious she supposed because she must have made him look foolish in front of his subordinates. He grabbed her shoulder with one hand and struck her hard across the face, then back-handed her with such violence that he knocked her out of his own grip to the ground. The bully who had first found her completed the treatment, hauling her to her feet again, and striking her viciously across the face with his rubber truncheon. She felt a great impact; there was no immediate sensation of agony even though later that night her exploring tongue would discover three smashed and aching back teeth. All around her she was aware of confused jostling, screaming voices, and hatred, vicious hatred.

There were bright lights in her eyes, coarse laughter. The blows had smashed both supports of her glasses. They were lost in the trampled mud. A gash had opened down the side of her nose. Blood poured down her chin and on to her night clothes. She was almost blind and absolutely helpless. In all this mixed confusion and violence she thought imploringly: 'The end must come soon. It must be soon.' And she welcomed it. But no! Someone found her spectacles and thrust them back at her. Trembling, as if the act might somehow bring her back from a preposterous world in which no grain of sanity remained, she cleaned them on her nightgown then popped them back on her nose.

Now they were urging her back to the house. She couldn't bear to feel them touch her so she tried to keep one step ahead. That was as far as thought went: to keep one step ahead, just to keep one step ahead and their hands away from her.

Reaching the small, square, brick-floored veranda the lieutenant shoved her up against the main pillar, his revolver in her face. She fell back against it, feeling the rough brickwork against her shoulders.

'Oh why didn't they finish it?' She was too exhausted and defeated to stand any more; she could feel the blood running down her face. 'Why didn't they finish it?'

She felt the hard muzzle of the lieutenant's revolver against her forehead.

'I'm going to kill you. I'm going to pull this trigger and blow your brains out.' His voice was hysterical.

'Thank God, it's the end,' she thought. Anything was better than this terrible, blinding, all-persuasive terror.

She heard other strident voices arguing and protesting.

'Pull the trigger,' she thought. 'Quickly! Get it over with.'

Whether in his drunken and drugged state the lieutenant would have killed her she will never know. It was Hugh, the young student nurse, who tried to save her. The other male nurse, Francis, had fled into the night, and Helen then, or later, did not blame him. But Hugh had waited on the veranda until she was captured; with terror-filled eyes he had watched them brutalise his doctor, seen the gun shoved against her temple . . . known they were about to murder her. It was more than he could stand. Yelling 'Leave her alone!' he threw himself between the lieutenant and Helen and his head struck the revolver and knocked it aside.

It was an act of instinctive and devoted courage, and it was precisely the action the lieutenant and his men needed to satisfy their anger. Killing a white woman could create a lot of trouble for them; even in their crazy, doped-up condition that realisation still penetrated. But this attack upon the divine Simba authority came from an African, a servile creature of this white woman; a miserable student daring to intervene against the invulnerable Simba power, which had already given them control of four-fifths of Congo, and which – they were certain – would sweep the National Congolese Army, the hated whites and all those who disbelieved in the divinity of Lumumba away in a sea of blood and revenge.

Now they had something to work on; a black body to punish. The heavy rubber truncheons which inflict agonising pain and damage crashed against his head and body knocking him to the ground. He uttered one sharp cry and then was silent. The boots thumped in; the sound they made and the crack of truncheons flailing against flesh made Helen physically vomit.

Outside, the night sky flared with stars above the darker outline of trees and palms. Cicadas shrilled with the insistent pitch of electronic tone, fireflies moved in the dark recesses of the banks, moths fluttered heavily across the gravel roads, and deeper in the rain forest animals, with eyes like little yellow lamps in the trees hunted their prey, killing in the primitive pattern of jungle law with quick and merciless efficiency.

On the veranda civilised man was beyond mercy. They kicked and beat the inert body with vicious ferocity until Helen knew he must be dead.

They kicked him down the shallow step of the veranda and outside on to the gravel. Their torches formed a pool of light in which he lay like some poor dying fish, the impact of boot on flesh sounding like the slap of angry waves.

Helen closed her eyes. 'No more,' she thought in agony. 'I can take no more. Please no more.' But there was more to come. Much more. With a brusque order the lieutenant stopped the game. Hugh did not move. 'Get back to the lorry,' the lieutenant shouted at his men. Then gesturing to Helen with his revolver.

'You. We're taking you back to town. You're under arrest. Get dressed.'

He shone the torch into the living-room and down the corridor showing her the way, following her with heavy strides. He kicked open the door and with the point of his gun motioned her in.

'Go in and put your clothes on.' Helen went in, stood hesitantly, then took off her dressing gown.

She hardly knew what she was doing and yet instinctively she knew what was about to happen. The ruthless beam of the torchlight ripped away all privacy.

'Get dressed,' he snapped again, and she was conscious that he was moving towards her. Of course there was no question of getting dressed. Hardly before she had time to lift her nightdress he was on her in savage crude attack. He forced her backwards on the bed falling on top of her. Whether she struggled or fought she scarcely knew. The will to resist and fight had been knocked out of her. But she screamed over and over again and no doubt the pitiful screams reached the ears of the soldiers laughing and joking at the truck.

The brutal act of rape was accomplished with animal vigour and without mercy. On the veranda a few minutes before Helen was certain that her Christian God had deserted her. The pitiful cry which she knew by heart but which she had never understood in its deepest significance now rang in her mind with tragic clarity: *'My God, my God why hast thou forsaken me?'*

If she was indeed forsaken, and poor Hugh's brutal death of a few minutes ago seemed to make this fact irrevocable then the entire edifice of her life had collapsed. Her belief, her faith, her work were all a sham and a hoax. There was no God. All the training, all the long years of teaching, all the joys, the prayers meant nothing. There was nothing . . . nothing.

This was the desperate sickness of spirit she carried like an iron weight down the corridor to the bedroom. *This* knowledge as she lay pinioned and spread-eagled under the rapist was the real horror. God had deserted her. The evil that lived in man had chosen her for rape and death, not for life. God had refused to answer her prayers, and allowed her to reach this ultimate abyss without answers and without hope. There was nothing in life and therefore nothing beyond death.

She was conscious that she was filled with pain. In her ear his breathing was stertorous. She could feel the cartridge-belt and revolver-holster pressing into her flesh; in his haste he had not bothered to remove it. And then in the middle of the bewilderment, the hideousness, agony, misery, shame and physical pain, suddenly into her mind flowed a peace – almost an exultation – which she had never experienced before.

It was an awakening of such clarity that the relief was overwhelming. The reasons formed themselves in simple logical sentences on the mental retina of her brain. To Helen, this was Christ's simple answer to her suffering. 'They are not persecuting you as you. You are only my representative here. This is my eternal Calvary, my age-old, never-ending death for all mankind. I ask you only for your body. The perpetual suffering is mine not yours. Stand with me. I accept responsibility for all this evil. It is being done to you because of me. Because I am in you. And I have not forsaken you.'

She was crying as the lieutenant clambered off her body and her rickety single bed. But the tears of relief were not that her ordeal was over, but because she had found her faith again.

The lieutenant, satiated now, was gentle; a possessive gentleness that women with sexual experience would understand, but Helen did not.

'You are my wife now. We are going in the truck. Get dressed.'

And even though in her own terms she had received a spiritual reawakening, the physical pain, terror, and numbed misery remained; she felt desperately unhappy.

She reached for the work-worn dress which hung over the back of the chair.

'No,' he said. 'Not that one. Get a clean one out of the cupboard. You're my wife. I want you to look smart so the others will admire you.'

In other circumstances his solicitude at the conclusion of rape might have been laughable. But Helen did not feel like laughing. She obeyed orders. She opened the cupboard door, extracted a clean dress and put it on. Obediently she walked by his side to the truck. She let him help her into the cab. He gave a curt instruction to the driver and they rumbled off into the darkness, their headlights wheeling over the gravel path and probing the bushes.

'My name' he said amiably, 'is George. Lieutenant George.' Even his tone of voice indicated how his attitude towards her had changed. He was her protector, he owned her, no one else was going to touch her. He put his arm around her shoulders and as they drove through the night Helen wondered what life in a Simba Army camp was going to be like. She was now his wife, a trophy, a spoil of war. There was no government, police, or magistrate of any authority who could intervene or to whom she could turn. No one in her mission could assert any physical or moral pressure. In any case no one would know where she was. Like thousands of others in this lawless period, she would simply 'disappear'.

She stared numbly through the window of the cab watching the truck lights flick past familiar landmarks. She was faintly surprised when they turned right taking the narrow road which led from Nebobongo to Ibambi seven miles away. Delayed shock made her feel exhausted and physically ill.

She couldn't understand why he kept asking her questions about the Ibambi missionaries; how many lived there, how many Americans? Did she know any Americans?

In Ibambi they stopped outside the store owned by Mr Mitsingas. Mitsingas was Greek, portly, middle-aged with greased dark hair, olive skin, two double chins and eyes which glinted through creases of fat. To Helen his throaty chuckle

[47]

always seemed to reach a new dimension as he extracted his margin of profit from the transaction in hand, and her reactions towards Mitsingas in person, and the local Greek community in general, were always tinged with the suspicion that she was being 'done'.

In her terms they were wealthy and exploited the poor. An allowance of just over seven pounds a month, most of which she gave away, meant that she numbered herself amongst those poor. The Greeks made a profit out of all of them including her Africans. She had come for God; they had come for money. Their positions as such were polarised, and ten thousand miles of philosophical space separated them. To add to her doubts, at this moment there were strong rumours that the Greeks kept themselves out of trouble by paying the Simbas to leave them alone. Helen did not approve of that particular practice either.

This did not mean for a single second that Helen did not do all she could for them; her friendships with many wives and children were intimate. She brought their babies into the world, attended to their aches and pains; she was their doctor and observed that responsibility.

But she did not have much chance to tend to their souls, for if they had any religion – and she was inclined to think they'd left such luxuries behind in Greece – it was something carefully hidden and suspiciously Catholic, called Greek Orthodox. And although she had heard how necessary it was to be suspicious of Greeks bearing gifts, her main feeling of disapproval concerned their apparent inability to exist in this life without a profit motive.

It is also true that she did not often stop to consider the social and economic hardships which brought the Greeks to Congo in the first place.

They had emigrated, which is really too fine a word for it . . . they had left their villages because of a grinding poverty which Africans born into their fertile, lush, rain forest, could never even comprehend.

The glowing clarity of light, the deathless philosophy, the marble splendours of tourist Greece did not raise a single radish from the barren earth, or put one piastre into the pocket of a peasant unfortunate enough to be condemned to scratching a living from such soil. For the Greeks, Congo was not Arcadia but it was better than home.

So Mr Mitsingas and his compatriots emigrated. They opened little stores in areas of equatorial Africa where no one else wanted to exist; 'exist' being the operative word. Colonial history in Africa confirms that the European powers parcelled it out to suit themselves, imported their own civilisations, laid down the laws, installed communications, made worthy efforts to educate the blacks, extracted fortunes from the top half of the profit margin – which Helen so instinctively distrusted – and departed swiftly and intelligently when they found they were not wanted or the going got too hot.

Usually they had homes and countries to go to. Mr Mitsingas, his countrymen, and a whole vast community of Arabs and Indians scattered about Africa through a hundred years of commercial endeavour had nowhere to go. Africa was their home.

They made profits, yes. Some made large fortunes. But many only survived. And if profit is honourable, then theirs was earned honourably through the sweat of their labour. And few historians in the regal march of empire builders across the continent have dwelt upon the importance of their role in the slow emergence of Africa from tribalism. They lived on the smell of an oil rag, a handful of rice, a stalk of bananas; they lived in remote areas where most sahibs would not survive for ten minutes; they made a living from the sale of half a cigarette, two pounds of dried coconut, a handful of coffee beans . . .

Helen, however, never saw them as pioneers or bringers of light. Perhaps God could calculate what margin of profit was honourable – or when it was. She couldn't. She thought Africa would have got on just as well without them; she was always guarded therefore in her observations about the Greeks.

That Mr Mitsingas had lost a large proportion not only of his profit but of his very livelihood, she could see at a glance as her captors walked her round the back and into the huge, dark store. The shelves were bare. It had been looted. Scattered about the large table were mugs and empty beer bottles. A dozen or so men – soldiers she supposed – the darkness making their rank or purpose hard to identify, slumped in chairs or sprawled out on the floor. A smoky oil-lamp lit the scene but she was far too distressed for more than a glance around.

Lieutenant George led her into a bedroom beyond this large room and her heart sank at all its implications. It was filled practically entirely by a large double bed and a man and woman were sprawled on the dirty sheets.

Lieutenant George swore at them angrily and sheepishly they scrambled away back into the store. He turned to Helen.

'These are my quarters. You can lie down there.' Helen glanced at the bed and closed her eyes in despair. So he had brought her here to start all over again? Possibly for the use of those other men next door? She couldn't bear to think about it.

A voice called: 'Lieutenant George?' and he said authoritatively, 'I've more work to do. Stay here. I shan't be long.'

With a sense of intense relief she watched him leave. The last thing in the world she wanted to do was stay in this filthy bedroom. In fact she simply couldn't stay alone; there must be some shred of safety in numbers. She peered out of the door. In one corner she saw an unoccupied rickety wooden chair. She crept out and sat down. Once seated her strength and will seemed to ebb away. Hunched there, arms clutched round her body, bent half forward to try to diminish the physical pain in her stomach, she clung to this small oasis of stillness separated from the dark threat of these men and their intention. She did not move, she just sat there rigidly.

The hours seemed endless. Men banged in and out from the street. Trucks constantly arrived and roared away again. Occasionally someone came close and peered at her and then moved on. Perhaps Lieutenant George had made it clear that she was his property.

She wondered if the Simbas had gone back to Nebobongo to search for Stebby and Elaine? Lieutenant George must surely have known they were there? And poor Hugh? Surely Francis would raise the alarm and they would go and find him. The thought of his battered body lying in front of her house filled her with pain.

Another thought was insistent. She had been raped. Supposing she was pregnant? What would she do if she had a baby? Her life would be finished. Where would she go? Who would have her?

Then, far away she heard the first cock-crow: an insistent evocative cry ringing through the stillness and almost immediately it was repeated by other birds. She knew then it must be four-thirty and close to dawn because in that part of

Congo the cocks were as reliable as alarm clocks, and somehow their raucous calls brought a glimmer of relief. Daylight must come soon and with it some residue of mercy, and a return to the things she found sane and believable.

A few minutes later there was a great clatter as they herded a batch of prisoners into the store and pushed them into one corner. When she dared look across, Helen could make out five Roman Catholic sisters, three priests, and a young layman from the Ibambi cotton factory. She longed to be able to join them, but she simply could not summon up the physical strength and courage to leave her chair.

It seemed absurd, but it was almost as if she was tied to the chair. All she had to do was get up, walk towards them and sit down again. But she couldn't, and she prayed that the Lord would give her His strength and faith for hers was quite used up. Half an hour later four local Greeks were pushed in amongst them and roughly ordered not to talk.

Then Helen realised that one of the Greeks was Mitsingas and he had seen her. He smiled – no one was going to stop Mr Mitsingas smiling – and he patted the empty chair next to him.

Perhaps it was the smile, perhaps it was the courage needed to smile which made the vital difference. Like someone recovering from a long illness she managed to stand up, then slowly she edged across and sat down. She saw the concern in his eyes and realised that with her broken glasses and blood-splattered face she must look a mess.

'Are you all right?' he whispered.

She nodded. She didn't dare try out her voice. Even his first tiny gesture of friendship almost brought tears.

Light was flooding in through the windows now revealing the sordidness of the room, when someone in authority – an authority asserted by heavy footsteps and a loud voice – returned. It was Lieutenant George, and with a new audience of cowed Europeans to bully he bristled with official ferocity.

'You have all been arrested by order of the government. You will be taken to prison in Paulis.' He glared at Helen with disfavour; obviously in his terms she should still have been in the bedroom. 'Radio instructions to this effect reached me at midday yesterday. All aliens to be arrested and transferred to prison.'

That was a surprise to Helen. So last night's episode hadn't been merely random house-search. Her arrest was part of a general pattern. That hadn't been made clear, or maybe she'd misunderstood.

The harsh voice continued. 'I've just returned from Wamba. All whites there are in prison. The arrest of all whites in the Babonde and Ibambi areas is continuing.'

He stamped out of the room. Five seconds later a Simba came in to collect Helen. The lieutenant wanted to see her.

On the veranda Lieutenant George glared at her. Last night's relationship was plainly at an end. The man who had put his arm round her in the truck had changed his attitude. Daylight had made her an enemy again. She preferred it that way.

'I have heard,' he said threateningly, 'that there is another "Miss" at Nebobongo? Is this true?'

So they hadn't found Stebby and Elaine yet? Well, there was no point in telling lies; they would be safer with the main group of captives.

'There are *two* girls in the house near mine,' she admitted. 'Two other misses.'

His face stiffened. Obviously he had failed in his job and blamed her. He was so furious that for a second she thought he was going to strike her. Instead he turned on his heel and marched across to his lorry. Seconds later it went roaring back towards Nebo.

His departure removed much of the tension. Everyone was tired, no one seemed very interested in guarding anyone any more. Helen asked one of the nuns if she thought they might leave the store. Then Mr Mitsingas intervened. 'Come to my house,' he said. 'It's only just across the street; they know we can't run away so the guards won't be bothered.'

He was right. Only a 'cub' Simba, a boy of about fourteen, bothered to follow them.

Mrs Mitsingas, plump and motherly, took one look at Helen's bruised and swollen face and instinctively seemed to know what had happened, and that in itself was an enormous relief. She was so gentle; she put her arm round Helen's shoulders and gave orders to her husband. 'You go away and make the coffee.' As he turned away she added 'There's bread and cheese in the pantry.' To Helen, 'Come on, my dear, we'll go to the bathroom and clean you up.'

In the bathroom, examining herself in the mirror Helen looked wryly at the destruction. Blood coated her face and was clogged in her hair. Her lips were swollen. There was a gash down her nose. With her tongue she could feel the three broken teeth at the back of her jaw. They hurt.

Mrs Mitsingas bustled about wiping blood away, tenderly dabbing bruises, and asking no questions.

Lorries still roared up and accelerated away, and more and more white prisoners were being brought in. A little later Helen overheard someone saying 'Yes the Protestants are here.'

That was all she needed. She rushed out to meet them. There were her friends. She could have kissed them. Immediately the questions started, 'Helen... your face? What happened?'

Later she realised she should have kept quiet, kept her own counsel, kept her mouth shut. But she could not. The relief of seeing her friends again, of being safe, of being able to confide, was too much for her. So she babbled; she chattered in a great rush of relief, and suddenly she realised from the stony, horrified faces around her that they didn't want to hear, that she was making them listen to something which they had been dreading and keeping at arm's length; didn't want it to be real, and now she was making it real.

She saw the look on Amy's face... And she let her voice dwindle away. Why should Amy understand, and why should she shock and horrify her in this way? Neither Amy's past nor her own had endowed either of them with the strength to accept or acknowledge the cruel reality of rape. How could Amy understand? How could she leap forward in sympathy when suddenly, something beyond the bounds of her comprehension was forced upon her? Helen had to bear this herself, but then Jessie Scholes who'd lagged behind the party came into view and everything changed. Jessie ran forward to hug her. 'Oh Helen!' she said, and by her voice Helen knew she understood everything. 'Oh Helen!'

This was the sympathy she needed. For years in Africa Jessie had been mother to her in all but name; here was the recipient to whom she could pour out her story, assuage her grief; here was Jessie who understood.

Soon afterwards Stebby and Elaine were brought in by car,

bringing with them one piece of news which gave her immense relief. Hugh was not dead. He had recovered consciousness, managed to stagger for help and Stebby and Elaine had been warned of events.

It was midday by the time the Simbas decided to convoy their prisoners to Paulis. All the Europeans were piled into lorries and driven away. They were told they were going to be shot. They arrived at two o'clock and were assembled in three groups: Catholic sisters, Protestants, priests and civilians; all lined up in the shade of the lavender-blossomed jacaranda trees.

The commander of Simba troops at Paulis drove up. He was a smart young African modelled on a long line of Belgian officers and he was not only bewildered, he was furious. Who in the name of Lumumba had ordered the arrest of all these people? Wamba? He had heard of no such orders emanating from Wamba. He had received no authority for their arrest. They must be returned to their stations and homes at once.

There was a sweeping panache about his authority. No one dared question it. The oracle had spoken and Lieutenant George did not seem to be around.

Chattering and singing, the lorry-load of Christians delivered, as someone jokingly remarked, 'literally from the lions' – drove back along the forest roads.

Helen simply could not stop talking. She talked about anything, to anybody who listened or not. The intense feeling of relief welled up like a spring bubbling out of the earth. The wind battering her skin, the heat of the sun, the lurch of the lorry so that she had to brace her muscles to hang on, were so marvellous. To be able to smile at people for no reason and receive a smile back in return, this was the very bread of life. You could not savour its flavour until you had brushed against the mindless violence and proximity to death of last night. No one knew this but Helen. No one understood this but Helen. Now she understood more about the small island of continuity, perplexity and agony which is the sum of one human being, than she had ever known before.

IV

Life at the convent settled quickly into a routine as each group of women decided their individual pattern of existence. The Protestants shared the same language, faith and communal bedroom. The Spanish nuns kept very much to themselves; they were large, indomitable women, mainly of peasant stock, wearing long cascading robes, their faces under the huge white wimples and trailing veils sharply defined, hollow-eyed, tight-lipped, seemingly chiselled out of walnut. Ferociously Catholic and independent, they muttered on their progress around the convent prayers which sounded to Helen more like threats than entreaties for God's mercy. Five hundred years of Jesuitical fanaticism had helped to fashion their faith, and there was no question to be asked regarding their courage.

The Italians were very different. Practically all were good-looking; several – in their snowy white robes enhanced by five crimson buttons, crucifixes hanging on long scarlet cords – were beautiful. Helen watched them touching their rosaries with such gentleness, and thought of them as stunned children unable to believe what was happening to them: indeed when they played with the children you could hardly distinguish their chatter and laughter apart; they made friends so quickly, embraced so easily; their love was so out-going. In the kitchen Amy struck up a deep and joyous intimacy with Sister Vitoria who, with conspiratorial smiles, whispers and giggles, taught her that the manufacture of spaghetti was an inspirational art suspected by people from the unromantic north.

The children belonged to the civilian Belgian women also held captive in the convent. Many more were still held at the hotel in Wamba, and quite early on Helen learned how deeply the Mother Superior was concerned with their welfare. Also, almost inadvertently she learned of other tragic occurrences.

'The Belgian women simply refuse to believe that their husbands are already dead,' said the Mother Superior shaking her head in concern.

Helen found this a little hard to follow. 'Perhaps it's better they should still hope,' she reasoned.

She already knew that the Belgian civilian women were the most difficult to get on with; they were used to attention; used to servants, a life of cocktail parties, 'sundowners', nannies to look after the children, and they made little effort to help with chores in the convent. Most of them were good-looking women in their early thirties, and when this life fell apart they had little faith or philosophy to fall back upon.

The Mother Superior was adamant. 'There is no hope. I was forced to witness.' She paused, glancing at Helen as if wondering whether she should continue and then adding, 'Five days ago they took us down to the town. They paraded the prisoners in two lines, the priests, the Belgians and the Americans in one line, the other nationalities in the other. Then they killed the priests, Belgians and Americans very cruelly, very vilely, making us watch – threatening that it would happen to us all very soon.'

Helen's throat was dry. She now understood the long, careful look the Mother Superior had given her. '*All* the Belgians and Americans were murdered?'

'All of them.'

'Not the English?' The Mother Superior's eyes flicked to hers confirming what news Helen was seeking.

'You are asking about the two boys from your Protestant mission?'

'Yes. Bill and Jim.'

Helen identifying the expression on the Mother Superior's face wished she had not asked, and tried to go on gabbling to avoid the truth she knew she now had to hear.

'Bill McChesney was American. I brought him out from England when I came back from my last leave. From Texas . . . Such a nice young man . . . Twenty-four.' Helen closed her eyes, her chatter dwindling away as she saw the expression on the Mother Superior's face.

Bill was American. They would not spare him. But surely Jim? She managed 'Jim as well?' The Mother Superior nodded. 'But Jim was English, not American,' Helen whispered.

Jim Rodger was slim, dark, quiet and deeply religious. In the early days he had once asked Helen to marry him but she had been too full of the Lord, her plans and the excitement of a new country even to consider accepting.

'The young American had been badly beaten up in the prison,' continued the Mother Superior. 'When they divided the prisoners into two lines – one for execution and one to be marched back to prison – he was too ill to walk, so the English boy put his arm round him and held him up. They called the roll and made the Americans and the other Belgians stand on one side. 'All the other nationalities in the other line,' they ordered. But the Englishman would not leave his friend – he would have dropped to the ground, this young American, had he not supported him.'

'But surely', Helen demanded in agony, 'didn't anyone call out? Didn't they tell the Simbas he was English?'

'Yes, they called 'He's not American or Belgian, he is English'. But the Simbas did not understand or care. And he would not step out of that line and release his friend. So they took him away and he was murdered with the others.'

Helen wanted to be sick. It was the nightmare back again. How could she stand like this hearing of the murder of two of her dearest friends without declaring her grief, exhibiting her desperation? Weeping was not enough. Poor Jim, who had so often doubted the quality and depth of his own belief, who had been so shy and humble, so deeply worried, not so much because he knew he could not leave any sort of mark on a missionary world full of zealous Christians and pioneer workers for God, but because he would not even be able to keep abreast of them. Now he would worry and doubt no more.

His Christian God had suddenly faced him with a view of Calvary. Common sense would say, 'Put your friend down and step away to safety. No one one will judge you harshly for this. You cannot save this American. If you die you will receive no medals; your own death will not alter or soften his. No one will think you a coward. In this arena of brutish killing no one will remember your isolated action. Many people will think you are stupid. You are English, it is not your turn. Step away to life.'

Helen could guess how these voices of reason and logic would whisper in Jim's ears. But she knew he would not listen. Bill McChesney from Phoenix, Arizona, was his friend. To stand by a friend was a fundamental Christian precept. How could he let him slip to the floor and step away? It would be stepping away from Christ, and from everything that enriched his life and made it real and worthwhile. How could he endure his own company ever again if he failed at this first cruel challenge, even though he knew full well that this vital juncture of personal history would make it his last.

Helen knew that his grip around Bill's waist would tighten. And he would not move.

Helen stood there, tears on her cheeks as she listened to Mother Superior sparing her nothing as she recounted how the Simbas killed all their prisoners using the terrible 'commande' torture; how they bent them backwards tying their wrists to their ankles, forcing them into agonising positions, kicked them about as if they were footballs, laid heavy planks across their bodies to make see-saws; mutilated and murdered them eventually with their heavy machete knives.

But it seems likely that the Mother Superior *did* know how deeply she was affecting Helen and was deliberately putting her to the test. It was essential that the strong ones should know what had happened and what might happen so that perhaps they could help the weaker survive in a future which was bleak and intimidating. 'We must have strength', she declared, 'and God will help us. Besides, the living matter now. They have need of our counsel and advice.'

The red brick buildings of the convent, attached schoolrooms and dormitories, sprawled over a wide area of grassland hacked out of the tropical rain forest. The grass was lush and green; in atmosphere the whole setting recalled the gentle orderliness of the French or Belgian countrysides. Only the heat, the blaze of sky, and in normal times, the hundreds of noisy laughing, little black girls with kinky hair styles and pretty gingham uniforms told you that this must be Africa.

The main convent building was built around an open-ended square, a stone-paved veranda lined the inner sides enclosing the flower beds and lawn, and beyond them falling away down a steep hillside lay the vegetable garden, chicken coops, the place for chopping wood, and at the very bottom of the hill the stream.

On December 2nd Helen noted in her diary, 'Just been sitting in the cloisters after a fairly savage time, new guards on patrol, in silence, nothing to do ... one dared not move ... a move or sound could engender a savage blow from a gun. I was between a twelve-year-old girl and a nine-year-old boy. The guards passed down the cloister and I nudged the boy ... we'd have two minutes before the guard returned ... and I showed him how I could wriggle my ears. For twenty minutes he kept quiet, straining his facial muscles into every grotesque position imaginable, trying to do the same. The guards passed again ... I nudged the girl and showed her how I could turn my tongue over – to right or left – and screw it up into a tube or flatten it out like a plate: for twenty minutes she laboriously practised and twisted and curled in hope of training her tongue. Meanwhile with a hair pin I unpicked ten inches of the hem of my dress, and after the guards passed for a third time showed the lad how to make a cat's cradle, and we kept quietly amused for another hour. We got cramped, the low cement wall we were sitting on was getting chilly as the sun passed away from the courtyard, and evening came.

We had kept silent and still for several hours – and so, suddenly, with the inexplicable change of mood of our captors, they brought out some large unripe pawpaw fruit and called the children to join them in a ball game.'

During this period, to keep the younger children quiet was difficult enough, but given an inch – like playful kittens or puppies – they sprang instinctively into action. Any Congolese guard was likely to turn a corner and find himself ambushed by a pugnacious six-year-old plus small sister, leaping from cover to point a toy gun and mow him down with a machine-gun rattle of burping noises. Some of the guards were not amused and these antics kept Helen in a state of perpetual nervousness. If familiarity had not been quickly established she thought it unlikely that any child would have survived. But then again many of the guards reacted with a child-like simplicity of their own; they were always likely to roll an orange in the path of the same desperado six-year-olds and engage in a quick five minutes of football. There was no rhyme, reason, or intelligent continuity about their behaviour. But even when the prisoners were allowed to move about more freely, to get books out of the library, write, sew, tend the garden, teach the children choruses, it was always necessary to be on the alert for an outburst of violence.

It was ironical perhaps that in a convent dedicated to God, to contemplation, to religious instruction and saintly introspection, Helen on so many occasions had to creep secretly into the laundry to console two stricken nuns, Sisters Dominique and Clothilde, and make her own philosophy plain to them.

She could sense their confusion about her own attitude. How could a woman after such a deep and fundamental humiliation as rape find sustenance in the world again? How could she, a missionary, a 'bride of Christ' in Catholic terms, ever face people with a smile in her mind or on her lips? How could the brutal possession of her body by a black rapist ever be forgotten?

She found it hard to explain that it could not be forgotten but that she could rationalise the ordeal; that her education and faith allowed her to set it where it belonged, in the past.

More to the point she instructed both girls: 'You must trust in God and know absolutely that the shame is not yours. You must believe that ultimately you carry no responsibility. You may carry the hurt of it but not the shame. The shame is the man's. You must believe that.'

Practically every day of that December of 1964 was one of continually sustained terror. In the second week, after breakfast, carrying her usual two buckets, Helen set off down the hill to fulfil her morning task of fetching water. A Simba guard, as usual belligerent and suspicious, trailed after her, and as they walked through the gardens and over the brow of the hill, Helen heard the sound of lorries arriving at the front door.

The noise made her feel anxious and she turned, trying to influence the guard. 'Can't we go back? It might be important.'

He obviously preferred the country walk. 'No,' he said sharply. 'You go on.'

They followed the track behind the convent, past the African sisters' dormitory which the Simbas invaded practically every night, and turned down the narrow path of beaten earth between the vegetable gardens and the wire-netted run for the chickens and ducks, Helen already conscious that even empty, two big buckets were quite heavy. She looked across the valley hazy in the sunlight towards the Protestant mission compound, glimpsing the top of the church and near it the roof of the mission house itself. She wondered how the three Protestant missionaries remaining there – Daisy Kingdon and the two younger ones, Pat and Elaine – were getting on? Why they had not been allowed to join them in the convent was a question which perturbed them all.

At the bottom of the hill she slithered down the last four yards of muddy bank to the water hole. It was no longer clean for the dry season had arrived and animals both wild and domesticated drank there. She used an enamel mug as a ladle to fill both buckets, then tried to struggle back up the bank.

Slipping and sliding, it was at this moment that the humiliation, pointlessness, sheer physical ache from what she was doing and how little she was achieving suddenly struck her. She felt tears welling into her eyes and despised herself for being such a weak-kneed, cowardly female. She slipped again and the water sloshed over the bucket's rim. Then she saw the hand reaching down to help her. 'Here give me one,' said the guard grabbing a bucket from her. His quick generous action undid her even more, and as her face turned up he must have seen the shine of tears in her eyes for not only did he carry that bucket to the top of the bank but returned to collect the second one.

On the return journey he carried one bucket, Helen struggling behind with the second. She was sniffing and weeping to herself, this gruff and unexpected kindness unsettling her far more than she thought possible.

So often this happened; she made inner resolutions never to trust these people again, and then just as the pain in her chest, the exhaustion, the giddiness and sickness almost overwhelmed her, one of them did something so unexpected ... protected her from a blow, stretched down a hand ... that she was left uncertain and unbearably moved.

At the top of the hill he told her that her ankles were puffy, her sandals torn, and she didn't look well at all. She said she didn't feel very well.

'All right,' he answered, 'you can sit down on that tree trunk and rest for ten minutes.'

He carried *both* buckets up the next incline but a hundred

yards from the convent, as she had expected, he assumed his professional face and abruptly banged them down, snapping brusquely, 'You carry them now.'

With that he marched on ahead reasserting his tough Simba image. This poise was abruptly shattered when a young Belgian boy came racing towards them gabbling in a mixture of French and Swahili. He belonged to one of the Belgian mothers, and startled, Helen said, 'Now calm down, what's the matter?'

'They've gone! They've gone!' he howled.

Helen put down the buckets as if their handles were suddenly red-hot.

'Who've gone? Gone where?'

'My mother, the sisters, all your ladies. I was playing behind the woodshed and they've left me behind. Everybody's gone.'

Filled with overwhelming terror and distress, Helen began to run, the guard and the boy at her heels. 'Please God,' she gasped as she ran, 'please God don't leave me behind. I couldn't stand it alone.'

The courtyard was silent and empty, the message of those droning lorry engines now clear.

'I've got to find them,' she cried turning to the guard. 'I've got to find them, d'you hear? If they're going to shoot them, they've got to shoot me too. I can't be separated, I can't.'

Her overwhelming sense of hysteria was frightening. Probably since the beginning of the rebellion she had repressed this fear of being alone; now some mental sluice gate had shattered and uncontrollable panic flooded her mind and intelligence. She raced out of the front door heading towards Wamba and preferably the first firing squad she might encounter. Two hundred yards from the convent with the puzzled but implicated Simba pounding along behind her, she saw a lorry driving up the gravel drive towards them. She stopped and stood to one side to watch it pass. Almost unbelievingly she gaped at what it contained, her face crumpling like that of a small child, tears blinding her as she saw Jessie, Elaine, Amy, Stebby, all her friends . . . all safe . . . oh thank God they were safe!

She began to chase back after it, in a sort of Kafka nightmare experience, the nightmare aspect continuing to the end for when she reached the lorry outside the convent door only Amy was sitting there.

'Amy?' she cried, 'Amy, what's happening? Where are the others?'

The guard had now caught up with her again. He grabbed her arm; there were other guards around; the time had come to exert his authority.

'They're inside,' he said angrily. 'They've been taken inside. You've got to come inside too.'

Amy sat in the back of the lorry her shoulders hunched, utterly dejected. She said despairingly, 'They asked me if I was the doctor and I said, 'No' but they wouldn't believe me; they've told me to stay here.'

Helen tried to drag away from the guard. 'But that's absurd!' she cried. Her voice was shrill and she couldn't bear to see her friend so distressed and frightened. 'I'm the doctor. I'll stay with you here. I'm the doctor. If they want me they can have me. But you can't suffer in my place. I'll stay here.'

The Simba guard realising that this was mutiny grabbed Helen by the shoulders, spun her round, propelling her towards the door. 'Inside!' he roared. 'You are to go inside!'

In the cloisters, Jessie, Elaine and Stebby were sitting huddled together; plainly what they had witnessed recently and what they feared, terrified them.

'Pray!' whispered Jessie urgently, 'pray!' Helen bent her head. She didn't want to pray. She wanted to know what they were doing with Amy outside. They knew as well as she did that Amy wasn't the doctor. 'Amy?' she whispered, unable to control herself any longer. 'What are they doing with Amy?'

As if in reply to her urgent question the main door opened and Amy came through and walked towards them.

'They just let me go,' she announced in a dazed voice, 'They just let me go.'

It was half an hour before Elaine felt it safe to tell Helen the whole story. 'They took us all down to the gaol. It was awful, they were pushing and jostling and hitting us. That dreadful little colonel arrived in his car, leapt out and knocked down several of the nuns, just punched them to the ground with his fists and that acted as a sort of signal – all the Simbas turned on them tearing off their veils and rosaries and screaming obscenities at them. The violence was terrible, absolutely horrifying . . .'

'What about you and your group?'

'We were collected together in a little bunch, one of the Simbas pushed us to one side.'

'So what happened?'

'The colonel knocked down Sister Marie Frances with his fists. He was just like a savage animal. Then he saw us and his entire attitude changed. "Who are you?" he asked, and when the guard told him we were the Protestants he was almost gracious and said, "You can go back to the convent. This is nothing to do with you." So they brought us back. But it wasn't funny.'

'But what were they doing with Amy?'

'I think the colonel tried to tell us we should say we were medical workers, doctors and then we shouldn't get beaten up.'

'And one of the Simbas got the message wrong?'

'I expect so.'

'Sister Marie Frances?' demanded Helen. 'D'you think she was badly hurt?'

'He knocked her down but I think she's all right. She's tough. Those poor sisters, they've still got them down there.'

At lunch time Sister Dominique and Sister Clothilde returned followed during the next few hours by the others. It was now plain that while Sister Dominique was still fighting for her own mental survival, Sister Clothilde had come to terms with her situation. The young Belgian nun, forced to endure humiliation beyond the boundaries of her knowledge or instruction, had adopted a very different course.

It was the Mother Superior who first told Helen of her fears, but the inclinations of Sister Clothilde had also been observed by the other nuns; they saw what was happening, and as gossip – even amongst women as saintly as sisters of the Church – is not uncommon, tongues were beginning to clamour.

It was clear that Sister Clothilde had taken Helen's advice at face value; that by suffering herself she could, quite literally, save her colleagues from rape. But there was more to it than that; what rustled tongues in the cloisters was the perception that this was no saintly sacrifice but an indulgence in carnal pleasure.

The introspective, silent young nun of no rare beauty or outstanding zeal had discovered the fierce attraction inherent in the

Dr Helen Roseveare, newly-arrived at Nebobongo
Station, four maternity nurses and John Mangadima

A crowd of Congolese villagers watch 'our doctor'
comforting an old man dying of cancer

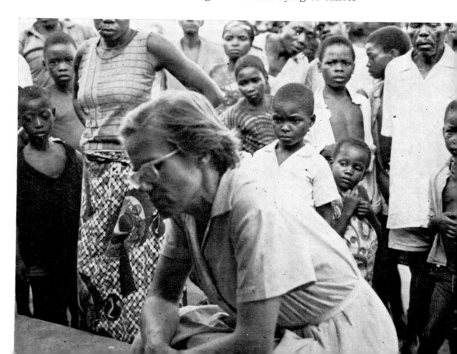

Helen Roseveare's long journeys to isolated villages
involved many incidents like this: rescuing a car
from a flooded road

Ibambi Main Street: the WEC missionary settlement
is two miles away

Helen helps bath her houseboy Benjamin's two small
sons

As doctor, surgeon, school-mistress and missionary
Helen found time to play games with the children
at the Leprosy settlement of Nebobongo

Simba recruits being trained during the northern rebellion against the central Congolese government
photo: Camera Press

Simba 'cubs': large numbers of these children were trained for service with the rebels *photo: Camera Press*

physical possession of her body by the male of the species. Events which had pushed her into the quiet backwaters of saintly contemplation and introspection had now revealed that in her bloodstream lay the surge of life itself; that the flesh, indeed, could be more, much more, than merely a housing for the contemplation of God in all His infinite mystery.

The rebellion had brought her sexual experience and somewhere in the unobtrusive shy female, desire and the need for fulfilment had awakened. A deep sensuality could now masquerade – for she had not enough self-knowledge or assertiveness to understand her discovery – as a defence of her fellow creatures. She offered herself; she was not abused or forced. And this offering was to black men! Creatures of God certainly, but nevertheless black men! And rapists and enemies at that! It was a situation outside Helen's comprehension and beyond any advice she could offer, as it was, indeed, outside that of the Mother Superior or the other nuns. They said she must be mad. These dreadful events which were destructive enough, God knows, to breed insanity in any woman, must have made her mad. But reluctantly, perhaps subconsciously, as women they sensed the betrayal latent in their own bodies, and this was disturbing, for their mutual preservations appeared to rest entirely on the premise that together they could survive but singly they were doomed.

During the next two days in small groups the nuns were allowed to return to the convent, but increasingly through December 1964 sudden raids took place.

Perhaps the most terrifying started at nine minutes past eight one Tuesday in December a time recorded exactly by Helen in her diary. The atmosphere in the convent was quiet and sane. As usual after supper the nuns were walking or sitting on the veranda, Belgian mothers were getting their children ready for bed, and even though darkness had brought its inevitable quota of apprehension and fear, a small sense of peace and security existed inside those red brick walls.

No warning bell this time; the front door bolts were shot back obviously by a guard at a pre-arranged signal. The door banged open and Simbas came bellowing into the convent screaming and capering like madmen.

The abrupt noisy attack was clearly calculated to spread maximum alarm, confusion and terror, which without doubt it did. The panic was heart-stopping; women screamed, children's faces puckered and dissolved in wails.

The Simbas, a few in uniform, most half naked and sprigged with the usual oddments of animal fur and green leaves, seemed both drunk and drugged. In a mass hysteria of rage they lashed out with rifle butts, spears and clubs their motive apparently to slaughter everyone in sight. The nuns cowered, the women sheltered their children in their arms and waited for death; Helen sitting next to Amy could only gape in fear.

'Stand up, stand up all of you!' Helen was grabbed by a wild-eyed Simba and thrust against the wall.

'Over there you! And you too.' Another grabbed Amy and thrust her in the same direction. Their plan was now becoming clear: a round-up of all the sisters. Kicking, striking them with rifle butts, tugging at their clothes the Simbas forced them into line. Helen caught the despairing eyes of Sister Dominique but could do nothing to help.

Within minutes they had scoured the convent and assembled the Mother Superior and her charges into a long file along the veranda. Some were bleeding, many weeping. The sight of the line of broken women, many elderly and grey-haired seemed to delight the Simbas. To Helen their jubilation was sickening. 'You are to be shot!' they shouted. 'D'you understand? You are to be executed!'

Hitting and jostling they herded them out into the night. They looked so piteous that Helen, Amy, Jessie, all of them including the Belgian women, stood transfixed, weeping and unable to help.

Were they being taken too? No, it was only the sisters who were to be executed. The door banged shut again and it was all over. Only two of their usual guards were left behind, and they hardly knew what it was all about. Fortunately they were two of the friendlier sort, and they conferred together for some minutes before the elder spoke up.

'We think it would be better if the five Protestants moved into the main dormitory with the Belgian women and the children. There are plenty of mattresses and we can guard you more easily if you're all together.'

Helen glanced from Jessie Scholes to Amy, Elaine and Stebby, seeking not so much leadership as security. Fear knotted her stomach. Was this another trap? They could trust no one. Reluctantly they decided to do what the guards advised.

The five of them quickly gathered their possessions together and scurried round to the large dormitory where the Belgian women and nuns slept. They each chose a mattress, not daring to ask 'Why them – not us?' Were they really going to shoot the nuns, or had they some other humiliation in store for them? No one dared or wanted to think about it, their own personal terror was as much as they could bear.

They had hardly settled down when the dormitory door suddenly opened. Breath was held, movement suspended. A guard poked his head inside, 'Will one of you go and turn the generator off?'

The balloon of tension subsided. Helen was now conscious of eyes on her. She had the reputation of being a mechanic who knew something about engines. Normally the generator which provided electricity for the entire convent compound was Sister Marie Frances' province. Helen knew nothing about generators of this size.

As she hesitated she saw Amy looking at her. 'I'll come with you,' she volunteered.

'Thanks', Helen murmured. Followed by the two soldiers carrying a storm lantern they walked the length of the cloisters which were now eerily quiet and deserted. The generator was housed in a small lean-to at the end of the kitchen. They ducked under the low doorway and faced the enormous throbbing machine. There were cobwebs overhead, oil on the floor, a panel of switches and dials dimly seen on the far wall, but as to which switch or lever turned the machine off there was no clue.

Helen stumbled over a length of rope in the oily sludge at her feet. She was still scared because she sensed that unless they managed to switch the generator off fairly quickly the young guards would suspect monkey business and jump to the conclusion that they were being mocked. They were both armed; they were both ignorant boys and, without officers or N.C.O.'s to command them, liable, after the violent precedent they had just been set, to turn nasty very easily.

Amy sensed the same danger and her voice was urgent. 'What do we do?'

Helen stared back. 'I've no idea. Watch this amp meter. I'll try every switch in turn. See if we can make that needle drop. Tell me what happens.'

She moved to the biggest switch she could see and threw it up. Nothing happened. She tried another. Same result. In a kind of desperation she turned and reversed every knob and switch she could see. Still nothing. The monster roared and whined with a vibrant life of its own. Helen could sense Amy's growing disquiet, the distrust of the guards, feel her own inner hysteria. During all her years in Congo she had always had to handle the engines; grease them, repair them, make them tick; she was the marvel who kept ancient, second-hand vehicles on the road long after they should have been abandoned in the jungle. She had a knack.

Now, not only was she beaten, she was *scared* of the great oily throbbing monster which seemed to threaten their very lives. She circled it in terror, took a step towards the darkest corner, slipped, and grabbed at a rag hanging on some part of the machine. The rag came away in her hand and the engine throb died away.

Amy's head turned from the ammeter.

'You've done it.' Her relief was enormous. Helen lifted her eyes to Heaven in thanks; she gulped; she couldn't speak. They backed away from the machine on tip-toe as if they might wake it up again, or as if it might suddenly blow up like a time bomb.

Outside on the veranda, the night was full of stars and so quiet, even the normally shrill cacophony of the cicadas seemed muted and far away.

Helen drew in a deep breath; they had defeated a malevolent generator; it seemed equivalent to ending a war. They hurried along the veranda beginning to splutter with suppressed, near-hysterical laughter. Then she remembered what had happened and prayed, 'Dear God, please help them out there in the darkness.'

Back in the dormitory Helen pulled off her sweater, kicked off her sandals and rolled them up as a pillow; always they followed the Mother Superior's advice not to undress. She pulled her blanket over her head to shut out the mosquitoes which invariably whined in her ears as soon as she settled down. The darkness was impenetrable now; the sense of fear and tension as unyielding as a brick wall.

But what was happening to Mother Superior, Sister Marie Frances and Sister Dominique? Was it to be the same sickening humiliations as before? She tried to switch off her mind as she had switched off the generator. 'Oh God, please protect them,' she whispered. She tried to will herself to find a few moments of relief in sleep but found herself straining to listen. What was that noise? A car? A man's footsteps?

Suddenly a baby whimpered, and immediately her throat constricted with fear. She pressed the angry 'Keep it quiet! Shut it up!' back in her throat. Poor mother and baby. How much worse off they were than she!

She lay rigid for a few seconds more, then sat up, pulled on her sweater, and fumbled round for her glasses. She felt better sitting up, crouched, her arms round her knees. The breathing all around her grew steadier, more rhythmic as they slept. The mother had quietened her fretful baby. Helen lay down again and tried to sleep when suddenly the door opened and a shaft of light from a storm lantern fell across her mattress. She grabbed her glasses. Fear choked her. She felt her heart pounding. She could not have screamed or spoken even if she had tried. The two guards peered in at her. They were solicitous. Was everything all right? She nodded and the door closed behind them. Her relief was so great that she could actually feel her muscles slacken their tension. How much longer could she go on existing under this strain? Nothing had happened except the two young guards had poked their heads through the door to see if they were comfortable. That was what was so terrifying. Nothing had happened, yet her heart had almost stopped.

Sometime during the night she must have fallen asleep for she woke at 6 a.m. hearing the sound of a key turning in the lock.

Her eyes saw the early sunshine moving on the pale walls, and she sensed unfamiliarity. This hard palliasse. These movements and sounds so different from the noises made by Elaine, Amy, Stebby and Jessie.

Elaine, Amy, Stebby and Jessie? Then she remembered the horror of last night ... The terror of that great throbbing engine; the guards would want her to restart it this morning, and how was she to do that?

She sat up. Oh yes, this dormitory was very different from their ten-foot-square cell with its two hard beds, desk under the window, wash-hand basin, and the upholstered mattress – softest place of the lot – on the floor for Jessie. Locked in from 8.30 p.m. until 6.0 a.m. meant one thing, a free-for-all sprint for the bathroom next morning competed for by seventy women, with Mother Superior saying gently they should really let the sisters have precedence as they had to hear mass at 6.30 a.m., and Helen as resident Medical Officer trying to counter the objection with the view that in this matter all their needs were the same.

No hurry this morning however; an orderly, dispirited procession.

Were they really going to murder the sisters as they'd murdered the priests and the other civilians? It was obvious that the female gender meant nothing to the Simbas; they'd destroyed hundreds of women over the past few weeks.

Then a gust of hope . . . a whisper suddenly went round. Someone at the door . . . not Simbas . . . friendly voices . . . two of the sisters . . . oh thank God for that! Helen could have wept as she confronted the broad grin of Sister Marie Frances. She had a cut on her head, a bruised face; as usual she'd taken as many blows as she could absorb. The two guards made no attempt to stop them talking and Sister Marie Frances's grin faded as she described what had happened.

'It was terrible. They beat us and punched us and tore off our veils. That wasn't so bad as the filthy cell into which they pushed us for the night. Human excrement everywhere. The stench made you sick.'

She caught Helen's eye and paused; she knew what Helen was going to ask. She nodded sadly.

'You mean that Sister Dominique . . . ?' Helen said quietly.

'She and Sister Clothilde. Both taken and abused again. The poor things, we could do nothing to help them. '

Marie Frances and the other 'grey' Belgian sister had been released to return to the convent to prepare food for the imprisoned nuns. They had to hurry. Sister Marie Frances gave Helen all her keys, took her along to the generator and instructed her how to start, stop, and service it; she showed her everything, adding with a wry smile, 'Just in case'. Then she went off to see how her little pygmy adopted daughter was getting on, and to feed her dog. Her warmth and vitality were so all-embracing that Helen watched her go out through the front door carrying the basins of food with a sense of personal loss.

At two o'clock that afternoon the front door bell rang again and the guards opened it to reveal another group of sisters gathered outside. They filed in slowly; almost unconsciously, in agonised suspense, Helen realised she was counting them. The Mother Superior, Sister Marie Frances, Sister Sylvaner, the old Spanish nun with a face like a wrinkled orange whose name she couldn't pronounce, Sister Dominique, her face as set as if it had been moulded in wax, Sisters Johannes, Gertrude, Wilhelmina, they shuffled in.

They were *all* back. Oh, God be praised!

They were filthy. Their robes were matted with mud and excrement. The snowy robes of the Italian sisters with their pretty little red buttons were covered with dirt and effluent. Their head-dresses had been torn off; their eyes were staring, their cropped hair tousled; there were bruises on some faces, blood on others. They were humiliated, bereft of dignity and they were cowed. It was heart-breaking to see their shoulders rounded, their heads bowed, the way they stood, so fearful and afraid. They had returned from the edge of destruction and they were stunned and shocked by the experience.

Helen knew they hated to be seen like this, wanted to creep away and hide. But standing there, poised for a second, facing each other like two hostile groups, and suddenly recognising in the other faces such anxiety, such compassion, such love . . . it was too much for all of them. They swept together mingling into one weeping, broken-hearted congregation; a crowd of terrorised women beaten into abject humiliation but no longer were they strangers, no longer Catholic, Protestant, civilian, Spanish, Belgian, Italian, British; merely women who clutched each other in a communion of grief, seeking in each others arms some scrap of comfort and coherence.

It was, as usual, the Mother Superior, tiny, dishevelled, bruised, who issued the dominating order which gave purpose and relief to the scene.

'We are dirty!' she snapped. 'We must all wash. This very minute we must wash our clothes. Do you hear? Everyone to the laundry to wash their clothes.'

There was a chorus of agreement. They must wash their clothes. They must cleanse themselves. Not for a second did they consider any sort of symbolism. One had to get clean. One had to wash. The stains must be removed.

Like a chorus of fallen angels they trooped along the veranda, many still weeping, some singing, all borne along by this compelling purpose.

Helen drew Sister Dominique into a quiet corner. Her hair was short and silky like a boy's. Dirty and bruised, her cheeks stained with tears she was still beautiful, and young and vulnerable. Helen who simply wanted to show that she understood and cared couldn't think where to start. 'I know.' she murmured, 'I know.'

Sister Dominique who had kept her face strong since she first came in through the door was completely undone by the sympathy. Her face crumpled and covering her eyes with her hands she began to weep uncontrollably.

Helen let her cry for a few moments then gently prised the fingers from her cheeks and drew Dominique's head down to her shoulder. As she held the young girl tightly in her arms she found that her own cheeks were wet and realised that there was a certain measure of purification as well as relief in their tears.

Part Two

I

In February 1953 when young Doctor Helen Roseveare sailed from England heading for Congo, she never forgot her elation as the ship so sleek and splendid in her colours of pale blue and maroon slid through the Mediterranean and the Suez Canal, and then down across a dark blue ocean.

Mombasa fascinated her, with its white colonial buildings shaded by the heavy branches of the mango trees, the slanting sunlight, heat, flies, noise, black faces and glinting teeth. On the overnight train to Nairobi she simply could not bear to sleep; she had to jump out at every halt so she could try and breathe in the very soul and spirit of Africa.

The steamer which crossed Lake Albert at night was stiflingly hot, but not even mosquitoes and the airless darkness under the mosquito net could disillusion her. The moon was reflected in the surface of the lake, the water slurred endlessly past the bows like skeins of black silk; everything was strange and beautiful. She was up before light. She knew that the turbulent sunset she had witnessed and this vast, quiet dawn represented nature in its most romantic chocolate-box mood, and the romantic Doctor Helen hugged the experience to herself in an exultation which was almost unbearable.

The great spiny ridge of Central African mountains barring the route to the west, slowly emerged from the white mist rising from the surface of the lake, high amongst them the Mountains of the Moon. Because of this enormous watershed the old civilisations far to the north had been born. From the pressure tank of these high and beautiful lakes of solemn and legendary importance, rivers flowing north, east and west, Nile, Zambesi and Congo, were thrust on their long journeys to the three oceans.

Beyond, deep in the rain forest, pygmies, gorillas, animals, birds and plants of rarity and beauty existed unaware of the polluted civilisation from which she came. Farther to the north she would see great herds of wild elephants, bulls, cows and calves, jet black, their huge tusks curved and shining as they stood belly-deep in the shallows of the White Nile, forking trunks-full of green lilies and water-weeds into their mouths, occasionally pausing to squirt jets of water over their skins, but mainly feeding endlessly, ruminatively, totally at peace with the world and their surroundings. And somehow their very placidity and the irrelevance of her presence gave her the feeling that this was indeed, a wild and primitive part of the world.

The event which brought the young lady doctor to this remote heart of Africa was simple but crucial: her conversion – strange as it may seem – to Christianity.

Not that she wasn't as far as her family friends and relatives were concerned a Christian to begin with. The family came from Cornwall. Great-grandmothers had remembered old Cornish rumours that when the storms raged and mist and flying spume hid the granite headlands of that long, isolated seaboot of England it was . . . 'fine weather for the Roseveares.' Fine weather for wreckers to place lanterns at wrong navigation points and lure sailing ships to their graves.

There is a Roseveare inscribed on a plaque in the ancient, once sand-buried church at St Enodoc's across the estuary. And Helen's childhood memories of Cornwall were uniformly happy. She had been lucky; she had so many things in her favour. She passed examinations without trouble, though she would much sooner have kept up with her adored older brother who could out-jump, out-run and out-fight her. Father had been one of the most brilliant mathematicians of his day, knighted for his war-time work with the Civil Service, so academic honours came easily to her.

She treasured those memories of long walks in Wales when she was at Howells, the exclusive girls' public school, and he would snatch a day or two off to visit her. They would tramp over the mountains he, while briefly acknowledging the great sweep of the countryside, the remoteness of war, the soft wind in their faces, patiently explaining some knotty equation to do with advanced mathematics.

She always remembered those three wonderful holidays in the thirties when he had piled her mother and the kids into the family car on top of tents, blankets and cooking utensils, and they had driven off to 'do' Europe.

All so simple then for a small girl. You ate, you slept, you laughed, you played, there was no time or room for emptiness, no need for reasons; growing up was a time for satisfying appetites.

Adolescence ended at Newnham College, Cambridge. She started off there doing all the things she was good at and liked. She was good at sports. She loved knocking balls about. She got her blue two years in succession for both cricket and hockey, though she would admit that it was largely a matter of simply being *willing* to play cricket which earned her that distinction, an honour which in her own estimation was slightly tarnished when she was out both times without scoring a run in the match against Oxford.

She also discovered that a medical education at Cambridge University contained many hazards for the young and ingenuous. She was the only girl student in a study group of six medical undergraduates. Every Wednesday morning they each took it in turn to act as 'guinea pig' while the others administered the experimental treatment and made notes. On this particular day Helen, nineteen and bashful in the presence of five belligerent males arrived in the laboratory to find out that it was her turn.

'Oh, is it?' she said mildly.

'Yes, it is,' replied the self-appointed leader handing her a glass of clear liquid. 'Now drink this up like a good girl.'

Helen smelt it and didn't like it. 'What is it?'

'Gin.'

'Oh!'

'What's the matter? Haven't you ever drunk gin before?'

'No.'

'Well, it's about time you did. And there's no backing out now. You've read your syllabus haven't you?' (Helen decided it was a bit late to admit she hadn't.) 'You know the subject: "The Effect of Alcohol on the Human Constitution." It's your turn. Go on, drink it down like a good girl.'

Helen drank.

'There! Didn't hurt, did it?'

Helen agreed it didn't hurt.

'Obviously no point trying this sort of experiment on this lot; they're ginned up to the eyebrows already. You're the ideal virgin subject. Now just knock back this next tot and we're ready to take a blood sample and measure the alcohol content.'

Rarely could a divine innocent have fallen into more cunning hands. By the time she had gulped down four large gins she was barely aware of voices saying, 'Better top her up with another double, Godfrey,' and 'If she has any more she'll float upwards of her own accord.'

Some two hours later with the ritualistic pomp of young knights bearing their dead queen back from a glorious battle-field, five solemn undergraduates bore a horizontal Helen – waving arms and legs in all directions like a disorientated spider crab, and roaring out incoherent verses of 'Onward Christian Soldiers' – back through the interested bystanders on the streets of Cambridge.

They deposited her gently at the front door of Newnham Ladies' College, an establishment noted for the decorum, gentility and educational qualifications of its lady students; they did not wait for the reactions of the Principal but scurried away breathless with laughter. Helen was sick. The Principal, wise to the ways and idiosyncrasies of young medical students, took no action over the episode, maintaining a tactful if frosty neutrality.

Work, music, amateur dramatics, sport and friends all engaged Helen's attention. But something was missing. The trouble was she did not know what was missing. The belief grew inside her that surely there must be something more to life than a passive or even active participation in a score of pleasant activities.

She simply could not just sit back and say, 'I'm all right!' and let the rest of the world go hang. She had to be implicated.

Reading philosophy was all very well but it was somebody else's philosophy. How did you create your own? She knew the world was in a desperate state: she had grown up in the most disastrous war in history; people were always starving, miserable, terrified or exploited. She tried the political parties. Power was the end product of all their rhetoric, argument and dreams, and history seemed to prove they abused power and were corrupted by it as soon as they attained their desires. It was all too glib, too self-righteous. You scored dialetical points like a tennis match; you argued until the dawn came up and went to bed convinced you had made a good case; and next day when you woke up, Russia, America, China, the Afro-Asian groups and the Europeans were all charging along their old chauvinistic paths, each certain that *their* philosophy and *their* way of life was the only well-paid and well-fed route to eternity; each certain, without doubt, that they alone had been chosen by God.

God really wasn't much help either. Ostensibly Helen was a Christian. She went to church; she paid lip service to all the good causes, but in the second half of the twentieth century how could you *really* believe in God? He didn't seem to have much to do with paying the rent, modifying the boss, soothing an angry wife or boy-friend; what had God got to do with fast cars, overdrafts, strikes or package tours? The Christian Church represented 'religion'. Religion made its ritualistic appearance at births, christenings and funerals. You could applaud the earnest 'telly-priests', the guiltless scientists disassociating themselves from primary responsibility, but it all had to do with 'religion' not any sort of personal God.

The word God seemed somehow to have become too powerful a noun to be accepted simply or naturally. People simpered to children about 'the little Lord Jesus'. God seemed to be taken over by those strange people carrying banners at race meetings.

To her slight astonishment some of her contemporaries at Cambridge seemed to have found 'belief'. How, Helen didn't know, or seem able to find out. She felt her own emptiness but knew no way of filling it, and it was not in her nature to join the 'in' crowd, and mouth empty phrases.

Something about the religious life, however, drew her towards it. Mainly perhaps it was because she was ready to 'try anything once', and she found herself slipping into the habit of joining in at Christian Union prayer meetings and Bible studies. She discovered – and this slightly astonished her – she loved singing hymns; she adored all those rousing swinging choruses, the plaintive melodies, the appeals, the confirmations of faith she didn't understand or expect to understand.

When she eventually came to the hymn which started 'More

about Jesus would I know'... the idea intrigued her; she was perplexed by the thought. People committed themselves to music, art, gambling, sport, sex, drinking, gardening, sailing... a hundred things. Was it possible she could commit herself to God?

She 'slogged', to use her own description, through the New Testament, and then found to her amazement she had been captured by the great mystery, by the clear compassion, by the simple message, but she was still bogged down by the dogma, the theology, the pomp, ritual and ceremony encrusted on Christianity like the varnish, barnacles, and coats of paint on the hulk of a great ship.

Christmas came with the news that her youngest sister had mumps. All three sisters had shared chickenpox and then measles several years earlier, which wasn't very funny really because Helen's eyes had been permanently damaged. Better if she avoided mumps wrote her mother and not come home until January.

Two friends told her of a vacancy at a Christmas house-party at Mount Hermon Bible College, Ealing. She applied, was accepted, and arriving felt at once lonely, bewildered and unqualified. On the second day her study group were led through the book of Genesis, shown how to annotate and summarise the message, and information to be found there. Helen with her logical, orderly mind thought it a fascinating exercise. Next day they were going to follow the same procedure with the Epistle to the Romans. Would they try and read as much as they could before tomorrow morning's Study session? She curled up on a sofa in front of the fire and began to read and make notes. 'Through its orderly array of facts I gripped the essential basic truth of man's need in his lost state of sin and depravity, and of God's provision to meet that need through the substitutionary death of Christ...'

When she finished she started off for bed. She met two girls just leaving the bathroom. 'You're late,' she said. 'You're early,' they replied. She looked at her watch. It was 6.30 a.m. The other two were on early kitchen duty. She had worked all night. To her intense disappointment she fell asleep in the study session she had prepared for with so much anticipation.

On the last evening she got into a vehement argument with

her associates defending her conception of Christianity. And as she argued she realised she did not know enough or understand enough; that too much was mystery, and that their theology was miles ahead of hers. She lost her temper and the thread of her argument. They laughed at her and she left humiliated and close to tears.

In her room she threw herself on her bed and wept. Despair and loneliness were all she seemed to have achieved in her search for God.

Then she raised her reddened eyes to the large printed text of a psalm on the wall. She didn't seem to have taken it in before though she must have read it a hundred times. *Be still, and know that I am God.*

Eight small words which drove into her heart and brain; eight small words which thrust like a searchlight through her despair. Suddenly she understood the essentially simple, elementary, contradictory conclusion that it was *not possible to understand*. Not intellectually. Not as you would work out an equation. Not as a matter of logic. To understand with the intellect as the single comprehending instrument was beyond the mind of man. To rationalise, logomachise, analyse, deduce and conclude were the normal activities of the brain and computer. An understanding of belief lay beyond their horizons. Belief was a colour unseen in their spectrum.

Be still, and know that I am God. The reasons and the finality were in His hands. At last she understood. There were to be many more emotional fences to surmount but now she had achieved an individual relationship. Other people may have found this easy. Helen had not.

That evening she went down to the meeting still overcome by her own almost incommunicable awakening. Their leader always asked for testimonies, and usually, once on her feet Helen could never stop talking. This time she couldn't speak at all. Eventually, feeling foolish, she managed to blurt out that she had met with God. It was difficult to explain that the great light which had blinded Paul on the road to Damascus had shone down for Helen Roseveare from a psalm on the wall of a bedroom in Ealing.

(2)

The Africans of the Congo rain forest are a pagan people.

Since the daybreak emergence of pre-historic man no one has disturbed them in the peace of their dark forest glades because nothing had excited the curiosity, avarice, or power-dementia of the outside world.

Gold, silver and precious stones were not easily available. It was far simpler to poach and transport ivory across the vast plains on the eastern side of the central African water-shed. No one searched for lost civilisations or Cro-Magnon man. Even when Europeans became obsessed with their nineteenth-century dream of empire, and the scramble for Africa – the carving of the continent into neat geographical joints – began, no one scrambled very hard for the clammy, fever-ridden jungles of equatorial Africa. The reason was lethally demonstrable for geographical, anthropological and medical reasons the white man could not survive there.

In 1482 the Portuguese navigator Diego Cao discovered the mouth of the Congo. He could hardly avoid it. Thirty miles out at sea the sludge emitted by one of the world's mightiest rivers stained the immaculate blue of the Atlantic a deep cocoa-brown.

Diego built a marble pillar on the southerly bluff, called with grisly justification Shark's Point. Seven miles away across the river mouth, a long fat yellow bank of sand, six feet high and liable to flooding, was called without any justification whatsoever – for no bananas have ever grown there – Banana Point.

During the following three hundred years, a succession of tiny outposts at the mouth of the river traded in slaves and ivory. But generally the great African bight and southern coastline between latitude ten degrees north and ten degrees south, continued to live up to its generic name: the white man's grave.

In 1816, the British Admiralty, unsure whether the Niger and the Congo were one and the same river, despatched Captain J. K. Tuckey R.N. in command of a well-equipped expedition to resolve this matter. Captain Tuckey penetrated less than a hundred miles up-river to Isangila just past the first rapids. There he, and sixteen other ranks, died very quickly of fever. They were speedily buried and with equal haste the expedition turned back towards the healthy ocean.

The first heartbreaking topographical obstacle to any exploration of the hinterland is revealed not far above Matadi. From the smooth and enormous reaches of Stanley Pool two hundred and fifty miles up-river – overlooked these days by the modern city of Kinshasa – seven foaming cataracts fall half a mile in height over a comparatively short distance. The seventh and last cataract, the first encountered coming in from the sea – there are also some thirty rapids – is the most dramatic. The natural terrain compresses three thousand miles of river draining the equatorial basin of Central Africa into a channel eight hundred yards across, most of which is occupied by a large island. The right-hand outlet is thirty yards wide and the roaring torrent emerges leaping and foaming like the freshly-severed carotid artery of the African giant.

The three European expeditions which emulated the ill-fated Captain Tuckey did not penetrate far enough to witness this spectacle. The combined deterrent of terrain, of insect-borne disease, plus that danger of cannibalism emphasised by the determined missionary Livingstone, who died exploring the headwaters of the Congo, and declared with dour Scottish candour that he had no wish to become 'black man's pot', reinforced the theory that there was no way in along this waterway.

Indeed long after the Americas, Asia, Australia, the oceans and islands of the world had been colonised or conquered, Congo sweating under its equatorial sun, drenched by its tropical rain, remained inviolate.

It was not until 1876 that H. M. Stanley, on foot, starting from Zanzibar on the east coast crossed the great central mountain barrier. He came down from the high grasslands into the unbelievable tangle of jungle, swamp and river. It was one of the epic journeys in man's long history of exploration and a stone set in the roadside a few miles away from Helen Roseveare's present medical school at Nyankunde, records that he set up camp there before beginning the descent into the rain forest, to follow for sixteen hundred miles the twisting river and so reach the place marked by the grave of Captain J. K. Tuckey.

The drama of Helen's first entry into Congo in 1953 was heightened by the first call upon her as a doctor.

At the border Jack Scholes, Jim Grainger, and two Africans were waiting to meet her with a two-ton truck and a three-quarter-ton pick-up. She helped to load her luggage and the supplies with which she had been entrusted and climbed into the cab.

The heavy tyres skidded on the gravel road as they toiled up the escarpment and it was dark when they reached the mission station at Nyankunde, a place which was to figure dramatically later in Helen's life, but was at that moment merely a cluster of huts and houses perched three thousand feet up in the high grasslands which slope down towards the vast rain forest.

They rested for the week-end and Helen was a little disappointed at the Englishness of it all. There was a tennis court and she played tennis; there was a sort of musical evening and she was asked to play the violin which she had brought with her.

Obediently scraping away the performance was interrupted by the news that a doctor was needed in the nearby village. The doctor at Nyankunde was away on leave; could Helen attend the case?

With an older missionary she climbed back into the truck and with headlights blazing they bumped along a winding track deep into the bush. They stopped near the village and Helen stepped out immediately aware of the enormity of the star-filled African sky, the fire-flies, the sense of loneliness and the high pitched monotonous shrieking coming from the cluster of conical huts dimly seen in the darkness.

The missionary said quietly, 'I think we're too late. That's the sound of the death wailing.'

There was no light in the village, and only a smoky fire in the hut which made Helen's eyes smart and water. On the earth floor lay the thin, emaciated body of the chief already stiffening in death, and around him half a dozen women, his wives, naked and keening their grief, already aware of what Helen was able to confirm by a cursory examination.

On the way back to Nyankunde, the missionary sensed her bewilderment and asked, 'Bit more primitive than you expected?'

'Yes,' Helen answered. To her it was a confused, barbaric experience in which she seemed to have no place or usefulness of any sort.

'You'll get used to it,' he said. 'Don't worry.'

Her arrival at Ibambi was far more reassuring. The truck braked to a halt under a wide banner of red bunting stretched across the road between two palm trees with the words 'Welcome to Ibambi' picked out in cotton wool upon it. An old man whom later she came to know very well and love, stepped forward to say with much emotion, 'We welcome you our child into our midst.'

Pastor Ndugu was grey, gentle and kind. He had started his Christian career as houseboy to the famous C. T. Studd who had first reached this part of Africa in 1913 and who, indeed, was responsible for the primary conception of the Worldwide Evangelization Crusade.

Charles Thomas Studd, English gentleman, famous cricketer, captain of Eton, and Cambridge University, hero of historic test matches against Australia, had been inspired by the American evangelists Sankey and Moody. In 1885 his announcement that he was giving away his inheritance, abandoning his mode of living and obeying the divine instruction, 'Go thy way, sell that thou hast and give to the poor . . . take up thy cross and follow Me,' had been received with consternation and disbelief by the British public.

He spent twenty-five pioneering years in China and India before returning to England. He did not intend to rest. Over fifty, in poor health, and with almost no money he set off for Equatorial Africa. Reaching the village of Nala, confirmation of Livingstone's reports that cannibalism was widespread was quickly available. Ten years prior to Studd's arrival the first white man ever to be seen, accompanied by thirty-five African soldiers, had entered the village. His declared intention: to subdue and control their district. Told to go away he refused. That night his force were surprised, overwhelmed, slaughtered, and with all the ceremony appropriate to such a rare occasion, eaten.

Studd trekked on through cannibal country penetrating deep into the Ituri forest to the kraal where the great chief Ibambi held omnipotent power. There, in a bamboo hut, Charles Studd, English cricketer and Christian gentleman, pioneered what he at first called the 'Heart of Africa Mission'. He worked tirelessly until his death in 1931 leaving behind instructions that his body should be buried in the forest in the green place where he had laboured so long and so hard for God.

Twenty-eight years old and apple-green, on her first arrival in Ibambi, uneasily aware that there was much more to becoming a doctor in Africa than the mere entitlement to a Cambridge University Medical Degree provided, Helen felt her feet very small to follow in such indomitable footsteps. But as she listened to Pastor Ndugu's welcome she felt the tears sting her eyes, and the response to her carefully rehearsed sentence in Swahili, 'I have great joy to be here amongst you,' was an immediate and spontaneous eruption of hugging, kissing, cheering and singing. She had never in her whole life experienced such an overwhelming emotional reaction. She came from a background where feelings were sublimated, ladylike, channelled into safe, calm reaches. In Ibambi she found that love and affection were treated as a normal part of the human relationship. And later, examining her own motives, she discovered that not only could she reciprocate, but enjoy an intimacy with her patients and parishioners which was inconceivable in a British society.

Next day in the large bare room which Jack Scholes had set aside for her work, the women and children had crowded in, all come to greet their *own* lady doctor who had come from so far away across the mountains. They had smiled at her, touched her and occasionally indicated a mysterious ache or pain. Indeed, in those first few weeks, with no drugs and no Swahili, if her patients rubbed their heads she gave them aspirin, and if they rubbed their stomachs she gave them Epsom salts. Nevertheless, at the end of that first day utterly exhausted with trying to cope, she was filled with an enormous exaltation. Christ had said, 'Go ye into all the world and preach the gospel to every creature.' She could preach, she could heal, and she knew intuitively that God had guided her to this special destiny.

II

When Helen arrived at Ibambi in 1953 the two people most
intimately concerned with her work and future were station
leader Jack Scholes and his wife Jessie, and they watched her
progress with a solicitous, kindly and sometimes wry smile.

'We loved her because we knew her,' Jack always said. 'She
lived with us for almost three years from the time she first came
out. And what a worker, a real worker. But she can't drag
everybody after her at her speed. You can't keep pace. You're
walking stride for stride and suddenly she's a hundred yards
ahead. And just when you're catching up she's off two hundred
yards in another direction.'

Jack, of medium height, hair already turning white was a con-
templative Lancashire man of farming build. A man whose
eyes were shrewd and watchful, who thought before he spoke.
A man of silences. He helped young Helen set up her dispensary
at Ibambi and before the year was out he was listening to her
plans to reform not only the enormous country of Congo, but as
far as he could make out the entire African continent from Cape
to Cairo. Few people outside Livingstone, Cecil Rhodes and
Zulu Chief Cetewayo could ever have approached Africa with
such all-consuming zeal.

When Helen discovered God, the idea of becoming a medical
missionary slipped naturally into her mind. Her affinity with
W.E.C., still known as the Heart of Africa Mission when she
first arrived in Congo, also fitted into her pattern of Christian
endeavour. Nine a.m. to five p.m. missionaries were not part of
the Worldwide Evangelization Crusade's thinking. You had a
vocation or you had nothing. They said: 'If you've got a vision

go and do it, but we're not interested in mere visionaries. You can expect hard, endless work. You'll go into the field with practically no salary and we'll expect you to live alongside the nationals of that country.'

Americans, Australians, British, Swedes, Swiss, half a dozen nationalities worked side-by-side in world-scattered projects. They recruited their members not only from the professional and university levels but mainly from working and middle-class people. They asked for devout belief. They asked for volunteers who were prepared to devote their lives to hard work in remote outposts without praise, attention, or reward. Their allowances were meagre. They paid their own fares if they had any money.

There were missions already established in the Congo they said, a Christian church, schools of many varieties but, in the province they suggested for her, W.E.C. ran no medical services. She would work under enormous disadvantages but the need for a doctor was desperate. That was enough for Helen. Congo sounded wild, challenging, far away, and there was a need which should fill her own emptiness.

At Ibambi looking round her empty room containing a tea chest, a camp bed, a camp chair she realised they had not exaggerated the difficulties.

Jack Scholes also pointed out with dour north-country candour, that if, as a young lady doctor, she thought her university education, medical degree or excellence of her church work conferred any sort of preference or favour upon her, or was going to make her a good missionary, then 'she'd better have another think coming.'

Humbly, Helen agreed with this diagnosis. She swiftly realised that you had to make a fundamental assessment about your *use* as a missionary, your *right* to be a missionary. You had to rationalise your impertinence at living in someone else's country and trying to alter their habits by shattering their beliefs in the old gods of sun, wind, rain, and the black spirits which whispered in the dark corners of their minds.

Jack came from the older school of missionaries. He'd been accepted for training at a missionary college in 1921. In 1922, with the aeroplane routes still waiting to be flown by their pioneer aviators, he left by tramp steamer from Liverpool for Alexandria. He travelled through Africa by river boat, lake steamer, and a steam train which plugged slowly over never-ending steel rails. Across deserts, plains and jungles he went, secure inheritor of that Livingstone legacy of belief that Christianity and commerce must push in side by side to bring God and civilisation to the barbaric inhabitants of the unknown African continent.

Two final days in a vintage car over a road which bore some resemblance to an elephant track took him and his two companions to the north-eastern corner of Congo. And that was it. The great tropical rain forest began. There were no more roads. You walked.

Long lines of African porters carried your boxes and bales on their heads; you smelt animals at night, listened to the chatter of monkeys by day. This was a country of heat, flies, dark rivers, suspicion, tribalism and witchcraft.

The Belgian District Officer gave them every help. He recruited the seventy porters necessary to ferry the three white men and their luggage to their destination. Every fifteen miles or so a rest-house had been established. It was a three-day journey to Faradje, another six days to Dungu. Then six more to Nala, and the first of the Heart of Africa Missions. Jack stayed there, the other two pressed on to Ibambi. Time had ceased to become important or precious. It stretched from sun up, to moonrise. It stretched through the cool night and the long hot day. It had a slowness, a cadence, and a rhythm which was full and satisfying.

Jessie left Blackpool on the 24th November, 1924, journeying by sea to Kinshasa – since then renamed Léopoldville and now Kinshasa again – which lay above the great rapids two hundred miles from the mouth of the Congo. It was then a small European outpost with a very flourishing mortality rate. She waited for three weeks for the up-river boat to take her to Stanleyville. She arrived in Ibambi on March 7th, a journey which had taken her three months and thirteen days. She had been engaged to Jack back home, and they were married in the following January.

There was something very rare and splendid about those early days of evangelical work in this almost untouched, and certainly unknown corner of Africa. There were no motor roads. You moved at the speed of your own two feet.

Even when Helen first arrived in 1953 it was still primitive to a degree paralleled only perhaps by the Garden of Eden, although there were of course all manner of 'serpents'. Diseases of every variety were borne by animal, insect, water and food. Biblical diseases such as leprosy were everywhere; tropical diseases such as elephantiais, yaws, hookworm, ulcers, malaria, yellow and black-water fever were commonplace. There were crocodiles in the rivers, snakes and leopards in the forest. Elephants could trample your crops, and locusts devour what was left of them.

Driver ants could arrive at your gates – as they did once at Helen's – in a wide, dark, endlessly-flowing river. With their bite they would kill every living thing which did not move out of their path: chickens in their coops, goats in their pens.

In the tropical rain forest there was a species of red fly, the chrysops, which stung like a horsefly, and every morning Helen would see several in her classroom. Its bite implanted in one's tissues larvae which developed into tiny hair-like white worms called filaria. These infested your body for most of your life. They crawled about inside you, often surfacing just under the skin like adventurous submarines so that you could observe their slow progress across your hand or arm. When they crawled across an eyeball or the lobe of an ear it was quite painful.

Getting rid of these parasites was a difficult job.

Helen tried the cure twice on successive home leaves. Both times she found its effects worse than the worms and did not take a third course of treatment.

Her patients from the rain forest were invariably original. Her first pygmy patient had been a pure delight: a ten-year-old boy, miniature but proportioned perfectly, with smooth, shining skin, and darting inquisitive eyes. He had broken his thigh, and in her mud and thatch hospital at Ibambi she'd reset it under local anaesthetic, building with the help of the carpenter a highly effective – if surrealistic-looking – trapeze of blocks and pulleys which kept the leg stretched and the bone correctly in place.

To the primitive eye, however, it must have looked too dramatic, for when she returned from lunch she found her pygmy patient gone. 'But what happened?' she demanded exasperatedly of the apologetic ward orderly.

It appeared that the boy's father, not much bigger than his own son, had suddenly arrived in the ward looking like a small startled fawn wandering through Piccadilly Circus. He had examined Helen's superb traction apparatus with terrified eyes.

'But was he frightened by the apparatus, or did he think we had already cured the boy?' demanded Helen.

'I'm not quite certain doctor, but I just couldn't stop him.' Father had unhitched Helen's contraption, gathered his son into his arms and carried him back into the forest never to be seen again.

As doctor to a parish covering several hundred square miles of territory Helen's cases were often of rare medical interest, their treatment highly unlikely to be found in any textbook.

On one early occasion a group of Africans carried in a man slung in a blanket between two poles.

'What's the matter with him?' Helen asked. The eldest African explained. 'There was a quarrel,' he said. 'A spear was thrown.'

'It struck him?' inquired Helen.

'Oh yes, it went in through his back and came out through the front of his stomach. It stuck out at least two feet.'

'So what did you do?'

'We pulled it out the other side.'

Helen said, 'I see,'

'What else could we have done?' It was a good question. Helen didn't know.

'We have brought it with us to show you.' As if it might be of some medical interest one of the pole-bearers stepped forward holding out the spear. It was a vicious-looking weapon nearly six feet long with a thin, pointed blade. He held it out hopefully as though its exhibition might aid her diagnosis. She touched the point gingerly. It was very sharp.

There was no possibility of Helen operating. The thought of trying to trace, repair, and antisepticise the track of a spear wound through the middle of a man's body gave her the shudders.

She dressed and bandaged the entrance and exit wound and put the victim to bed. Less than a week later he got up and walked home. In many ways the people of the rain forest were a hardy race.

By the end of her first week at Ibambi not less than one

hundred and fifty patients a day were pouring in with terrible ulcers, running eyes, septic wounds, earaches, abscesses – the bewildering range of afflictions never ceased to astound her. On her very first afternoon she had to pull out two teeth without any anaesthetic.

Returning from Wamba one day a party of villagers had waved her down. She was a doctor, they declared, and they needed a doctor immediately. How they knew her identity Helen never discovered but she'd protested in her painstaking Swahili, 'I've been shopping in Wamba. I've no medicines, no drugs, no instruments, not even a thermometer.'

Their spokesman had brushed aside the excuses. 'You are the doctor. Our village elder is dying.'

'I'm sorry,' said Helen and spread her hands. 'But I have no instruments, no drugs.'

'You are a doctor.' That was enough for them and their voices were softly imploring.

Helen made one last effort. 'Listen, I'll come back as soon as I get my equipment from my dispensary.'

'He will die before that. You must come. Please come.'

There was no alternative so she'd trudged for more than an hour deep into the dripping forest along overgrown trails, half dreading what she could find: the last stages of T.B. perhaps, an inoperable cancer, a strangulated hernia? What could she do then?

By the time they reached a clearing amongst thatched huts and she saw the silent crowd gathered round the fire it was almost dark. Before the fire an old man twisted and turned in delirium. She touched his forehead. It was fever-hot. Nervously she looked round at the orange firelight flickering over dark, absorbed faces. They were all strangers and it was a long way back to the road and the car. Supposing the old man died while she was trying to help? What would they do? She pushed the thought abruptly out of her mind and examined the feverish emaciated body. To her relief the source of his illness was immediately obvious. An enormous inguinal abscess. Immediate medical aid was necessary even though it had to be of the Girl Guide, instant first-aid variety. This time her patient wasn't a small girl pretending she'd broken her arm, but an old man on the verge of death. Helen had no instruments, no instruments at all; that was the crux of her dilemma; the abscess had to be lanced.

Then she saw the small group of pygmies who, in their strange intuitive manner, had somehow scented drama and drifted into the clearing to watch. Tiny, lithe figures, naked except for loincloths, skins shining as if made of dark chocolate, utterly still, they clutched their bows and bundles of arrows, their eyes wide and fascinated.

Helen nodded at the pot bubbling on the fire and said: 'I'll need that boiling water,' She walked across to the pygmies. Even at five foot three she towered above them and they drew back nervously. She smiled reassuringly, reached forward and touched an iron-tipped arrow belonging to the nearest man indicating that she wanted to borrow it.

With a quick darting look he handed it over. She walked back to the fire, lifted her skirt, tore off several strips of petticoat, and dropped them into the boiling water. She thrust the iron arrow head into the flame. It began to glow red hot and she heard the speculative murmurs of her audience increase. They hushed as she approached the old man. She motioned to two of his friends to hold him steady, then deliberately she stabbed the arrowhead deep into the festering swelling. A torrent of pus emerged. The hiss from the crowd sounded like a bicycle tyre bursting. She used the boiled strips of underskirt to clean the wound, drained and plugged the hole, and with more strips of petticoat bound up the abscess leaving instructions as to how it should be treated until she returned.

Rarely can a doctor have enjoyed such a swift, total, and remarkable victory. With a few moans and groans the patient changed from a delirious, dying old man into a weak but quite coherent human being. By the time she had returned the arrow to its owner and rinsed her hands his temperature had plummeted. Before she left he was talking softly but clearly to his audience.

The walk back to the car was slow and tiresome. But she was conscious of an intense feeling of relief and triumph. The British Medical Association might not have awarded her treatment unstinted praise but she hoped they would have understood its necessity. Thank God it had been effective. So often over the years in Congo she did all she could for her patients, but realised so often, that when their lives hung in the balance God had to decide the final issue, not she.

The young African boy had stood uncertainly before her, his eyes wary, his face buttoned up to hide his nervousness. His clothes were clean but well-worn, and generally he gave Helen the impression of a school truant suddenly surprised by the headmaster. Six months at Ibambi however, had blunted Helen's capacity for surprise.

'God has sent me to see you,' he said. It was at least an original and promising start.

'I'm glad.'

'My name is John Mangadima. I am a Christian.'

He intrigued Helen with his determination that the interview should proceed logically and at his own pace. 'How old are you?' she asked.

'Sixteen.'

'I see. And what can I do for you?'

'You are a doctor?'

'Yes.'

'Will you teach me to be a doctor?'

'Is that what you came for?' She was taken aback.

'Yes.'

She wondered how she could explain in her rapidly improving Swahili how long and complex a task it was to become a doctor. First of all there was the necessity for vocation or calling. On reflection, considering the way she had entered medicine, she decided not to labour this point. But she could explain that even becoming a trained male nurse took quite a long time.

He was, however, one step ahead of her.

'I have already worked for one year at the Belgian Red Cross Hospital at Pawa,' he announced abruptly.

'Oh, have you?' said Helen surprised. The hospital lay fourteen miles to the north of Ibambi, and as part of her government medical education to fit her for work in Congo Helen had spent a month there shortly after her arrival, cycling backwards and forwards each day. Mainly she had worked under Dr Kadoner, a fine doctor of the old school who had spent twenty-five years in the Belgian Colonial medical service. Helen admired him greatly. He taught her much surgery in twelve

[94]

hectic days, performing a daily average of two hysterectomies, eight herniorrhaphies and several other minor operations between 7 a.m. and two o'clock in the afternoon. She also became acquainted with the tropical diseases endemic to their area, studying the diagnosis, treatment and laboratory tests connected with them. She also met Dr Swertz.

Dr Swertz was younger than Helen, short, square and dark, his gaze direct and hostile. He was a capable leprologue and laboratory pathologist, under whom she was expected to spend two weeks instruction. Dr Swertz plainly did not like women, and in particular women *Doctors,* and as he never uttered one single word to Helen – preferring a monosyllabic grunt – during her stay, the period was non-productive.

Helen looked at young John Mangadima with new interest. 'Why did you leave?' she inquired.

He said simply, 'I reprimanded one of the Belgian doctors.'

It did not seem to have occurred to him that for an African to reprimand a white doctor working for the Belgian Colonial regime was roughly equivalent to anarchy.

Helen carefully replaced a roll of cotton wool in the drawer, and screwed the top back on her fountain pen.

'I see,' she said thoughtfully, '*You* reprimanded one of the Belgian doctors.'

'Yes.'

Helen had no doubt at all which doctor he had reprimanded. Dr Swertz always considered a swift kick in the backside or a clout across the head to be routine and necessary disciplinary procedure with any African staff, patients, or students who happened to get in his way.

'What had the doctor done?'

'He kicked a leprosy patient.'

'What did he do after you reprimanded him?'

'He struck me across the face.'

'What did you do?'

'I turned the other cheek.'

'Very Christian,' said Helen. 'What did he do then?'

'He struck me across the face again.' Helen nodded understandingly. 'I thought he might,' she said.

'Then he kicked me out of the hospital.'

'So you came here?'

'Yes.'

Helen knew there was no point in trying to take the matter further; kicking Africans was currently acceptable in Congo. Some of the doctors were good and conscientious men, and she understood their practical difficulties. There was never time for the kindly advice, the good-natured suggestion. A slap across the face often merely indicated that the African concerned had transgressed and must do better next time. Certainly from watching Dr Kadoner she knew he always had ten times too much to do. They were vastly overworked and incredibly understaffed; demand always outstripped the bounds of human time, strength or patience. She'd cycled past a queue of Africans half a mile long the first morning she arrived at Pawa hospital; she cycled past a queue of the same length on her last morning. And whilst she could never approve or subscribe to physical abuse of Africans she understood how it could happen.

She had learned many things in those early months – not all of them palatable or creditable.

While she was under training at Pawa an old man from Ibambi, a good church worker and a respected elder, arrived for an operation escorted by his two teenage grand-daughters, both pretty girls. He was not operated upon, but sulphonamide pills were prescribed every four hours. When the local male nurses arrived at 6 p.m. for night duty they took one look at the pretty grand-daughters and gave the old man an ultimatum. No pills unless the grand-daughters spent the night with them. Indignantly the old man refused the trade and sent the girls away. Because they all came from Ibambi Helen was informed of this occurrence, and she confronted Dr Kadoner with her disapproval. He shrugged non-committally, his face expressionless, his interest minimal. It was obvious that he considered the retention of his trained male nurses to be more important and of greater good than the virginity of two local girls. 'After all, this is Africa,' he remarked, and took no action.

The fact that the old man died the following morning increased Helen's feeling of bitter injustice and started a sequence of events which was to concern her for the next twenty years.

Her relationship with Jack and Jessie Scholes was strengthened in those first months when Jessie fell dangerously ill. For week after week Jack and Helen nursed her as cerebral

Helen Roseveare revisiting the convent at Wamba where she was for weeks a captive of the Simbas

In a remote village Helen instructs a group of women in hygiene and maternity welfare

Nuns being rescued by
mercenaries
photo: Camera Press

Two mercenaries rescuing an
injured child
photo: Camera Press

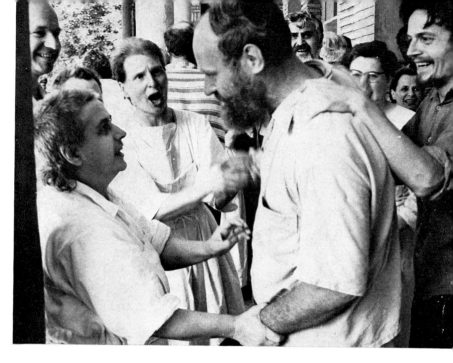

The joy of deliverance as nuns, priests and civilians are rescued
photo: Camera Press

A rescued priest and companion journeying to freedom
photo: Camera Press

The moment of deliverance:
Dr Roseveare with Lieutenant
Joe Wepener of 54 Commando.
Helen left immediately on a
plane with this Polaroid print.
Wepener was killed shortly
afterwards

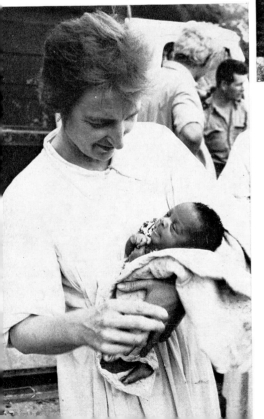

In the midst of turmoil a nun
cares for an abandoned child
photo: Camera Press

malaria turned to blackwater fever and her life hung in the balance. When she eventually recovered, the friendship – a love as deep and true as a mother, father, daughter relationship – between the three of them was firmly established.

But those long night hours she spent at Jessie's bedside also demonstrated to her how greatly needed were trained nurses in Congo and how little she knew about that skilled profession.

She knew already from her visits to other isolated Protestant mission stations scattered about the province that a clinic, a dispensary and one trained African could be a godsend. Now here was a boy called John Mangadima . . .

'Where do you come from?'

'The rain forest. I was born in a village deep in the forest. We were very poor.'

Helen could imagine it. She had already seen many such places: huts of mud and straw thatch; you worked in the cleared land from sun-up until darkness, you ate enough food of a sort; the chief and the witch-doctor ruled your life. You never earned enough money to buy even a single cow so the purchase of a wife was always beyond your reach. You were born, existed and died in the rain forest as oblivious to life and the outside world as a worker ant in a rotted tree stump.

'Parents?' asked Helen.

'My mother and father are lepers. They had to leave the village and go to a leprosy camp.'

'I see,' said Helen, accepting that piece of news as calmly as she thought she was expected to accept it. 'Now to be working as a student nurse in Pawa means you must have had some education?'

'Yes,' said John Mangadima. 'But not enough.' He explained this in detail, neither glossing over nor adding to his background. By Western standards his education was rudimentary: about equal to that of a British eleven-year-old. But he had done a year as a student nurse. Surely that made a difference. He looked at her appealingly.

'I will work very hard, do all you instruct me to do.'

The large brown eyes in the earnest face were filled with perplexity and anxiety. The voice quavered. He had failed through his sense of Christian justice at Pawa. This might be his last chance.

Helen made one of her normal and quick intuitive decisions. 'All right John. If you're willing to work, I'm willing to teach you. It's a bargain.'

She knew at that moment that John Mangadima's appeal was the catalyst to her own need. His spirit and determination matched her own exactly. 'Teach me,' he had pleaded, and by heaven she was going to teach him! She was going to teach the Africans to run their own medical services so that no one in the world would have the right to hit them in the face because they did not understand.

The arrival of John Mangadima in Helen's life was momentous in its far-reaching consequences. It completely altered her vision of what she was going to do in Africa.

From an early age she had suspected that the world inhabited and organised by men was one which in her opinion could do with a great deal of alteration. If marriage and dependence were a natural commitment of life, and all she was going to get was Jeremy worrying about the mortgage on the semi-detached, or Richard dashing off to catch the 8.10 to town every morning, then *those* prospects didn't really excite her very much. Far better for all concerned, she decided, if she used her female intelligence and talents to chart a life of her own.

Nothing inspired her about entering the medical profession. There was a reasonable proportion of reverend gentlemen – bishops and missionaries – hanging on the family tree, but not many doctors. One fact, however, which undoubtedly influenced her, was that at the end of the war an emergency measure existed enabling medical students to compress a nine-term university course into two years. Besides, what else was there to do? As a university graduate she seemed to have a choice between doctoring and school-teaching. Telling your friends that you were going to be a doctor sounded the superior of the two; most people raised an eyebrow with interest and performed a little mental genuflexion at the idea.

So she became a doctor, but it was young John Mangadima who influenced her change of direction. From the very first at Ibambi she was determined to remove all language barriers between herself and her patients and was already studying Swahili with a fanaticism worthy of a Marxist disciple. Now, with John to coach her she quickly became fluent; within months she lived and dreamt in the language, and later passed a proficiency test to her own satisfaction when, after a severe bout of fever she was told she had raved in Swahili for two days.

Ibambi provided Helen with her first experience of being doctor in charge. At the beginning in the empty room where she did her work – the crowd of patients waited out on the veranda – she used assembly-line techniques: all the 'coughs' in this line, the 'headaches' in that, the 'ulcers' here, the 'unknowns' over against the wall. Then she'd check the 'coughs' to see if there was any pneumonia, treat those that showed any symptoms and ladle cough mixture into the others.

She kept her case histories on pieces of paper torn from an old exercise book, and for those first few months she had no help from either European or African.

It quickly became clear that if she was going to make any impact upon the medical scene she had to have besides patients, a hospital with wards and nurses. With John Mangadima's arrival the need to teach and train became paramount.

Building the hospital was probably the simplest part of her programme. There were many skilled and willing workers amongst the African Christians at Ibambi, and within a few months they had built two large mud buildings with thatched roofs and shuttered windows, the walls whitewashed, each filled with wooden beds. She now found herself in possession of a twenty-four-bed ward for women, an eight-bed-ward for men, and various small rooms for maternity, minor surgery and special cases. They were filled almost overnight.

With difficulty Helen recruited seven other boys to train with John Mangadima; the idea of training female nurses at that time was completely impracticable; very few girls had any education at all. Half of the boys were educated to the standard of English eleven-year-olds, the others to that of eight-year-olds. On the credit side however, they had a specialised knowledge and awareness unknown to the Western child: they knew about agriculture, forest craft, about birth and life and death.

On the debit side they had no notion of science, not even a primary conception; they or their parents had never thought in a scientific or logical manner at all, and after those first few lessons she wondered if she would ever be able to overcome this daunting disability.

When on that very first occasion she stood up in front of her class looking down at the eight shining, expectant faces she had no conception of the troubles which lay ahead. She held up a thermometer. 'Now,' she asked, 'what is this?'

The faces remained clear and untroubled. Only John Mangadima knew.

'This thermometer,' she went on, 'has a Fahrenheit scale so we have to turn it into a centigrade scale.'

She paused, realising that if she had spoken in Sanskrit or Mandarin Chinese she would have stood just as good a chance of being understood.

Seven blank faces stared at her. To conceal her slight confusion she turned to the blackboard, drew a picture of the thermometer and began to mark off the readings at the side: 98.2, 98.4, 98.6.

One of the boys inquired very politely:

'Excuse me madam, what are those little dots between the figures for?'

Helen put down her chalk and sighed. It looked as if she was going to have to preface her medical course with a short foundation in mathematics.

'You don't know what a decimal point is?'

'No madam.'

'Do you know your twice-times table? Twice one are two, twice two are four . . .?'

'No madam.'

Helen put the thermometer back on the table. She was certainly going to have to start with mathematics.

They spent hours, days, weeks – sometimes to Helen it felt like light- years – on the thermometer.

'Inside this glass tube is a metal which expands.'

In Swahili she couldn't translate metal. 'John,' she asked, 'what's metal in Swahili?'

'There is no such word as metal in Swahili,' he answered politely.

She found a small metal ring and a metal ball. She demonstrated that the metal ball would not go through the ring. They tried pushing. It would not go through. She boiled the metal ring and showed that now the ball went through quite easily. Metal expanded when it got hot. 'Here, hold it and see.'

They exclaimed, 'Ouch!' and dropped it. 'Now do you understand? That's 'metal', and that's 'hot', and when it's *hot* it expands and we can get this *cold* metal ball through it. 'Expands' means it gets bigger. Now that drop of metal in the thermometer which we call mercury gets hot when you put the thermometer under the arm of someone who's got a fever. It has nowhere else to go upward, except *up* the ladder. It walks up the ladder.'

The whole thing was rough, the whole thing was elementary but she knew you could not teach eight boys – and they shrank to five fairly quickly when faced with the exigencies of education – such subjects without many rudimentary simplifications. Yet she was going to teach them, come what may. And in teaching them, to her astonishment, to her joy, to her great excitement she broke through into new regions, new worlds, new experiences she did not dream existed inside her own heart and brain.

For the first time in her life she understood why she had sat as far away as possible from the surgeon in the operating theatre, kept her eyes closed as long as possible when he did 'the nasty bits'. She hated being a doctor; she knew that having committed herself she had no alternative, and she steeled herself to the thought that for the rest of her life she would have to go on being a doctor. But she was not going to like it.

Medicine involved her emotionally. Watching people suffer through sickness or injury worried and upset her. She would become so involved she could not sleep. When a patient died in hospital she grieved as though it was a close relative. She realised it was a terrible weakness; she knew she had to be detached clinical, aloof, but she also knew she would never be able to train her heart to adopt this attitude.

She discovered teaching as a young girl discovers her first love. She was no longer hesitant, nervous and afraid as she was in medicine; she soared over the obstacles like a top-flight steeplechaser. All right, if the boys could not think in a logical Western way, they certainly thought in a logical African way, so she would find out how to use their logic and harness that to her teaching methods. She had come to Africa with no 'vision' of teaching in her blood, yet if she considered the subject the 'teaching gene' was spread liberally through generations of her family; her own father had been a teacher.

Teaching obsessed her. She began to feel that there was nothing she could not teach; she became convinced that *anybody* could learn *anything* if the teacher could teach, and suddenly her life and outlook achieved a direction, an impetus and a fulfilment she had never expected.

In those early months of schooling she had one stroke of great good fortune. She had started with only a Red Cross First-Aid and a Home Nursing Guide as textbooks. Then one of W.E.C's outstanding senior missionaries Arthur Scott returning from leave heard of her plans. He had been trained in Belgium; his notes for training African health-workers had entailed years of sweat, toil and patient observation. Now, with love and good wishes he passed them all over to Helen. A goldmine! She knew she would never be able to thank him enough.

She based her teaching on his notes; through the years she added to them, built them up, subtracted from them. Nothing as valuable to her teaching curriculum was ever offered to Helen than Arthur Scott's unselfish gift.

She found that her own method of teaching obtained through practically every one of the twenty-four hours, and sometimes her methods of necessity were primitive.

She would march through a ward trailing students in her wake and stop by a bedside.

'This patient,' she would announce, 'has pneumonia. How do I know she has pneumonia?'

Five pairs of eyes were mystified. No voice answered.

She draped her stethoscope round John Mangadima's neck and told him to plug in. She placed the end of the stethoscope against the patient's chest.

'You hear that noise? You can hear its rhythm, its depth?'

'Yes, madam.'

'Right, now put it against your own chest.'

John Mangadima did as he was told.

'There is a difference?'

'Yes, madam.'

'Now put it against Yokana's chest. See if the noise is different or the same as your own?'

John's eyes opened respectfully as he listened. 'It is the same as mine.'

'Right, now listen to the chests of these next three patients and tell me if you think any of them have pneumonia.'

John did as instructed and selected the third. 'This one has pneumonia.'

'Correct,' Helen confirmed triumphantly.

It was basic, it was rough, it might seem crackpot, but it worked.

'Listen,' she said. 'You are going to learn about the ten basic diseases in this part of Africa. You are going to learn how to recognise them and learn what to do about them and how to treat them. Now, let's start with malaria . . .'

In Congo there were always thousands of people with malaria in various forms. She showed them how you pricked the finger of a patient and took a drop of blood on a microscope slide; how you smeared it round and let it dry; how you used the little bottles of stain, and how you slid the tiny pane of glass under a microscope. There, through the magnifying lens, you saw the evidence you were looking for; the type of malaria the patient had which confirmed or disproved your diagnosis. She taught them how to stain slides and to do ten basic laboratory procedures: how to bandage, take a temperature, give an enema and injections, how to recognise bacillary dysentery, intestinal worms, tuberculosis and pneumonia, how to treat wounds old and new, tropical ulcers, yaws and syphilis.

Her immediate aim was simple. To become accepted as a trained male nurse in Belgian Colonial Congo you had to have a diploma issued by the Government which gave you the title of Aid Nurse. The examinations were held once a year in the Red Cross Hospital at Pawa.

In October, eighteen months after she started the school, the day arrived for the great test for which she had prepared her pupils. Shortly after sun-up she piled five taut and nervous youths into the back of her Chevrolet truck and set off for the town. She had secured freshly pressed khaki shorts and shirts for all of them, and they looked very presentable. There was practically no talking on the drive through the lush tropical forest for Helen was far too busy praying for divine support to make polite conversation.

She parked at the back of the hospital and led her posse inside. The doorman was uninterested.

Examinations? What examinations? This was a hospital not a school house. It took half an hour to sort that out. Yes, the examinations were going to be held in the laboratory at the back of the hospital. A government doctor was driving specially from Wamba for the event. Would they please assemble in the lab.

Waiting in the ante-room next to the laboratory were twelve other students trained by the Red Cross hospital. They looked at Helen's class with contempt. Didn't the boys from Ibambi speak any French? No? How ridiculously gauche and primitive. So Helen's five only spoke Swahili? Indeed! How quaint! It meant they were obviously jungle boys. The arrogant twelve did not inquire what she – a peculiar white female – was doing with such youths: *that* defied imagination. They thought themselves very grand; they laughed, they chatted gaily in French, and Helen could almost hear the confidence seeping out of her pupils like air from a slow puncture. She wished she could have struck up a slightly militant hymn to aid morale but as it was a Catholic hospital she decided such a course would not help their chances.

Helen was allowed into the examination room with each of her pupils to help with necessary translations; and once work started her pride began to grow. The examination was entirely oral and she saw at once that the hospital-trained students were parrots, making glib rehearsed answers to set questions, utterly lost when a different or subsidiary question was asked.

John and Yokana and the others listened when it was their turn, they considered each question; their answers revealed that they *knew* what they were talking about and were *thinking* before they spoke.

When the examinations ended Helen sat in the ante-room her nails digging like small knives into her palms, and she would have been quite unaware if her hands had been dripping blood.

The examining doctor cleared his throat. 'First with ninety-five per cent is Yokana from Ibambi . . .'

No mother has ever felt more pride than Helen at that moment. She took off her glasses and polished them industriously to remove the dampness which had settled on them.

The doctor's voice droned on. John Mangadima was third with eighty-five per cent. Two of the others had passed with high marks. The fifth was put back until next year.

Four out of five had succeeded magnificently; the first male student nurses to be trained at Ibambi.

Had a military band headed their journey back to Ibambi, Helen would have thought it perfectly natural. As it was, the drive back was as glorious as any in Helen's whole life. They cheered, they sang, they chattered incessantly, and when they got back to Ibambi to Helen's intense disappointment and disillusionment, no one was the slightest bit impressed.

Helen wanted a celebration; she wanted a church service, a diploma-award day; it was all so important, the first nurses trained in Congo by their mission in all their history! She wanted the Congo flag flown on the lawn, a band playing and the Governor General in white uniform and a plumed hat. Didn't they understand that all those months of work – not alone by her but by the boys who had come out of nowhere yearning to accomplish something – had succeeded? For the boys it was a journey to the moon! Yet no one was interested.

She felt certain that Jessie and Jack would have celebrated with her if they had been free to express an opinion. But Jack was mission leader, Jessie was his wife; they had to be impartial.

Next day he came to see her. 'Helen,' he began bluntly (Jack although patient and kind was inevitably blunt in his approach), 'Helen, as you know, the Mission's Field Committee are in session at this moment in Ibambi.'

'Yes,' said Helen, still sore from yesterday's reception, and not trying to conceal from herself the wish that if the Mission Field Committee fell into the lake it would do them no harm.

'They've asked me to tell you their decision.'

'Yes?' said Helen.

'They'd like you to move your entire medical centre to Nebobongo.'

Helen's breath seemed to stop for about five minutes. So this was her reward!

'Nebo?' was all she managed to get out.

'It's only seven miles down the road. And there's a hospital – or a sort of hospital – there already.'

'There's nothing there now except an old leprosy camp!' Her voice was an outraged squeak.

'It's the committee's decision Helen.'

'But I've already started here. Ibambi's ideal. We've built our first hospital. You know the first-ever students passed their exams yesterday.'

'The committee feel it would be better for everyone.'

Helen made a noise rather like the 'blow' of a surfacing whale. It expressed her feelings. Although she sensed that Jack was certainly on her side, she knew that many others were not. A short time earlier a similar committee had been held at Ibambi and Helen received one of the biggest shocks of her missionary career. Missionaries were just like other people; while many disagreed with her – she expected that – they disagreed with everybody else too.

When Helen, with only nine months experience behind her, stood up to talk about her vision of *training* Congolese, to her astonishment there were all sorts of objections. Training, particularly medical training, should, they said, be the work of government not of a Christian mission. Training was not their job.

'But Christianity must be teaching . . .' she began, then faltered and sat down bewildered and confused. Nevertheless, encouraged by Jack and Jessie she had gone ahead with her plans, and now that she was really making headway, they sprang this on her. The idea of moving to Nebobongo was ridiculous!

'Can I make my views felt to the committee?' she demanded hotly.

'Helen, you'll only start a big row.'

'Yes, I expect I shall.'

Jack pursed his lips. 'All right,' he agreed dubiously. 'Come across this evening.'

She seethed all afternoon. One by one she marshalled her arguments. Point by point she rehearsed them. She bathed, changed her dress, combed her hair, and marched across to the committee room waiting for the trumpet call which would sound the charge.

Jessie was waiting for her in the outer room. Helen could hear the voices within.

'Helen,' said Jessie. 'Shall we pray together?'

'Pray?' exclaimed Helen. Pray, when her mind, soul and heart were poised for instant raging controversy? She was ready to strike argument aside with the fury of her rhetoric, the justice of her cause, the passion of her belief. Pray?

'No,' she said.

Jessie eyed her solemnly. 'Then I'll pray for both of us.'

She knelt and prayed that Helen should find grace, humility and understanding; she then delivered a little homily on pride and its fall, on the virtues of Christianity and brotherly love. Helen sat stony-faced.

Jessie got up and went on talking. There were two, three or even half a dozen sides to this question. Surely Helen must realise that? The mission had been started to bring Christianity to the Africans; that was the main purpose of Ibambi and all the other mission stations: to teach the word of God. Many missionaries thought that training and various forms of education were outside their sphere altogether; many believed that starting a hospital and training-school at Ibambi would change the character of Ibambi; hundreds, possibly thousands of people would be pouring in who weren't even Christians . . . .

Helen did not feel it necessary to interrupt at that point to mention that this idea crystallised practically her entire conception: through healing you introduced a vast new audience to Christianity.

How would they feed all these people? Jessie asked. New departments would have to be set up. The Heart of Africa Mission would take second place to the Heart of Africa Hospital.

Helen sat and listened. No missionary in all Africa possessed more kindness, and love for her fellow-man and woman than Jessie Scholes. Helen could not – and did not – doubt for one second her motives or her sincerity. Therefore if Jessie could make this strong appeal perhaps she should examine her own motives.

If she looked into her own heart she knew that if she went to Nebobongo she would be faced with an immense challenge; the place was an overgrown wilderness enclosing a tiny maternity centre, an orphanage and a leprosy camp, all that was left of a huge government scheme of ten years ago. She would have to assume station leadership and all the responsibilities that such leadership entailed: drains, hygiene, rations, roofing repairs, orderlies' wages, a hundred and one calls upon her time and attention. And if she was honest with herself she knew she wanted to be free to follow her heart's desire: to train nurses, to set up a successful hospital and medical school sheltered under the umbrella of Jack's experienced leadership.

The door opened and a senior missionary from the north smiled at her. 'Hello Helen,' he said. 'Sorry to have kept you waiting. Please do come in.'

She felt Jessie's X-ray eyes on her back as she walked through the door. She listened politely to the committee's point of view. They were certain she would have great scope at Nebobongo; it was a big problem but under her leadership they were confident that she would be successful. They realised she might be disappointed after having made such a fine start at Ibambi, however, all things considered . . .

'Yes,' she agreed meekly, trying not to smile at the dumbfounded expression on Jack's face. 'Yes, I'd like to give it a try. Thank you for the confidence you have in me.'

A week later with John Mangadima and her students, Evangelist Agoya, his wife Mama Taadi, and six children, she loaded all her possessions into a truck and headed for Nebobongo. Her apprenticeship served, she was on her own.

III

Upon 31st October, 1955, the day after her arrival at Nebobongo, Helen started work. With two African helpers, she walked backwards and forwards across her new terrain, measuring, plotting, sketching and discarding, her mind absorbed in problems of draining, sewerage and building.

The feeding, clothing and other logistics had to wait until after dark, and indeed, for the next few years her days started at 5.30 a.m. with hospital ward rounds, and finished – after dealing with paper work and administrative details – at about 10.30 every night.

Her first task was to decide what could be rescued from the jungle, what abandoned and what rebuilt. She drew up her list of priorities. A new workmen's village in a healthy spot to the west of the hospital site. Adoption for many of the orphans and a practical experienced teacher for those who remained. A new hospital and all that its construction entailed: clearing land, digging waterholes, starting new food gardens, providing toilets, building a kiln to fire the thousands of new bricks . . . the tasks were endless.

On the credit side she had a small brick maternity unit run with loving attention by Florence Stebbing; an orphanage for thirty-eight happy juniors, and a few houses in reasonably habitable condition.

But the water ditches were muddy, overgrown, full of mosquitoes and perfect breeding grounds for disease; the leprosy colony had all but disappeared in encroaching jungle. What remained of the African Protestant community eyed the 'new-broom Helen' with deep suspicion, and she realised that one of her first jobs must be to gain their respect and trust.

Medical work of course never stopped. The patients merely transferred to the new site. Attending to their needs was not always easy; sometimes it was unmitigated disaster. Certainly God *had* to come to her aid that night of the first Caesarian, and Stebby had been there to witness the panic. Dear Stebby! Clichés like 'salt of the earth,' 'faithful unto death', 'solid as a rock', jumped into Helen's mind whenever she thought about her. She was short and homely; there was a durability, a security, a matter of factness about her which had helped hundreds of patients as she comforted them before an operation. When Stebby entered a ward common sense and sanity prevailed. Older than Helen, Amy or Elaine, she was a trained nurse and midwife.

And it was Stebby who at that most harrowing and traumatic midnight hour had uttered words of such rare incisiveness that even Nelson, Washington or Napoleon might have envied them.

Stebby had warned her with the urgent news. 'Pregnant pygmy mother just brought in. Far gone. Dying probably. Think she needs a Caesarian. Better hurry.'

Helen uncurled. The light of the hurricane lamp deposited with a bang at the side of the bed hurt her eyes. She fumbled for her glasses to peer up at Stebby to see if she were serious. She was. 'Hurry up!' urged Stebby and was gone.

In those early days for some obscure reason Helen found Stebby's admiration for her a little embarrassing. Probably it was because she was a doctor. Possibly because she'd been to Cambridge. Perhaps because she'd got a father who was a 'Sir'. Helen hated to disillusion her, but she knew she could never live up to the inflated reputation which Stebby built up around her, and to be summoned so abruptly to perform her first solo Caesarian filled her with terror, Oh yes, she'd read all the textbooks about Caesarians. She'd got the books with her; she should be able to proceed from A to B and on to Z without difficulty. But the difference between theory and practice was now about to be painfully revealed. In the calm, antiseptic security of a London hospital she'd listened to the lectures but had never actually attended nor assisted at a Caesarian birth. And this was not a well equipped London hospital; this was wildest Congo in the middle of a dark and tropical night.

Helen sighed and slid her bare feet out on to the concrete floor. It felt cool. Nothing else did. As she slipped on her dress and walked along the corridor into their living room and out on to the small veranda a cloud of insects were already dive-bombing the hurricane lamp. Outside, the air was hot and humid, the moon large and white behind the trees, the cicadas as shrill and constant as a radio signal.

The gravel was sharp and crunched under her feet, the lamp making swinging circles of light as she walked the seventy yards to the brick shed with a corrugated iron roof bearing the high-flown name of maternity block. She quickly closed the door behind her and went into the labour ward. No, this was certainly not a well-equipped London hospital. Mosquitoes and night-flying insects battered at the wire-screened windows in competition with the hiss of the pressure lamp. Grotesque shadows blotched the whitewashed walls like some early British horror movie. And there on the table mute, shocked, naked and vulnerable lay the small nut-brown pygmy woman swollen with child.

She examined her carefully: temperature, pulse rate, heart beat and shook her head.

'We've got to try,' said Stebby stiffly.

Helen nodded. She looked at Stebby without speaking. Both knew that the little pygmy woman hovered at the edge of death.

Stebby said, 'We might save the child with a Caesarian?'

Helen agreed. Then she added, 'I've never done a Caesarian before.'

It was Stebby's turn to nod. 'Now's your chance then.'

Stebby was already wearing her mask and gown. Helen went into the outer room to scrub up and change.

A few minutes later she began to operate. Half an hour later, hopelessly confused in a sea of blood and amniotic fluid she delivered a malformed dead baby. She looked at what might have been a human being, certain now that she should never have tackled the operation. Even conceding the fact that she had no alternative, the sense of failure was bitter.

Drenched in sweat that formed a pool about her bare feet, she stared in anguish at Stebby.

'It's hopeless. I'm lost. She's going to die. I've no idea what to do.'

Stebby's voice was commanding. 'Don't be silly! You've got to do something. We can't let her die on the table.'

'It's no good. I can't find any landmarks. I can't even find the uterus.'

'Listen, I'll put my hand up from below. Feel for my fingers and sew round them.'

'But I . . . .'

Stebby's eyes above the white bandage of her mask caught and held Helen's. Her voice was clear and imperative. 'You work. I'll pray,' she said loudly.

The precise, Cromwellian instruction spurred Helen on. Afterwards she would admit that in the history of unsurgical procedures, unsterile conditions and unrecorded methods the next hour broke all records. With no suction apparatus, no proper retractors, with nothing but faith and determination they continued. Helen sewed the ruptured womb back on to the cervical stump. The little pygmy woman survived the surgery but ten days later she died from overwhelming puerperal infection.

A few years afterwards, with the introduction of multiple antibiotics, they would have saved her. But not even a veteran Helen – with hundreds of the Caesarian operations she would eventually perform behind her – could have altered that final outcome.

She was saddened and wiser from her experience. She understood more fully one of the fundamental truths of her profession: a death diminishes you. Often those you attend and hope to cure will die. She could reproach herself for her first moments of panic; but she knew in her heart that if she had performed a thousand previous deliveries she could not have saved the pygmy woman. She also knew that no matter how expert she became, the death of one of her patients would always cause her sadness and self-reproach.

It took her a year to get things going and every day provided a new experience from which to profit. Her ideas about an airy dispensary with a roof supported by brick pillars, cool, simple, and utilitarian, had to be somewhat revised when the first hurricane blew the roof in the direction of the Indian Ocean. There were smaller, personal irritations: letters from other missionaries saying they had need of her services also; after all she was not only in Congo to look after Nebobongo's affairs was she? They were under the impression that her function was to act as the *mission* doctor.

Blithely she had already decided she could almost exist without food, sleep or holidays; a belief she retained for most of her years in Congo. Food had never interested her; she managed on native food, including plantains, cassava, bananas and coffee, without any difficulty during her twelve years at Nebo. She never saw fresh meat; she used a tin of corned beef once a fortnight, and if she opened a tin of Kraft cheese that had to last for three days. As a doctor her interest in food for her own nourishment was minimal; she would eat if she felt hungry but more often than not she was too busy to remember she was hungry.

The result – and in retrospect she admitted this herself – was that occasionally she grew impatient and irritable, and on one occasion this earned her an admonishment from John Mangadima whose candour grew rather than diminished through the years.

She had finished her weekly eye clinic and cleared away, ready for ward rounds, when an orderly came in to tell her that an old lady was waiting on the verandah wanting her eyes tested. Helen was exasperated. The eye clinic was finished. She would have to come back next week.

An hour afterwards John Mangadima burst in upon her accusingly.

'You would not see that lady.'

Helen was defensive. 'She can come back next week.'

'Didn't you know she was blind? Even to get here at all was a tremendous trial for her?'

'No, I didn't know.' Helen answered but she realised immediately that this was no excuse. Because of her irritation and impatience she had rejected someone badly in need of her services, and John was right to admonish her.

'She waited at the roadside all morning asking if someone would please take her to the Christian lady who heals people. She waited there for many hours; she couldn't find the way by herself. She is a soul for whom Christ died – and you have harshly turned her away. Would He have done so?'

Helen stared at him, her eyes full of contrition not knowing how to reply. That the boy born in the rain forest of leprous parents should lecture the Cambridge graduate on her duties to mankind was ironic enough, but perhaps equally original was the fact that she could accept his admonishment and profit from it. Never again did Helen fail to see someone who needed her help no matter what the hour nor how tired or distressed she might be. The memory of John's rebuke always remained with her.

Twelve months after her arrival Nebobongo was flourishing. In the maternity department they delivered some forty babies a month; twelve pupil midwives were in training, three qualified girls in charge, with Helen and Stebby keeping a careful shop-steward's eye on the scene. There were two hospital wards and often fifty patients needing medical attention. People came in for outpatients' treatment from miles around; a hundred and fifty a morning on average. She also trained twenty male student nurses in a two-year course; there were thirty children in the primary school; there were acres of land growing peanuts, rice, manioc, plantains, pawpaws and pineapples. All this meant that administrative work was a never ending headache: government forms in duplicate and triplicate, accounts, enquiries, correspondence all needing attention.

She knew there was criticism about some of the activities she undertook. Many of her colleagues reiterated that missionary activity should begin and end with the Gospel. It was true that W.E.C. did not reckon to put any of its funds into either educational or medical projects; Helen ran all her medical activities from the funds she received from her friends in Britain.

Her outloook was simple; the need was there, therefore she would fulfil it. If it had been left to the government to provide medical and educational facilities in the enormous province of the north-east, then thousands of children would have grown up without schooling of any sort, and thousands would have died because of a lack of medical attention. Help them to help themselves was her credo and it still is.

She was obsessed with Nebobongo. As leader of a huge 'family' of workmen, teachers, students, and nurses, she was confident that they had made something out of nothing; and she believed that the pride she felt was not the sin of pride, but the pride of achievement. Surely God would see no harm in that?

She knew she was overworked and she accepted the criticism

that she was dictatorial maintaining there was no alternative. Her reaction – and there was possibly a trace of 'If you can do it any better please go ahead,' arrogance in her attitude – was 'I would be very pleased to have more trained medical help.'

When this became a distinct possibility during the Missionary Conference at Ibambi in 1957, Dr Harris a young British surgeon working in the north with his wife wanted to move. Helen replied in true Christian spirit, 'Certainly. Dr Harris is a better surgeon than I am. I can learn an enormous amount from him. Of course he must take over leadership of Nebobongo; he's a man and naturally must be in charge. We shall be able to expand and I shall really be able to get moving on my pet scheme to set up a whole series of out-station clinics.'

She smiled happily, said all the right things and at the time thought she meant all the nice things she said. She certainly had no conscious awareness that somewhere deep down in the Rose-veare body or high up in the Roseveare cranium a short fuse leading to an explosive charge of deep frustration had just been lit.

Four months later Dr Harris and his wife arrived at Nebo and Helen welcomed them cordially, insisting they live with her and share her home. From the first she had known that meticulous book work was not one of her strongest points; she was aware that her method of fourteen account books carefully cross-indexed to match fourteen carefully labelled porridge-oat tins would never gain favour in either Wall Street or the London Stock Exchange, but *she* always knew where she was even though Dr Harris did not seem to like her system at all.

Anyway, he could get on with that mundane side of the work; she had progressive ambitions. She had worked out a plan whereby she would spend one week at Nebo training her students and doing her routine jobs, and with the blessing of the W.E.C. Committee use every other week for the scheme which excited her: the establishment of forty-eight village clinics spread in a wide figure of eight around Nebobongo. She envisaged each clinic staffed by a trained male nurse – what else was the point of all the training she was doing? A supply of drugs sufficient to treat the diseases endemic to that area; each clinic to consist of a single-roomed house with a big verandah, the village headman to be cajoled into providing this; and in the room, a bed, a table, chair, utensils and cupboard. One unpaid church worker – the village evangelist – to look after the clinic if no male nurse was available. Basic drugs: quinine solution for malaria, Epsom salts for constipation, a kaolin mixture for diarrhoea, eye drops, boracic powder for ulcers, a more powerful mixture for deep tropical ulcers, potassium permanganate crystals for snakebite, aspirins, cough mixture, antiseptic solution for disinfecting wounds, and a special H. Roseveare formula for treating both hookworm and round worm. More important still was the fact that Helen herself, on her rounds, would be able to identify the beginnings of tuberculosis, leprosy, malnutrition and other diseases, and remove those affected to hospital before they became too ill.

So began what were really the most exciting and thrilling years of all she spent in Congo. She visited each of her forty-eight clinics once a month; twenty-four in the first week, and twenty-four the following trip. Twenty-four villages a week meant six a day, so she started at 5.30 in the morning and finished in the dark at the last village, where she spent the night.

She made the journeys in her old International three-quarter-ton pick-up truck, already spluttering towards a scrap heap when Helen bought it, and kept roadworthy by faith, hope and continuous attention. Inevitably it was always heavily loaded with medical supplies and drugs plus passengers going on some journey deep into the rain forest. She carried a set of surgical instruments for minor emergency operations, a microscope and a pharmacy balance; stock medicines of four to eight times their required strength to be diluted into the mixtures, creams and powders necessary to restock each clinic when she called.

Beneath a large sun-helmet, wearing an outsize printed cotton dress – utilitarian rather than fashionable – which ballooned round her slender figure, open-worked leather sandals over bare feet, the eyes behind the spectacles candid and concerned, Dr Helen Roseveare of Nebobongo always looked more like a slightly nervous butterfly collector than the intrepid heir to Dr Schweitzer of Lambarene.

Invariably at each village a reception committee met them. The talking drum would sound, the crowd would gather and work would begin. Worm medicine had to be administered to primary school children whether they had worms or not; expectant mothers had to be examined; those who needed surgery identified and told which day they had to arrive at hospital in Nebobongo. Endless queues: the eye treatment queue, the T.B. queue, the leprosy queue . . .

And of course the handshake queue; at each village people would come in from every hut for miles around – very often even shy little pygmies would emerge from their tiny cone-shaped leaf shelters deep in the forest to produce a sick baby or exhibit an arrow wound. She shook hands with everyone. There were rarely less than five hundred – and more often a thousand – people to greet her. It was part of their lives. Perhaps only a hundred might need medical attention but everyone needed to shake the hand of this strange female creature in the funny hat who seemed to be able to do more for a sick baby than all the witch-doctors in the province; it was part of the social ritual of rain-forest Congo. By the end of each week Helen had shaken hands many thousand of times and her fingers felt like jelly, but those scenes, and those incidents, and those wearisome, sleepless, bone-jolting months were the most evocative and rewarding times she ever experienced in her whole life; she was doing her job!

The condition of the roads was usually beyond belief: tracks of beaten earth through jungle of varying density. When it was very thick she could drive for fifty miles or so without a sign of human habitation. The giant trees branching across the roads dripped water constantly: before storms, during storms and after storms. All the bridges across the endless streams consisted of planks laid over tree trunks – two planks in line, which hopefully, were centralised under your wheels; and often it depended entirely on the choice of the local bridge-builder – who might favour American, with a wide wheel base, rather than European transport – as to whether you drove across or drove in.

Everywhere she went the Africans wanted to give her and the team a meal, and the team were always anxious to have a meal: it was discourteous to refuse, they said. 'Discourteous, nonsense!' Helen retorted, 'We're not eating five meals a day, we're eating *one*! And that will be after the last patient has been treated.' Invariably this was after dark at about eight o'clock at night.

'Our job is medical aid,' she insisted. 'We're fulfilling a need which has never been met before. Now Daniel,' (Daniel was the chauffeur who drove the truck) 'you will line up all the leprosies. And Susan,' (Pastor Ndugu's foster daughter, a great friend) 'you'll get the mothers and babies ready for the ante-natal.'

When she found a seriously ill person who needed immediate treatment she would send a runner to Nebo and arrange for transport to take the patient back to the hospital.

The wet season was worst of all: lakes of mud, rain pouring down day after day, roads impassable to all but Helen, and sometimes even impassable to her. Keeping the truck running was a life's work and she lost count of the hours she spent lying underneath it or probing beneath the bonnet. Broken springs, filthy plugs, dirty carburettor, exhaust pipe dropping off, punctures, these were the commonplaces of her motoring life. Cost? She paid for the entire operation – forty-eight clinics, drugs, petrol, out of her donations. Sometimes she would receive as much as thirty pounds a month although even in the best year the overall total never came to more than two hundred pounds. On that sum she managed.

Rows? Certainly she had her share of these and would admit that practically all were caused by her own impatience and weariness. She wanted to get things done five times quicker than anyone else; she was always glancing at her watch; they did not even know what a watch was.

She never forgot the embarrassing scene at the village of Deti which stood on the top of a steep muddy hill. She reached it towards the end of a long day at the end of a long week; and the road up to the village was composed of liquid glue. She tried to climb it again and again; she churned from one side to the other; she tried every gear; she even tried reverse but over the last one-in-five incline the wheels simply would not grip in the mud. Eventually, frustrated and weary she slid down to a lower level and sent a willing passer-by up to the village to tell them that she would hold the clinic at some accessible spot near the bottom of the hill.

Within minutes the village evangelist, Peter, had descended followed by a crowd of villagers. Helen got out. She was cold, wet, tired and irritated beyond endurance by her vain attempts to manoeuvre the filthy old beast of a truck up the hill. Peter immediately set her nerves twitching.

'But what's the matter? Why don't you drive up to the village?'

Helen said bitterly, 'Can't you understand that for the last half hour I've been trying to do just that?'

'But they're all waiting for you. Why can't you get to the top?'

Helen controlled her desire to scream. 'Because the road's too slippery and you didn't send anyone down to give me a push.'

'Well we didn't know.'

'You should have known. It's pouring with rain. Haven't you any sense at all? You knew when to expect me.'

'Doctor, we simply didn't know you'd arrived yet. Everyone is willing to help.'

Irritation and frustration overwhelmed her. 'Well it's too late now. They can come down here. I'm not going to try again.'

The argument continued loudly and forcefully.

Thinking about it afterwards, Helen realised that the spectacle of the local evangelist and the lady missionary standing in the rain haranguing each other was neither dignified nor useful. The eyes and mouths of the collected Africans were round and wide; it was unlikely the two of them would have come to blows, but only the arrival of Pastor Akawa from the village ended the quarrel.

'Doctor Helen,' he called loudly, 'shut up!' It was the first time Helen had been told to shut up during the whole of her time in Congo. To her own surprise she shut up – instantly.

The pastor was an older and capable minister. 'Now you go straight to the top of the hill on your own feet,' he said sternly. 'We will meet you there.'

Helen was defeated. 'All right. But if I can't get that thing up the hill you can't either. I might have done if I'd been pushed, but there was no one to push me. But now I won't be pushed and it can't be done!'

She turned on her heel and squelched off up the hill. She knew she was wrong to quarrel with Peter; it was not his fault, it was hers. But she had done it now and it could not be helped.

There were tears on her cheeks and she felt solitary and alone trudging up that muddy slope, before she became conscious that someone was walking alongside, and she realised it was Mama Taroli one of her friends from the village. An arm was slipped round her waist in support, and she sensed rather than saw that a dozen village women had formed themselves into an escort group to take her up the hill. *They* understood how she felt; their hands and arms and sympathetic murmurs told her that; let those unfriendly men push that ancient truck up the hill, that was all they were good for. Hot coffee awaited her in the huts and she could sit by the fire to dry herself.

But of course she did not sit by the fire and dry herself. She sniffed a few times and wiped her face. She drank hot black coffee and shook hands six hundred times, and when the pastor and Peter arrived, their faces displaying the usual insufferable signs of male superiority as they directed the villagers pushing and manoeuvring the truck into the square, she shook hands with them too, said she was sorry and started work.

At least that quarrel lasted only half an hour. The one with Dr Harris lasted a week.

It started so stupidly; but what quarrel did not? Daniel, her chauffeur had been told by Dr Harris to collect a patient and bring him to Nebo. If the patient's house was near Adzangwe – where Daniel lived – then he could visit his parents, if it wasn't near, he could not. Daniel collected the patient, visited his parents and returned. Dr Harris examined the kilometre gauge and declared it wasn't *near* at all; it was miles away. Daniel had no right to go. It meant he was untrustworthy. He was therefore dismissed.

When she heard this news Helen was furious, 'No!' she blazed. 'He's *my* chauffeur and I haven't dismissed him!'

'It was dishonest,' Dr Harris replied mildly.

'No, it wasn't,' Helen insisted knowing she would get the worst of the argument because as usual she was growing furious and as always Dr Harris was keeping his temper. 'It's such a piffling little thing. Daniel used the word "karibu". All right it means "near". But how near is near? You can say the earth's near the moon, can't you?'

So it went on. The row was not just a quick flare-up reached and resolved in seconds; it was the explosion point reached after weeks of simmering conflict between two people of utterly incompatible personalities. Dr Harris had arrived in Congo five months after Helen. He had married a fellow missionary in Congo and his first two children had been born out there; in temperament, in ambition, in everything he was vastly different from Helen. She, at heart, was a pioneer; she liked to start from scratch and build up; Dr Harris was thoughtful where Helen was impulsive; he was slow whereas Helen was precipitate never quite certain whether she was coming or going; his attitude to the Africans was completely different from hers. His deepest interest was leprosy and Helen held conflicting and provocative views about that also. She knew that back in England if you stood on a platform and talked about the needs of lepers, pygmies, Eskimoes if you like, but lepers in particular, the contributions would roll in. But if you drew attention to syphilis, tuberculosis, yaws, hookworm, malaria and the other unpleasant but not so dramatic diseases from which a far greater proportion of the Congolese population suffered, then the money did not roll in and no one liked you very much.

So Harris and Helen inevitably rubbed each other the wrong way. For a week after their quarrel no word passed between them and Helen bottling up her fury, simmered. She thought he misjudged the Africans, was unkind to the Africans and didn't trust the Africans. She'd always lived on a system of trust; nothing was ever locked. *He'd* put padlocks on everything; *he'd* changed everything so quickly; *he* hadn't even got used to the place before he'd changed everything! Everything as Helen had done it was now done differently! And this stupid business about the chauffeur . . . it was the straw which broke the Roseveare back.

When Mr Coleman, a missionary from the south, arrived at Nebo for medical treatment he bumped straight into Helen.

'Hello, Helen,' he said in his friendly Christian manner, 'How are you, and how's Dr Harris?'

'I don't know,' snapped Helen in an utterly exasperated un-Christian manner, only just preventing herself from adding, 'And I don't care!'

It needed no extra-sensory perception on the part of Mr Coleman to discover that in the heat of the midday sun the relationship between the lady and gentleman doctors in the far-off

Congo outpost of Nebobongo was at freezing-point. Each ignored the other's existence. Partition was an accomplished fact.

'Now you can't go on like this,' protested Mr Coleman. 'It just doesn't make sense. I'm driving you both to Ibambi and you're going to have this out with Jack Scholes.'

He marched them out to his car and opened both doors. Helen got in the front, Dr Harris in the back. It wasn't that Dr Harris wouldn't sit next to Helen; Helen wouldn't sit next to Dr Harris.

In Scholes's office Jack nodded wisely while Helen made it plain what an awful person she thought Dr Harris was, and Dr Harris said how much he admired Helen and how perfectly sweet she was . . .

At the end of an hour Jack said, 'This is perfectly ridiculous. You're both out here for missionary purposes and all you're doing is destroying the essence of our cause. What you're trying to preach doesn't make sense any longer: if you can't make peace with each other, how can you instil peace in anybody else's heart? Now we shall all pray about this matter.'

Jack Scholes prayed, Jessie Scholes prayed, Mr Coleman prayed, Dr Harris prayed. Helen did not pray. She knew she could not say to God all the things she'd been thinking . . . that Dr Harris was a beastly old nut . . . well, a beastly young nut – he was two months younger than she was . . . and even though she accepted the fact that he was a good doctor and a fine surgeon she disliked him intensely . . .

Even in the middle of all her un-Christian thoughts she could analyse her conflicting emotions clearly. She knew she hated Dr Harris's take-over. She accepted that she had brought it on herself, but that only made it worse. In her terms he'd 'just taken over' Nebobongo, *her* place, which she'd built up out of nothing, out of her dreams, out of her heart, out of the money she'd raised; the place where she'd dug the water holes, cleared the ditches, fired the bricks. All right, she had acknowledged the fact that you could not have two people in charge; that he was a man, and in Africa a man was the superior being, so she had handed over the keys. Then she found she couldn't take it. Perhaps she had been her own boss too long. But she had lost everything. She had always taken morning prayers; he took them now. She had always taken Bible class; Dr Harris took it now. Dr Harris organised the nurses and Helen had always done that. Everything that had been hers was now his. Of course, she knew she was wrong, that she was being un-Christian, idiotically feminine and uncharacteristically selfish. But she could do nothing about it. She knew it was the sin of pride but she couldn't do anything about that either.

Jack Scholes, however, by this time knew Helen rather well. He had learnt from years of experience amongst Africans that you took your time. You let things quieten down. You were patient. He took his time now. And Helen simmered down. Eventually she prayed. Eventually she shook hands; eventually she climbed into the car and they all drove back to Nebobongo. On the surface things were all right again.

(2)

Helen also realised that by this sort of behaviour she was not doing her own cause any good. She knew that while the African members of the Church wholeheartedly applauded her idea of clinics, many of the white members felt that she was wasting her time. She was not going so much against their wishes as against their inclinations. They felt the work was so hard and exhausting that she would probably work herself to death – which quite possibly she would have done and which she would have been quite happy to do. Indeed some of her journeys around Congo during those years were so adventurous that only a Helen Roseveare with a serious contempt for personal safety – if not for life itself – would have undertaken them. On many occasions she was desperately afraid but fear was always an emotion she managed to live with.

One midnight on the road near Boyulu she was scared literally speechless for probably a whole sixty seconds, and to keep Helen Roseveare speechless for that duration of time needs a shock of quite extraordinary proportions.

She had turned off the main road on to a narrow winding forest track, heading for the isolated mission station at Opienge. Enormous trees, dripping and dark, lined the endless miles of switch-back road crossed by at least forty plank bridges. Baboons and monkeys swung between the trees. It is wild, uninhabited, animal country.

Susan sat in the cab with her, Matthew, a student nurse,

two Africans, their wives and families slept peacefully under the canvas in the back. Great black bolsters of cloud loomed over the mountains as darkness closed in. When she switched on the lights, nothing happened. She stopped the truck and after fiddling under the dashboard and bonnet for twenty minutes she still could not raise the slightest gleam. A storm was imminent and moonrise was not due for hours. Therefore even though the chances of another vehicle approaching were minimal, the safest thing to do was to stay put. However, she decided they would not be safe without some form of signal indicating that their truck was blocking the so-called road; Congolese lorry drivers invariably blundered along with no more than a cursory glance through the windscreens, and Helen had no wish to be bashed aside by one of their vehicles.

There were two hurricane lanterns in the cabin. She lit them both and leaving Susan in the cab placed the first about fifty yards away in front of the truck. She had just returned for the second, reached the truck door and turned the handle when Susan's shrill horrified squeal of 'Danger!' compelled her to rapid action. Without conscious thought or decision she shot through the door and slammed it behind her, petrified now by the knowledge that the whole window area was blacked out by an enormous impenetrable 'presence'. A presence of fur or skin which moved! An immense black thing had crept up behind her as soundlessly as a shadow, and in that brief second before Susan screamed 'Danger!' had towered over her. Wordlessly, stiff as if rigor mortis had set in, Helen watched a great hairy black arm rise in the air, a huge hand plop gently down on the cabin roof, and then – ultimate horror – a giant, beetle-browed, yellow-eyed face stooped to stare in through the window at her.

She could neither move, breathe nor think. For perhaps ten seconds her face behind the glass window was no more than twelve inches away from the monster's. Her mind was frozen. She suspected her hair was standing on end.

The thing then slowly shambled round the front of the car. It was an unbelievable creature. It walked on all fours, but the front arms were mighty pillars fastened to giant shoulders which supported an enormous dangling head. When it reached Susan's side of the car it stood up to a height of what appeared to be about eight feet so that once again it had to stoop to look at Susan through her window.

At that moment Helen could not marshal her thoughts; in her innocence she did not relate this great segment of Equatorial Africa, where the Mountains of the Moon fall swiftly into the dripping foothills of the rain forest, to one of the last preserves of that mighty and rare beast, the gorilla. Later she realised it must have been such an animal. Afterwards she worked out that the eyes in the vast head stooping to peer in at them had probably been full of amiable curiosity. After all, gorillas live on green shoots of trees and he had probably never encountered anything so ludicrous on all his mountain peregrinations as these two peculiar humans, one white, one black, enclosed in a sort of see-through hut. He examined them with avuncular curiosity, decided they were only worth his passing attention and shambled off into the darker shadows.

Helen could only remember that they sat there in petrified silence. A few spots of rain pattered on the roof, then abruptly became a slashing deluge, the loud drumming on the cabin roof blotting out the few words they exchanged. It was cold. The roof leaked. They became wetter and wetter. Naturally she did not place the rear hurricane lamp in position; the entire lorry force of south-west Africa could smash into their truck for all Helen cared; she was not getting out to risk meeting that thing again.

The hours passed slowly. They dozed; they were wet and miserable. At about 2 a.m. a bright round moon rose over the trees and Helen saw that they were perched on the top of a slight rise and that the rain had run into other tyre tracks leading ahead forming two silvery guide lines which marked the road they had to follow.

'No point in staying here any longer,' she said to Susan. 'If we go slowly I can see the trail. Anything's better than waiting here.'

The engine started fairly easily and they moved off. Although she was tired and cramped it was not really very hard to follow the tyre marks. They had probably travelled twenty miles; they had crossed three swollen streams on plank bridges stretched over tree trunks. She crawled down a steepish hill, swung round a bend and this time a wider, deeper stream faced her. The tyre tracks ran to the edge of the river apparently precisely in line with the planks. But the river had swollen so that it just covered them; the water swirling across like a smooth silken platform. There was nothing unusual in this; you simply crawled across, your tyres half submerged. She ground down into bottom gear, pointed the bonnet in the right direction and accelerated.

There was one snag in her calculations, one missing link . . . the bridge. It had been washed away. She drove slowly forward straight into the river! The bonnet disappeared under the swirling water. Helen and Susan were flung against the windscreen; the sleeping passengers in the back slid forward against the wooden partition between them and the cab. The children began to wail. Fortunately the truck stuck in its upended position, the cab half full of water, the back perched on the bank. Swinging open the door Helen tried the river for depth; hanging on to the door handle she touched bottom at six feet which meant the water was over her head. She crawled up the bank, muddy and soaked. The two Africans, their wives and children, plus Matthew, had now scrambled out of the back. They joined her.

'The battery,' she pleaded. 'We must get the battery out. All our acid will drain away.'

She was not quite certain of her facts but it sounded the most practical thing to do; without a battery the truck couldn't move.

It was now about three o'clock in the morning. The moon was lunging in and out between great masses of dark cloud. Some of the time they could see and then suddenly they were blacked out. Helen found the tool kit, took a spanner, and all four of them dropped into the water and pulled themselves round against the force of the river. Helen took a deep breath, ducked under and fumbled for the bonnet catch. At the third attempt she managed to prize it open. The engine was completely under water but with difficulty she managed to unscrew the two battery leads. Jointly they heaved the heavy case on to the bank.

That was all they could manage. 'That's enough,' Helen gasped. 'Nothing more we can do until dawn comes. Let's light the primus and see if we can brew some coffee. You women must go and collect wood, so that we can start a fire. In fact we must light several fires to scare off any animals.' She made no mention of the animal they had recently encountered. Already in the cold night air the smell of elephant was acrid, the sound of elephant quite plain to hear.

They brewed Nescafé, sipping it gratefully. Cupping their hands round the hot enamel mugs and crouching near the fire. Helen knew that the mission station at Opienge lay some twenty-five miles ahead. It was better therefore, if they could move the truck to try and get across the river rather than attempt a return journey. There was no possibility of traversing the river except by swimming it or finding the planks which had formed the bridge and replacing them. It seemed to Helen that finding the bridge planks came first on her list of priorities and as soon as the first greyness appeared in the sky she announced her plan.

'First,' she told the two Africans, 'we'll see if there's anybody around to help us; one of you can swim across the river and go forward for a couple of miles, the other can walk back a bit; it's possible we could have passed a hamlet in the darkness. Meanwhile the rest of us will try and find the planks to rebuild the bridge.'

The rain had stopped and in the two hours which had elapsed since their plunge, the level of the river had dropped considerably. Up to their waists, sometimes their necks, and sometimes swimming, they struggled down stream to find the timbers. All Congo's rivers are infested with crocodiles but Helen decided this was no time to reflect upon such a negative eventuality. Anyway, finding a huge wooden plank sodden with water, and then propelling it back in front of you, up stream, took all your strength and determination.

In this manner they had collected about half a dozen planks from the reeds at the river's edge when one of their Africans appeared from the road behind them. He brought good news; a gang of half a dozen road workers whose job it was to keep bridges intact and the road open were nearby. He had found their camp and wakened them. To Helen's delight they carried axes, saws and adzes. Using slender tree trunks from the forest they levered up the front of the truck and dragged it back on to the road.

The whole gang joined Helen's expedition salvaging planks from down-river, but it quickly became clear that they were not going to recover enough; the torrent must have taken many of them miles downstream. Helen pondered, then she said, 'We replace the planks as far as the middle of the bridge and we push the truck out that distance. Then we take the planks from behind the truck and relay them in front of it across to the other side. At least if we get the truck over I can strip down the engine and see if we can get her started.' The plan worked well and, they manhandled the truck across. Helen had heard by this time that there was a village not far away, and she sent off the women and children to buy native food, borrow or buy a saucepan and make them all a meal.

With Matthew she went to work on the truck, stripping down the carburettor, petrol pump, everything that looked as if it might be waterlogged; the battery fortunately seemed to have survived in reasonable condition. The only thing which worried her was a part of the steering which she identified as the direction rods. One was still fixed to the car but bent; the other had been forced out of its coupling – which appeared to consist of two steel balls surrounded by a kind of semi-circular ball bearing – and had disappeared.

Several dives into the muddy water failed to locate it so Helen decided she would simply have to manufacture a replacement.

From a bed of stones on the river bank she selected two pebbles in the rough shape of the two balls which were missing. When the two African women had finished preparing the meal, she sat them down with orders to grind out the stones until they were roughly hollow in the centre. She gave them a sample of what she hoped the finished work would eventually look like and grinding one stone against the other, they started work. The women had been grinding corn and native foodstuffs almost from birth so their patience in such matters was phenomenal. Work on the truck continued until dark then fires were lit again and they all slept in the truck.

Early next morning Helen discovered in her replacement that one pin was missing. She contrived to twist a hair-pin into the right shape, and after she'd fiddled with the choke the engine fired and they were ready to start. That they had spent two nights on the road was not unusual in those pioneering days of Congo motoring.

When they arrived at Opienge the two male missionaries

there were considering sending out a search party. But they were not really worried; it was easy to be three or four days late on the sort of journey Helen had undertaken. Besides, there was a pride of performance in arriving under one's own power.

Helen spent three days at Opienge. The two missionaries serviced her car and tried to remedy some of her improvisations, but they could do nothing about her stone ball-bearing on the traction rod.

Winnie Davies, the mission nurse and an old friend, welcomed her warmly. During the next few days Helen saw all Winnie's patients, admired the maternity wards and accompanied her on several trips to outlying villages to visit the sick.

But Helen's adventures were not yet over. On the return journey she visited two more mission stations, and approaching the third she found another bridge washed away. That meant waiting several hours before a road gang could be found to repair it. Then she had a burst tyre. This entailed removing the tyre, patching the split and banging it back on the wheel rim.

The following day, the journey to Bomili was appalling. Ninety kilometres of rough, switchback forest road separated her from the mission station. The first sixty were through deep mud, and she crossed two wide rivers conscious that if her muddy tyres slipped on the wet planks there was no parapet to prevent the truck from plunging into the river. On the other side, the exhaust fell off. She picked it up, tied it to the roof, and continued, sounding rather like a Sherman tank.

She reached a rudimentary ferry made of huge logs bound together on top of dugout canoes, the only means of crossing the wide, fast running river. She drove the lorry aboard, the boatmen cast off and they were swept down current until the oarsman managed to pole them to the other bank. Helen was very thankful to leave that obstacle behind. She clattered over twenty-five miles of fairly flat country and then began to climb into the mountains, along a wild rocky track winding through thick forest. As she took a sharp corner the steering gear assisted by ground down stones and Helen's hair-pin, disintegrated. The wheel spun uselessly in her hands. The truck lurched across the road

E

and dropped down three feet into a mountain stream. Helen looked at Susan and said 'Bother!' In this area there was no chance of a road gang coming along to haul them out. As usual it was pouring with rain and every stream was swollen to twice its normal size.

'There is,' said Helen trying to be cheerful, 'a white man's house about eight miles from here on top of the mountain. I don't know him, but I think he's Belgian and he runs the gold mine here. I'm sure he'll help us. Come on, let's start walking and ask him.'

They climbed from the car and waded out of the stream. Before setting off Helen tied together the laces of her sandals and draped them round her neck. Shoes were precious; it was difficult to obtain replacements and she decided she would sooner wear out her feet than her shoes. It was now almost dark so she lit the hurricane lantern and led the way up the mountain making not very funny jokes about Florence Nightingale and the 'Lady with the Lamp'. At the beginning the climb was quite easy; they had experienced so much trouble on this journey that surely nothing could exceed what they had already endured. Helen led a sing-song but it was all up hill and the singing soon petered out. The rain kept pelting down and that did not help. Instead of singing Helen began to count her footsteps; every time she reached a thousand, she called 'That's another kilometre gone.'

They were now intensely aware now that they were in real elephant country. They knew that wild elephants will charge immediately if they don't like the look of you, and they don't much like the look of anybody. The muddy road was almost obliterated by pad marks, and they could hear a herd moving through the forest not far away. Coming upon a patch of forest which had been mown flat did not improve their morale. But strangely enough, although there were tracks everywhere, and they could constantly hear the huge beasts moving in the forest, they did not glimpse a single elephant.

It took them three hours of hard and painful slogging to reach the top of the mountain. At ten o'clock they stood outside the white man's house to find it locked and deserted.

'Well,' Helen said with her last weary attempt at cheerfulness, the church and our evangelist are only another half mile on.

He won't be able to pull us out of the ditch, but he may know someone who can help.'

Her feet were hurting so she decided to put on her shoes, only to realise her elementary mistake: her feet were so swollen and painful that she could not get them on. By the time they arrived at the evangelist's house she could scarcely hobble. The evangelist and his wife made them welcome. They built up the fire, for it was cold on top of the mountain, and produced a bowl of liberally salted hot water in which Helen could soak her feet. The brine stung but her feet felt better for it. The evangelist's wife did her best to be helpful; she carefully cleaned and bandaged Helen's feet, then cut off the tops of her shoes – Helen did not like to tell of her vain determination to preserve them – so that feet plus bandages fitted in comparative comfort. Ironically the Belgian had left that morning and gone off to his other house at the gold mine, only about two miles from the place where their truck had plunged into the stream.

'Fate,' Helen observed philosophically. 'So the sooner we get back to ask his help the sooner we get the truck out of the stream.'

The evangelist was worried. 'But won't you wait for the morning light,' he urged. 'The sun will be up very soon.'

Helen shook her head. 'No, if he's at that other house we'd better catch him before he leaves for somewhere else.'

The evangelist volunteered to show them the way. After a meal, a rest and several cups of hot coffee, Helen felt ready to start. Nevertheless, by the time they reached the foot of the mountain both she and Susan were worn out; they had walked roughly sixteen miles that night.

The evangelist led them through the sprawl of the gold mining compound to the Belgian's house perched in a pleasant spot on a hillside.

It was now 2 a.m. When they reached the verandah Helen sat on the steps too tired to go any further.

She was quite prepared to curl up and sleep. The idea of waking a stranger and giving all the necessary explanations was too much to contemplate.

To Matthew and Susan she said, 'Go round the back and see if you can knock up the houseboy. He'll find you some place to sleep. I'm all right here.'

Matthew and Susan went away. Five minutes later the Belgian's houseboy opened the front door. 'The master will see you,' he announced. Just as Helen was saying, 'Please don't bother. I'm quite happy here,' the lights came on.

A large man in a dressing gown regarded her in unfriendly fashion. 'Who is it?' he demanded.

'I'm sorry to bother you,' said Helen, 'I'm a missionary from Bomili. My car's broken down; the steering has gone and it's run off the road into a stream about two miles from here.'

'A missionary from Bomili?' repeated the man with the same sort of intonation he would have used for 'an escaped convict'. He then added, 'I must tell you I have been suffering with malaria. I have been very sick.'

'I'm very sorry to wake you,' said Helen. 'Please go back to bed. I shall be quite all right here.'

The man's attitude was very strange. In Congo there is a camaraderie amongst whites; help is given freely and quickly, even more quickly when a white woman is concerned. This man seemed quite indifferent to the idea of her spending the night on his verandah. Charitably she decided it must be because he was Belgian, she was British, and her French was not very good.

The evangelist had been lagging behind, but, observing him, the Belgian brightened immediately. 'Hello. What are you doing here at this hour of the night?' he asked.

The evangelist sounded surprised. 'I'm with my missionary.'

'*Your* missionary?'

'Yes, the lady sitting there. She's our doctor. She's from Nebobongo.'

The Belgian turned to stare at Helen. 'You said you were from bomili,' he said accusingly.

'I left there today. I'm doing a tour of missions and clinics.'

'My dear young lady,' said the Belgian, quite overcome, 'please come inside. I'll get my head man out with the truck and chains at once.'

Helen, surprised, could not understand why his attitude had changed so suddenly. With a crowd of workmen roused from their beds they drove down the track. With his heavy equipment it was a fairly simple matter to haul her vehicle out of the stream. The head man towed her back through the mud to the Belgian's residence.

When she walked into the bungalow she realised at once he had left instructions for her to be given the royal treatment. Hot soup, milk, sandwiches, clean linen on her bed ... oh, and such a lovely bed! She fell into it. Next morning she woke at nine to find an enormous breakfast waiting and the Belgian so kindly and avuncular, begging her to stay for at least another day and night; he felt she must be exhausted and in need of a rest.

Helen thanked him and said she must press on for she was due back at Nebobongo. And she discovered why he had been so boorish the night before. His gold mine employed local labour which divided spiritually into three different Christian groups. The community guided by Helen's evangelist was apparently his favourite: they never demanded time off for prayer meetings or Bible classes; they were conscientious, hard-working and impeccably honest. None of them objected to working overtime; if he needed a difficult job done it was always to the workers from the evangelist's flock to whom he turned.

The other two groups reacted differently. Christianity as a species of religious trade union operated for the benefit of the believer. To the manager of a gold mine willing labour made all the difference between profit and loss, and this attitude did not improve the relationship between him and reluctant workers.

When he heard that Helen was a missionary from Bomili, the headquarters of these surly Christians, he reacted accordingly; it was difficult to be charming towards the architect of his difficulty; especially at two in the morning; especially when one is shuddering from an acute attack of malaria.

Three days later Helen arrived back at Nebo, discovering en route that she had acquired an inbuilt nervousness about crossing plank bridges. She insisted on her passengers walking over while she navigated the crossing alone.

At Nebo Dr Harris met her outside the house. 'Oh, back again,' he said cheerfully. 'Yes,' said Helen.

'Jolly good. Did you have a good trip?' he enquired politely.

'Not bad. Everything all right here?'

'Quite all right, thank you.' With such banality do the English, on certain occasions, describe the incredible adventure, the ascent of angels and the fall of empire.

At the end of her first five years in Congo Helen had reached the conclusion that she was a complete failure; she had succeeded neither as a doctor, a missionary nor a woman; she had antagonised many of her contemporaries, and she had messed up her social and professional relationship with Dr Harris.

In an agony of indecision she wrote constantly to Norman Grubb, a senior missionary at W.E.C. headquarters in Fort Washington, Pennsylvania, U.S.A., recounting her spiritual doubts and agonies. It was a warm, father-daughter relationship; he tried to reassure and guide her and answered, in reply to one of her more strenuous bouts of heart-searching in which she felt certain she was of little use either to God or missionary endeavour, 'I have a deep conviction that you are a precious instrument of the Lord.' Helen replied sadly, 'Oh, how far from the truth this is. If you only knew all the meannesses and littleness and pettiness of my heart you'd be shocked. The pride – it makes me sick to look at myself – the rotten pride in achievement. No wonder He had to take the leadership away and give it to Dr Harris . . .'

From the first moment of her arrival in Africa she had been troubled by these doubts. From the very beginning, despite the adventure, the triumphs, the achievements, there was this . . . emptiness . . . this lack of lasting spiritual peace. She stuffed her daily hour-bag with work, ignoring the divisions of daylight and darkness, ramming it as tight as a housewife's laundry basket. But there was still no peace.

Others like Jessie and Jack Scholes, Stebby, Elaine and Amy seemed to have arrived at a haven and a completion in their Christianity; they were requited. Why wasn't she fulfilled in the same way?

Sometimes she wondered if marriage, a husband and child might perhaps be the answer to that sort of fulfilment? But she knew this was a hypothetical solution, so meanwhile all she could do was to go on working with a fierce and dedicated concentration. In every letter she wrote to her mother and to her friends she declaimed her loyalty, belief, and love of the Lord, but in her own heart she could not grasp what seemed to exist just beyond her reach.

In the tropical heat and glittering deluges of the rain forest she looked out at the beauty of the night, the bright dust-bowl of the moon, the silvery scrapings of the stars, through the eyes of a small and insignificant woman who believed desperately in God but could find no spiritual security of tenure. And because God, in her terms, must be that security, this, above all, disturbed her. She did not doubt God; she doubted herself. Somehow, she decided, her own communication system must be at fault; somewhere a switch was not turned on, a fuse had blown. She looked for miracles, she discerned miracles; in some people's eyes *she* created miracles, but it was still not enough and she did not know what would ever fulfil her, and she realised that her belief in God would have to suffice until death provided the final answer.

Early in 1958 she was considering whether she should leave Congo and W.E.C. altogether. She had reached the conclusion that as pastors, preachers and good shepherds the whites were not needed any more; the Africans could take care of that aspect of Christianity by themselves. She wrote: 'To hear Pastor Ndugu preach does my heart good ... they have a spiritual grip and deep discernment that just humbled me to the dust. It's not what I can, or have done, for *them*, but what they are doing daily for *me*! There's a fierce, fighting spirit of independence inside me that just won't bow the knee to any old Tom, Dick or Harry – but with the Africans I discovered that it isn't there – rather the reverse, a deep, hungry dependence, a longing to lean on them, to confide in them, to receive their advice, to be received by them into their families in a oneness that knows no racial barrier – I almost hate my white skin at times, and this makes me separate when I long to be united.'

Helen's disillusionment increased when she heard what some of her missionary colleagues had said about her: 'She knows everything, therefore she is impossible to work with.' She was also in very bad health and she did not object, therefore, when her name was placed on the leave rota two years before it fell due. Most W.E.C. missionaries went on leave after seven years; Helen was leaving after only five years in the field.

Before going to England she completed one last task which had occupied her attention for several years: the typing and stencilling of the pages of a medical textbook in Swahili for use in training male nurses. In the middle of 1958, feeling that it was unlikely she would ever return to Congo, she started the long journey home.

She arrived in London, outwardly smiling but inwardly perplexed about her future as a woman, a missionary and a doctor. She spent a month in Cornwall with her mother, and then went into the Tropical Hospital for treatment for chronic amoebic dysentery. Her health improved and she set out on a series of deputation meetings travelling all over the British Isles.

Ostensibly one of the reasons she had been granted early furlough was the fact that her training was incomplete; she needed more surgical training if she were to fulfil a useful medical role in Africa. In February she applied for, and was accepted, as houseman and Casualty Officer at the Mildmay Mission Hospital in Shoreditch, East London, and to her slight surprise enjoyed the job enormously. The work, the regular hours, and a salary cheque at the end of each month meant that for the first time in her life she could buy clothes for herself and gifts for her mother. And one other thing: the presence of a good-looking senior houseman into whose company her duties constantly led her, and who watched over her progress with a keen interest turned her mind in another direction.

The thought that perhaps marriage was the only real way of ensuring happiness as a missionary in the field now hardened into a certainty, and with typical Helen impulsiveness she decided that the young houseman was just the man for her. Mentally she began to prepare for the marriage, day-dreamed about the welcome they would receive when they returned to Nebo, the house they would live in, and the work they would accomplish together. Her plans had to be considerably modified when she discovered that he had no desire at all to go to Congo on missionary service. He was a good Christian but not as Christian as all that.

Helen decided she must alter her approach. She needed more time. Collecting a husband took longer than she thought. She bought herself new clothes, had her hair permed, applied to W.E.C. for a year's leave of absence and set out to lay her loving traps. She even considered the possibility that perhaps her new career as a young bride might rule out missionary work altogether?

She had, however, made one major error: she had not ascertained whether her passion was returned. And slowly, to her dismay, she discovered it was not. Obviously he liked her, clearly he enjoyed her company, but he had no inkling of the web of romantic intrigue being woven around him. He was a handsome, healthy and hearty young doctor who patted her cheerfully on the head and said, 'Well, old girl, I suppose you'll be off to the Congo soon?'

When the old girl replied, 'No, I've decided to ask for a year's extension of leave to get more medical and surgical experience,' all unsuspectingly he continued, 'Oh, jolly good show, old girl. Well, let's get back to work.'

After some months it eventually got through to the 'old girl', her hair waved, her feet – blissfully used to spreading sandals – now crammed into something much smaller, that her love was not only unreciprocated but circulating beyond his orbit. He thought she was 'a very nice girl', but the idea of marriage did not come within measurable distance of his understanding or intentions.

As this fact slowly, inevitably and painfully dawned in her mind, she had to accept the truth that he had not given her the slightest encouragement and that the love affair had existed solely in her own heart.

Nevertheless, she was bitterly hurt. She was aware that not only had she humiliated herself, she had failed God. While she should have been thinking about a lifetime spent helping others, she had gone instead hurtling selfishly towards self-gratification and personal achievement.

Colliding head on with a brick wall not so much of indifference as of sheer non-comprehension, dispersed the smell of orange blossoms like a gale-force wind. She saw clearly what a fool she had made of herself, and realised that she had to forget, survive and start again.

As a move in this direction she applied for the post of House Surgeon at Newport Hospital, Monmouthshire. She was confirmed in the post and journeyed westwards determined to work as she had never worked before.

At Newport she discovered that the medical routine encouraged the speedy healing of her broken heart.

She assisted in the obstetrical department and although she

had performed more than twenty Caesarians since that first traumatic night at Nebo, now she accomplished her first solo Caesarian in Britain.

For three weeks also, while the Medical Superintendent was away on leave, she was allowed the privilege of taking over as Acting Registrar and learned something of the difficulties of running a large hospital.

Also, she had time to reflect upon her years in Congo, and realise how acutely she missed Nebo and Ibambi. With the new knowledge and confidence she had acquired at Mildmay and Newport, surely she could now return without making the same mistakes, and find that peace of spirit and body she so urgently needed.

She wrote to Mission Headquarters. Would they please have her back? John and Elsie at Nebo would be seriously in need of leave by this time. Would they allow her to take over at Nebo again? If so – and she desperately hoped that it would be so – could she leave quickly. If possible, at the latest by May of next year – 1960?

Obviously some people at Headquarters possessed the same perspicacity as Norman Grubb. They said 'Yes.' And as a result of their decision Helen suddenly found herself humming as she walked along the utilitarian corridors of Newport Hospital and only with difficulty preventing herself from breaking into hymns of triumphant praise.

She had won that most precious of opportunities so rarely achieved – a second chance. This time she was determined she would not mess it up.

Part Three

I

In the middle of 1960 Helen set off for her second tour knowing that getting back into Congo itself might prove to be the most difficult part of her journey. At sea a cablegram from W.E.C. reached her and her travelling companions, Elaine de Rusett and Bill McChesney, suggesting that with the approach of Independence and the hurried departure of the Belgian Colonial Administration it might be better to wait in Nairobi and see how events turned out.

Helen turned Nelsonian eye and a deaf ear to this advice, but there was more trouble awaiting them at Mombasa. Travelling to Congo? Were they mad? They would not be allowed to disembark until they had deposited return fares with the Immigration authorities; and even having gained this surety the officials still felt it their duty to lecture them with force and clarity. Did they not know that all hell was about to break loose in Equatorial Congo? Were they unaware that hundreds of white refugees were already pouring out of Congo into Kenya?

'Congo is my home,' Helen replied mildly. 'There is still two weeks to go before Independence is declared, and I intend to be at my hospital in Nebobongo before that date.'

It could be asserted that the modern history of Congo began when Stanley made his historic east to west traverse of the central African continent in 1877 and the man most intrigued by Stanley's determination to exploit this territory turned out to be King Leopold II of Belgium. Even in an era when princely domination of Europe still presumed claims of 'divine right', it was something of a surprise – acknowledged by a nod of acquiescence from Britain, France, Germany and Portugal – that Leopold could annex the Congo as his own private domain. He administered it as such for the next twenty-one years oblivious of the many vociferously critical voices who alleged that the conditions of the African workers in the rubber plantations of the Upper Congo were identical with slavery and that forced labour, floggings, brutality and mutilation were commonplace. Leopold was forced eventually to appoint a commission of enquiry. It confirmed 'great abuses', and it became evident that the Belgian State itself would have to take over responsibility. This it did in 1908 'assuming its heavy task with a determination that as a colonial possession the Congo territory should be honestly governed, and in real agreement with the humanitarian principles which Leopold II had never ceased to profess'.

The beginnings of the sequence of bloody episodes which ravaged the work of Helen Roseveare and hundreds of other missionaries in Congo, destroyed the economy of the country, killed scores of thousands of people, and ushered in a decade of lawless violence, might be traced to comparatively insignificant speeches such as the one made in 1955 by Belgian Professor M. van Blisen who proposed that in thirty years' time Congo should be granted independence. The proposition raised the temperature in Brussels to such a degree that the shout of horror which greeted this radical heresy could almost be heard in Leopoldville itself. While Britain and France were shedding their African colonies with the resolute speed of nations who understand that either you go gracefully or are expedited by a revolutionary kick in the rump, the Belgian authorities seemed hardly aware that such a thing as Congolese nationalism existed, and most certainly they made only rudimentary attempts to train African doctors, lawyers, teachers and professional men to replace their own functionaries.

It was Patrice Lumumba, a left wing politician returning from a Pan African Congress in 1958 who demanded immediate independence. He was ignored. Accordingly in 1959 when the Colonial Government tried to ban a public meeting in Leopoldville fifty people were killed in the ensuing riots, and African mobs surged through the European neighbourhoods, firing, looting and destroying property to the value of millions of dollars.

The point was made. King Baudouin of the Belgians reacted quickly by promising independence without delay.

To Helen's great relief Frank Cripps was waiting at the Congo border with the mission truck and they crossed without difficulty. She was welcomed rapturously at Nebo and John and Elsie, very tired after seven years of intensive effort, were pleased to hand over the station.

But the unsettling mood of approaching Independence had infiltrated everywhere. In that first week she was requested to attend a meeting of station elders and male nurses, and one of the most senior, Joseph Bumukumu, made his point clearly. 'At the Red Cross Hospital at Pawa, Dr Kadoner has already handed over his authority to the senior African medical worker and Dr Kadoner has become the new executive director. Should not something of the same sort happen here?'

Helen sat quiet, a little tense, not quite knowing how the situation could be resolved. John Mangadima was in no doubt at all how it should be settled. He got slowly to his feet. 'I am the senior African medical worker, but let me add at once that I am not a doctor. I don't mind being in charge of the nurses and the general administrative work, but we can't do without *our* doctor and I certainly can't be over her.'

So that was that. On 30th June, when Independence Day arrived, the headman of the nearest village and senior men from the district all arrived at her front door wearing native dress and carrying presents of fruit and little bouquets of flowers. The headman made a short speech. They would like it very much if the 'strangers in their midst' would agree to join them and stay with them in this new independence?

Helen was very moved. It seemed that Independence was going to usher in a new spirit of co-operation between everybody.

A week later she sensed an altered mood as they watched cars trundling backwards and forwards from Ibambi. Every African knew about it and told Helen that something important was happening.

It was nearly dark before they came for Helen.

'Everyone's collecting at Ibambi. You've got to come too.'

'But what's the matter?'

'Haven't you listened to the radio?'

'I haven't got a radio.'

'There's trouble all over Congo. Just outside Léopoldville the missionaries have been knocked about. Several of the white ladies have 'suffered'. It was the first time Helen had heard the word used in this manner.

'The feeling is that all white women should get out while there's still a chance.'

'Oh!' Helen exclaimed. 'Is that so?' She did not add, 'If you think you're getting me out when I only got back in by the skin of my teeth, you're quite mistaken.'

Twenty missionaries were crowded into the room at Ibambi and Helen sensed it was going to be one of those fraught occasions; fraught with anxiety, suspicion, nervousness, indecision and occasional outbursts of anger.

A tall missionary with a long sad face began: 'The reports that drunken Congolese troops are raping, murdering, and looting in Leopoldville are undoubtedly true.'

'This isn't Leopoldville,' said Helen quickly, speaking out of turn. She was ignored. A short sunburned missionary from the south took over when the first had finished.

'The trouble is obviously going to spread all over Congo. All American missions have ordered their personnel to evacuate across the Ugandan border as quickly as possible. I think we should do the same.'

The argument started. Rarely did twenty missionaries from the Central Area – and some of these had driven in some hundreds of kilometers – meet together. Those in the extreme north or south could not reach the meeting but it was still a comparatively large group.

Helen already knew exactly what she was going to do. Although she was one of the younger ones there she was a second-termer if only by a matter of days. And she was firm in her conviction. God had called her out. God had not told her to go home; it was as simple as that. And whoever else was going to be needed, a doctor would certainly qualify for a post. She also felt very strongly that at this time of crisis the mission they had started in Congo badly needed their support and presence.

When her turn came to speak she made her position clear and

knew at once that general reactions were unfavourable; the men felt that she was making it harder for them.

One of the married men said huffily, 'It's all very well for you, but you're not responsible for a wife and children.'

'I accept that,' admitted Helen.

'And how shall we be able to protect you lady missionaries when it becomes necessary?'

'You won't have to.'

'It's all very well you saying that, but in the long run you'll be our responsibility.'

That made Helen furious. She hadn't been anyone's responsibility since she left college. This was pure male chauvinism. 'Not at all. We're out here on God's calling not yours. You're not responsible for us. God is. Surely this is a case for a free choice.'

The argument grew more heated and Helen noticed that the three senior lady missionaries, Margery Cheverton, Agnes Chansler, and Daisy Kingdon in their forties, fifties and sixties respectively, were sitting together on one side of the room. They had already made it clear they were not leaving.

Helen rose and went across to sit next to them. 'Excuse me moving but this looks more like my side,' she said. It wasn't until much later she realised what a formidable quartet they must have looked, and how unfair really it was on the men with wives and children to consider.

Those who decided to go packed their cars and streamed out at four in the morning. They arrived at Paulis where a plane was supposed to be coming to fetch them. They waited all day. No plane arrived. That night in convoy they set off for the Ugandan border and crossed without incident.

Helen returned to Nebo alone, went to bed in her own house, and somehow, suddenly it was all different; her recent arguments had left her full of a strange fear. It was quite an uncanny feeling and she could not sleep. By 2 a.m. she was exhausted listening to every tiny noise – the sound of a nightbird, a rat scurrying across her bamboo ceiling. Then she heard a tapping on the front door and she approached on bare feet, almost expecting to open the door to her own murderers. From the

[145]

reassuring whispers outside she knew that she was safe. Mama Taadi and Mama Damaris, her two wonderful friends, rushed in and hugged her.

They lived at different ends of the village, but each, making her own independent decision, had reached the same conclusion: Helen should not be allowed to sleep alone in that house. Tip-toeing through the darkness they had collided at her front door.

Helen made them hot drinks. Next day Agnes Chansler and Margery Cheverton, two maiden ladies whom Helen always thought of as her 'aunties', arrived from their mission station at Egbita about eighty miles away. They had made a similar decision: the medical work and Helen's safety were of prime importance; they had decided that for the time being they would abandon their own mission and come and work with her. What needed to be done? Agnes was very good with children so she could take over the children, couldn't she? And Margery would act in a general capacity. As Helen now knew that within a two-hundred-mile radius, where only a few weeks ago there had been seventeen doctors, there were now only two: Dr Swertz leprologist and pathologist, and herself, she was very glad to welcome them. She kissed them and gave them a cold drink. It was good to have friends.

During those next four years of Independence life in her part of Congo changed beyond recognition. A few weeks after her return she wrote home: 'Today is Sunday evening and it has been such a quiet and lovely day with the mass of yellow acacia blossoms brilliant against a clear blue sky; doves cooing, hens clucking, birds humming; all the sounds of peace and beauty – I listened to the kiddies, some thirty-five of them sing-ing hymns in the children's ward opposite, a lovely vase of yellow dahlias beside me on the table.

'Congo still writhes in the convulsive grip and tempestuous storm of political unrest and intrigue. How one's heart longs to see an end to it all, and peace restored to this poor republic. Economically, even without this political upheaval, the country is in the depths of the most abysmal need – there are just *no* technicians, no doctors, no senior school teachers – *none* – and U.N.O. says that even with the most rigorous programme of intensive training, it will take five years to produce enough for Leopoldville alone. Drug shortage is growing acute. Already I have had to start to refuse treatment to adults and conserve supplies for acutely ill children. Also food is becoming a problem – no more rice or salt or flour available locally, nor matches, and milk will be running out again soon . . .'

Independence had indeed got off to a bad start. In Leopold-ville a thousand miles away it was accompanied by rioting, mutiny amongst the Belgian-officered *Force Publique*, the near collapse of the hurriedly assembled and unprepared African government, and under the leadership of Moise Tshombe, the al-most immediate secession of Katanga, the wealthy copper-rich eastern province without whose financial support no central government could hope to function.

Because of the spread of violence Belgium rushed in thou-sands of troops to protect her nationals. Patrice Lumumba, appointed first Prime Minister, appealed to the United Nations for assistance, and later to the U.S.S.R. an action which added a political ingredient to the stew already simmering in the black pot of international intrigue.

The United Nations military intervention was instigated by Secretary General Dag Hammarskjold and whether or not he believed this might be the beginning of a new international role for U.N. it was spectacularly unsuccessful. Troops from many countries were flown in; the secession of Katanga was prevented by force, and the U.N. operation on a level of high-flown in-competence and expenditure learned that no one could feel either affection or loyalty towards an international army. Cer-tainly the episode discredited the idea of physical intervention by the United Nations in the arena of world affairs.

Helen viewed the disinterest of U.N. troops at close quarters and was not impressed. Her reactions to the more commonplace perils of Congo remained essentially practical: she swatted the flies which stung her; she biffed – to use her own terminology – the things which threatened her; she slaughtered the things which attacked her. She had no time to dote on the mysterious flora and fauna of Africa. She was too busy with God, her medical work and her pupils.

On one occasion she was surprised in her bath. The house at Nebobongo was built of red bricks fired in their own kiln.

The roof was corrugated asbestos painted red. The rooms were square and utilitarian, the windows shuttered to keep out the glare. The furniture was practical, looking as if it had been built under Helen's direction by a local carpenter who had never seen a Western set of drawers. It had.

The bathroom was a gloomy place half filled by the bath, a huge, square, concrete rectangle which over years had become discoloured to a dark grey. It took ages to fill with water and Helen in those busy days had no time to waste on such extravagance. Every evening she placed a large zinc bathtub in the middle, filled it with hot water and sat in it. There, for a divine minute or two, she would slosh soap and hot water all over herself and emerge fragrant and refreshed ready to eat what food was available and get on with writing up her notes, marking the papers and arranging the curriculum and medical programme for next day.

On this occasion, alone in the house as the houseboy had left for his own home, perched happily in her tub, she was suddenly surprised to feel the zinc tub begin to rock beneath her. Her reactions were instantaneous. She leapt out of the bath as if the water had suddenly become scalding hot. Simultaneously from under the zinc tub emerged the angry head of a black mamba snake, whose bite almost inevitably ensured a quick death. It had slithered up the waste pipe, and found the cool damp recess under Helen's zinc bowl a perfect place to coil in siesta. It must have been mildly curious when the hot water pouring into the bath raised the temperature – and absolutely enraged when Helen sat on it.

Her reactions were as rapid as the mamba's. Naked she fled into the living-room and grabbed the machete left there for such crises. Scurrying back to the bathroom, she found six feet of black snake hissing and coiling along the length of the bath preparatory to writhing over on to the floor. Helen flailed into action.

Next morning, when the houseboy returned, he goggled in admiration. 'You certainly chopped up that mamba good, missus! There was mamba blood on the ceiling! Yes, right up on the ceiling.'

Snake bites of all varieties were commonplace at Helen's hospital. Every sort of snake from boa-constrictor to adder were normal occupational hazards of life in the rain forest, and it was always possible to step on one in your darkened bedroom. On another occasion, delirious in the middle of a particularly bad bout of malaria, the male nurse observed, as Helen lay under her mosquito net, that her eyes were rolling round in the most peculiar manner. So peculiar was their rotation that he called his colleague to observe the phenomenon.

It was then they discovered that her eyes were following the gyrations of a large mamba circling the supports of the mosquito net overhead as he attempted to find some aperture in the net to join her in bed.

But there were other and even more obnoxious irritations. Permits were needed for practically every mode of transport, and every aspect of living. You would be stopped in your car for no obvious traffic offence; you never felt quite safe. The fact that so many Europeans had left gave one a feeling of insecurity. Under the Independence Government one was never quite sure what was going to happen, and during the next four years, in Helen's terms, everything began to fall apart.

When she first arrived in Congo in the early fifties the separation between black and white was finite. One did not so much accept, as tolerate the Government's attitude that the Africans were incapable of doing almost anything. Therefore they were given no authority though the missionaries tried to give the Africans both authority and direction. It was clear to Helen that most certainly in the district in which she lived, justice for any African barely existed. Bribery and corruption eroded all aspects of law; there was no point in a black man trying to take a white man to court; the result was a foregone conclusion – the white man was always right, the black inevitably wrong.

Another abrasive aspect of public life concerned religion. The Government's official faith was Catholic, therefore Catholic influence, patronage and authority permeated all aspects of public affairs; the hospitals were run by Catholics, the nursing staff were Catholic sisters, and it was for this reason that when the Simbas' rebellion started they identified anything Catholic with a despotic Government and reacted with horrifying brutality.

From the very first moment Helen arrived in Congo violence was a natural corollary of government and to life generally in the country. She would never forget her first experience of in-

[149]

stant crime and punishment. She had left Nebo to walk into the village to buy plantains for the patients. In the shade of the trees at the edge of the road, traders were selling limes, breadfruit, manioc, papayas, fat yellow bananas, stalks of plantains, and she wandered from one fruit pile to the next, enjoying her encounters and bargaining in her elementary Swahili.

The man she chose to do business with seemed no different from the others, a fat cheerful, ingratiating character, his vegetables apparently the same prices as everybody else's. In the crowd she failed to notice the arrival of a Belgian official and his two uniformed African constables who stood behind her listening to their conversation. The vegetable seller, however, saw them quickly enough for his eyes became furtive, and he was frightened.

Helen's first awareness of action came when she heard the abrupt order behind her and felt the two African constables shoulder past her to grab the man. The harsh exchanges between the white official and the frightened African meant nothing to her, but she could scarcely believe it when the two constables flung the man on his face on the grass and beat him with long plant sticks.

The noise as the sticks swished through the air cutting through the man's thin clothes was sickening. He screamed as they continued flailing him; there seemed no end to the punishment, ten, twenty, thirty strokes. Helen turned wildly on the Belgian official protesting in a mixture of English, French and Swahili. Suddenly in the sunshine, in her own quiet village she was forced to witness a scene of appalling violence. 'Stop it, stop it,' she shouted, 'What are you doing? Stop it, do you hear?'

The official's voice was peremptory and contemptuous. 'He was overcharging for third-rate produce. He knew he was cheating; he knows what the penalty for cheating is.'

That the man was being flogged because of her was more than she could bear. 'But he wasn't overcharging me; we were just discussing prices.'

The official waved an impatient hand dismissing her. A crowd had gathered now, watching in silence while the vicious flogging continued. Then the Belgian issued a sharp order and the blows stopped. 'That will be a lesson to everybody here,' he declared in a loud voice.

Helen turned away, the thought of trying to buy anything now quite repugnant to her.

Whether the Belgians were responsible for introducing flogging as a means of law and order, or whether they found it already established when they arrived, Helen never discovered. Certainly African chiefs trained in Belgian administration used flogging as a general antidote to all forms of petty crime, and after Independence the brutality of Congolese in power towards their fellow-countrymen was much worse than anything she ever witnessed under the Belgians.

All through those early years of Independence, she treated men brought into her hospital flogged almost to the point of task.

Shortly after Independence she was asked by the new civil authorities to act as visiting doctor to the Wamba hospital. Although this was inconvenient and meant giving up two days a week which she needed for other things, she agreed. Then she discovered that included in the office was the duty of medically inspecting the prison.

Her first arrival at the prison coincided with a sudden flurry of beatings in the prison yard, though this activity, she was told later, was part of the normal risk attached to being in prison. Certainly the smells sickened her. In one part of the prison she was shown a series of cells roughly nine feet by twelve each holding not fewer than twelve men, with no sanitary arrangements, no water, and half the inmates suffering from dysentery or malaria.

She did what she could administering tablets and medicines, knowing that these were of no lasting use for sick men in such conditions. Then she demanded to see the prison commandant.

'It's absolutely disgusting,' she stormed. 'You have cases of malaria, and dysentery; you have lepers, you have all sorts of diseases yet the prisoners are incarcerated like animals. You have no hospital facilities at all. How can I treat them when there are no beds for me to put them into?'

The prison commandant's face was hostile.

'This is a prison,' he said bluntly.

'I know they're in prison. But they haven't been condemned to death. Should they die because they're serving their sentences?'

'They are wrong-doers, they have committed crimes.'

'They're still human beings.'

'They're criminals. This is a prison.'

There was no way round this stony-hearted logic.

'Then what is the point of my doing a medical inspection at all?' she demanded.

He did not bother to answer that question simply reaching for a square card lying on his desk. It was divided into columns. Against the appropriate column he appended a tick. It was headed: 'Medical Inspection.'

'You have done the job,' he said tersely.

Helen did what she could for a year, hating every visit she made. Even the thought that she might be helping or alleviating the condition of some of the prisoners was quickly dispelled, because she was soon aware, and made to be aware, that her visits coincided with particularly brutal beatings for many of the men; the prisoners were beaten because she was there, simply to illustrate that she had no authority; the prison officials had authority; they placed the tick in the column marked Medical Inspection, they made a fool of her and enjoyed it. A year later an official Medical Officer was appointed to Wamba and she relinquished her detested position.

Acting as visiting doctor and surgeon to Wamba hospital was much pleasanter. She quickly established friendly relationships with the Catholic nursing sisters whom she would meet again as prisoners in the convent, and the African staff, although there was little hospital discipline in the sense she understood it, and very little professional conscience towards patients or in the administering of drugs.

The weekly journey was irksome, she had to admit that; it meant leaving Nebo at five thirty in the morning to be ready to start ward rounds at 8.0 a.m., and she was never home until after 10.30 p.m. on the day she returned.

It was on one of these journeys, the back of the truck as usual loaded with passengers hitching a lift to Wamba, and John Mangadima along to act as medical assistant, that the truck was flagged to a halt at a village about eight miles from Wamba. A group of Christians she knew very well gathered round.

'Doctor Helen, you must not go into Wamba today, it is too dangerous.'

'What do you mean? There's an operative list as long as my arm expecting me. People can't wait for operations. Some of them might die.'

'It is too dangerous, Doctor Helen. Wamba is in chaos. All the white people are either under house arrest or in prison. You might be killed if you're seen on the streets.'

'Nonsense,' retorted Helen flatly. 'I'm needed at the hospital and I'm going in.' As an afterthought she added, 'Anyway, what's all the trouble about?'

There was a despondent air about her friends. One announced 'The news has come through that Patrice Lumumba has been murdered.'

All Helen knew about Patrice Lumumba was that he was just another politician operating in Léopoldville. In her estimation the world would be a much better place if it contained far more Christians and far fewer politicians. She did not state this opinion, but turning was surprised to find that the news had emptied the back of the truck with disconcerting suddenness; not a chicken, pig, squealing baby or pregnant mother remained.

'John,' she said, 'I must get in to the hospital. You can stay here and I'll pick you up this evening when I finish. I think I'd better . . .'

She tailed off as she saw the cold look on his face.

'Don't you know me even yet? If you're going into Wamba then I'm going with you.' He held up his hand as she started to speak. 'And there's no argument about it. Shall we get in and start off?'

Helen blinked behind her glasses. She'd been thoughtless again.

'All right,' she said. 'Sorry.' Three miles from Wamba soldiers stopped them at a road block with levelled rifles, and Helen realised *they* knew all about Lumumba's murder and what it signified.

'Out of the car! Where are your papers? Where d'you think you're going?'

The first exchanges were in Swahili, but John, serene and calm, knew that the soldiers were local Wabudus. He replied very sharply in their own dialect.

'You are not to talk to this lady in such a rough fashion.

Do you understand me? This is *our* doctor. She is one of us. She is of our blood. If you wish to interrogate us take us at once to your senior officers and be quick about it.'

Helen knew enough Kibudu to understand most of what he said, and had difficulty in preventing herself grinning as the abashed soldiers drove with them into Wamba to the local administrative offices. Their discomfiture increased as a small crowd gathered, amongst whom Helen recognised several of her patients, who demanded loudly why 'our doctor' had been arrested.

The exchanges were noisy and the Administrator came out of his office to see what was going on.

The corporal in charge of the squad explained his predicament. 'We stopped this lady, sir, knowing that all the whites in Wamba are either under house arrest or in prison. This man with her, sir, says she is a doctor on her way to hospital in Wamba.'

The Administrator looked at the crowd and said politely, 'Perhaps you could step into my office, Madam, and we can see what this is all about.'

Half an hour later, equipped with credentials making it clear that she was indeed 'our doctor', and authorised to move wherever she wanted, she left his office bound for the hospital. When she returned to Nebo the same evening the guards at the road block saluted her.

Three weeks later 'our doctor' was not half so self-assured driving through Wamba, this time without John Mangadima. The police jeep which ranged alongside, hooted at her angrily and drove her into the side of the road.

The policeman swore at her. Didn't she know she had made a right turn without signalling with her traffic indicator? She was under arrest.

'This is absolute nonsense,' Helen began and stopped abruptly as she realised that the policeman had a large ugly revolver pointed at her head.

She was driven to the police station and marched in front of an officer. For a few seconds he continued working at his desk then glared up.

'What's all this about?' Helen had no intention of allowing them to get their version in first so began her side of the story.

The officer stood up, leant forward and struck her hard across the face.

'You'll speak when you're spoken to,' he yelled. Helen's hand went to her cheek; she was more shocked than hurt.

'And stand to attention in front of me.'

Helen stood to attention. She stood to attention for two hours, and any attempt to defend herself was met with abuse and threats. The 'our doctor' scrap of paper was pushed aside contemptuously – she doubted if they could read, anyway – while they harangued her on her duties towards the new regime. Did she think just because she was white she could drive through Wamba ignoring all the traffic regulations? Did she think she could behave like a white colonialist? Those days were over, and the sooner she understood that the better!

When she drove back to Nebo, this time there were no guards to salute her.

Even Nebobongo, usually a haven of rest compared with the irritations she encountered elsewhere, inherited its share of problems. One almost cost her her life.

She had returned from her weekly visit to Wamba bringing back bales of cloth to make uniforms for the infant school and student nurses. As usual it was after ten at night and she was exhausted. A student nurse and a workman helped to unload the goods into her lounge. Then she carried her lamp into the kitchen to collect the plate of food the houseboy had left for her supper. As she sat at the table she was conscious of the cold, anticipatory nose of her young Alsatian puppy pushing into her lap to remind her that he too was interested in what lay on her plate.

She took one mouthful, sighed and gave up; she was far too tired to eat. The puppy sensing this gave her a second predatory nudge and she said, 'Oh, all right,' and put the plate on the floor. The food was eaten, the plate cleaned and polished by a long appreciative red tongue, in about twenty seconds.

She did not remember getting into bed, but she remembered the hideousness of the next three days: the vomiting, dizziness and burning in her mouth and stomach. Benjamin, her houseboy, had found the puppy stretched out stiff and dead on the floor when he arrived next morning, Helen in an unconscious delirium.

The house had been stripped bare: all the cloth she had bought, household goods, curtains at the windows, foodstuffs, all her clothing, her watch which she kept by her bed, even the blankets, sheets and pillow on her bed had gone. The violators had calmly eaten a meal at her table and left only the dirty crocks.

They had poisoned the food with native berries of a particularly deadly variety, and two mouthfuls would probably have killed Helen as effectively as it killed the Alsatian puppy. The local police arrived and made a beautiful plaster cast of one footprint they discovered. Even Helen had to admire this fine example of their craft, and no doubt it is still being exhibited today in some police college in Province Orientale as a perfect demonstration of the art. Naturally it had nothing whatsoever to do with catching the criminals. That was far more Congolese in subtlety.

Susan with her friend Eleanor were out at Pastor Ndugu's village running the clinic when a young African walked in wearing a highly patterned sweater which Susan recognised immediately as belonging to Helen.

Eleanor was injecting patients in the next room when Susan surprised her by whispering, 'There's a youth next door with a sweater I want. I'm writing out a prescription for him to be injected.'

Unsuspectingly the youth handed over his sweater and marched in to see Eleanor. When he returned to find his sweater missing he began to complain.

'It's over at Pastor Ndugu's house,' explained Susan blandly. 'If you want it you'd better go across and fetch it. '

In the living-room there Susan cross-examined him with the ferocity of a prosecution counsel at a murder trial, as indeed, but for a twist of good fortune it would have been.

'Where,' she demanded, 'did you get this sweater?' The youth was taken aback. 'I bought it at a shop.'

'Which shop?'

'A shop in Wamba.'

'What was the name of the shop?'

'I've forgotten.'

'But you know where it is ?'

'Oh, yes.'

'Then we can take you there and you can show us.'

'Oh, I've just remembered. I'm confusing this sweater with another. My brother bought this from a shop in Stanleyville. There are a lot of shops in Stanleyville.'

'You are a liar,' stormed Susan. 'If you don't tell us where you got this sweater we're taking you to the Chief and he'll know how to get the truth out of you.'

The youth was weak and easily brow-beaten. He admitted he'd bought the sweater from a man in the village next to his. Yes, the man had all sorts of things to sell: bales of cloth, household goods, knives and forks, they were very cheap and he asked you not to tell anybody else.

The evidence was presented by Susan and some of Nebobongo's senior African staff to the police. Nothing was done about it. The bent wheel of Belgian colonial justice had turned to another position but it was still bent. Congolese judicial procedures still operated in the same blindly prejudicial manner as before only this time the black man was always right, and it was clear that in many African minds the freedom word *uhuru* implied a specific right to rob, plunder and dispossess the whites.

There was occasionally even a flash of macabre humour in the sequence of events. On one occasion the local chief wrote to her saying that if ever a thief broke into her house, on no account was she to challenge him because the thief would undoubtedly be armed, and he would be much more skilful at killing her than she would at killing him. This disconcerting information removed all peace of mind as she lay in bed with a machete on one side and a spear on the other, thinking how dreadful it would be if anyone came in to kill her, and how even more dreadful if she should strike back and inadvertently kill *him*.

She was in this state of mind one night when she woke conscious of a soft sawing noise at her shutters. Someone was trying to get in. Tense with fear she put on her glasses, grabbed her machete and with a torch in the other hand crept forward. Standing silent at the shutters she realised that indeed someone was trying to force them open. Summoning all her courage she switched on the torch and bellowed, 'Go away!' She heard a noise outside as if the surprised burglar had fallen backwards in fright, and then someone scrambling up and running away. She then became aware that two inches away from her nose the point of a long sharp machete projected towards her. On reflection she had at least gained one extra machete out of that night's work.

The most astonishing experience occurred when John Cunningham, a missionary from the north, arrived with his pregnant wife for the birth of their baby.

The evening she started in labour Helen decided to apply a little common sense to the proceedings.

'It will take quite a few hours,' she observed, 'so while Elaine gets everything ready I suggest we all rest as much as possible to be ready for the real work when it begins.'

Helen put her feet up on the couch in the living-room, Mrs Cunningham retired to bed, and Elaine started sterilising instruments and boiling water because it was never very easy delivering a baby under bush conditions.

The rest period was interrupted by a loud scream from Mrs Cunningham. Everyone rushed to the bedroom. 'There was a black man in the room,' she declared in a panic. 'I'd just dozed off, woke up, and there he was at the foot of the bed!'

There was no black man in sight. 'Now calm down, calm down,' Helen soothed. 'It was probably only a bad dream due to your condition. You go back to sleep and we'll search the house and make certain that no one's here.'

A house search revealed that indeed no one was there, except the five whites: Mr and Mrs Cunningham, Helen, Elaine and Stebby.

Two hours later the baby began its journey into the world. In the middle of the process Helen needed something from the bathroom and Elaine volunteered to fetch it. As she passed Mrs Cunningham's now vacant bedroom she glanced inside to see an African just scrambling out through the window carrying a briefcase in his hand; (later they decided he'd probably hidden under the bed the whole time.) Elaine dashed back, her reactions frantic.

'An African! In the bedroom! Just jumped through the window carrying a briefcase!'

John yelled, 'He's got the briefcase. He's got my briefcase!'

Helen trying to cope with the arrival of a baby shouted, 'What was in it?'

'Everything we own in the world. Passports, documents, all the church money.'

Metaphorically Helen dropped everything and dashed for the back door. Mounted outside was her own personal talking drum placed there by friends for an emergency like this. Trained by them to use it, Helen grabbed the heavy drum sticks and began to bang away. A talking drum does not give a Morse code message, it imitates the sound of human vowels. In the early days she had learnt to send a couple of messages: 'Come to prayers,' 'Surgical team needed,' half as a joke. One side of the drum played a light tone, the opposite had a heavier resonance. You kept a regular beat going with your left hand and stroked rhymically with your right. Now into the midnight air went Helen's exhortation, 'We need help ... we need help ... we need help ...'

From the first tonal outburst the compound and indeed the whole village was alerted to the fact that 'our doctor' was in peril. The village men decided she was certainly under attack from a band of outlaws. Mainly naked they leapt from their beds, grabbed spears and clubs, and hurtled down the road towards the hospital ready for battle. John Mangadima and his band of student nurses, nearer at hand, interpreted the message differently. The birth had gone wrong; a full Caesarian must be mounted at once, the entire surgical team were needed. Pausing only to leap into white surgical gowns and caps they raced for the house. The time it took them to dress and the villagers to run, meant that both teams arrived outside the house in a confused crowd at precisely the same moment, naked villagers brandishing spears, surgical team waving stethoscopes.

Helen directed the emergency with a few quick words and they spread out to search the compound. The thief and money were never seen again, though most of the documents were recovered next morning thrown down by the roadside. The net result of these episodes, the attempt at poisoning and the burglaries was that until the Simbas finally arrested all of them, never again was she really out of sight and sound of her followers. Practically every mouthful of food put before her was tasted by her cook. Her male students in pairs and in shifts, slept at the house and maintained guard. 'Our doctor' was an essential and precious part of the pattern of their lives.

Part Four

I

Doctor Swertz's expression was as usual impassive, watchful, and seemingly hostile. As always there could be no doubting the seriousness of his statement. 'Doctor Roseveare,' he said bluntly, 'I think you should leave Congo at once.'

Helen who had been into this already with Jack Scholes and the others had her answer ready.

'Thank you very much Doctor Swertz but I didn't leave in 1960 and I don't intend to leave now.'

Doctor Swertz's expression did not change and his eyes did not move. 'This is not 1960. This is 1964. It is much more dangerous. I think you should go.'

Helen had already decided against offering him coffee. Doctor Swertz had no time for such social frivolities.

'Are you leaving?' she inquired.

'No, but I'm a man.'

'And I'm a doctor.'

Helen was slightly puzzled why he should be so concerned about her, but then she never had, and never would understand this enigmatic Belgian physician.

'I've got my car outside,' he urged. 'I'd like to drive you to Paulis so that you can catch a plane to safety.'

Helen would admit that Doctor Swertz's contacts at Pawa amongst the Africans were probably more sophisticated than her own. He probably knew more than she did about this new rebellion, but he didn't seem to understand that she was driven by reasons of faith not of personal survival. It really was most astonishing she thought, how the passing of the years changed one's opinion about people. Doctor Swertz had figured briefly, morosely, and silently in that very first training period at the Red Cross hospital at Pawa, impressing himself on her memory by ignoring her completely. Certainly his brusque reaction to John Mangadima's protest – swift slaps across the face – had been responsible for delivering John to her. But apparently, over the years, for some reason known only to himself, he had decided if not to like her then at least to accept her and of course he had one good reason to feel grateful towards her.

Helen could not understand him but she could admire him for his dedication: she knew that as a doctor he gave his life and skill wholly to Congo for a pittance of a salary. Their acquaintanceship, after seven years of mutual hostility, had really started in 1960. At Independence all Belgian civil servants had been ordered home. Before leaving he had come to visit her at Nebobongo.

As usual he came abruptly to the point. 'You know I have married a Congolese wife?'

'You also know that she has contracted tuberculosis?'

'Yes.' Helen had heard this disturbing news but had also been told that in his own taciturn way he treated her with tenderness, love and respect, and was never unfaithful to her. This side of his character was so diametrically opposite to his usual face-slapping methods with Africans that Helen could scarcely believe it.

'I am ordered back to Belgium, but I intend to return as soon as I can. The newly independent regime want me to go on working at Pawa for them.'

This was news to Helen and pleased her immensely. She was delighted to discover that behind the kicks and slaps administered by Dr Swertz existed a man of such humanitarian ideals, and even more delighted to hear that the Congolese also recognised these qualities and wanted him back.

For once in his life he now seemed at a loss for words. 'Would you . . .' he began hesitatingly. 'Could you . . .'

'Yes?' encouraged Helen.

'Would you look after my wife until I return. She is very sick and she will not get better.'

'Of course. I'll do everything I can.'

The story ended tragically for he returned only to help nurse an incurably sick woman who eventually died at Nebobongo in 1963.

In that August of 1964 when the missionaries at Ibambi and Nebobongo heard that Stanleyville was in the hands of rebels who called themselves Simbas, Helen had no clear idea what sort of rebels they were or what they wanted. And twiddling the knobs of her radio set didn't make it any easier to understand. She received half a dozen versions in English: the Russian and Peking spokesmen predictably asserted that this was a popular uprising of the downtrodden Congolese people against Leopoldville's imperialist-dominated puppet government, a line followed by Brazzaville's Communist regime on the northern side of the Congo.

The B.B.C. were cautious, the American stations excited, but the rebellion was sufficiently disturbing to halt Helen's impending thousand-mile journey across the border to Kampala in Uganda to procure supplies of badly needed drugs. She reasoned that if rebels were roaming about the countryside, it was likely they would either steal the truck on the outward journey, or steal both truck and supplies on the way back; and there was the added likelihood that she might not be able to get back.

During those four years of independence Patrice Lumumba had been assassinated and become the first pan-African martyr, and Dag Hammarskjold had died in a mysterious air crash near Congo to become the first senior United Nations martyr. In those first years the Central Government, bolstered by the U.N. had been dominated by President Kasavubu and exhibited the instability usually associated with the governments of some Latin American republics. When, in September 1963 Kasavubu abruptly dissolved parliament, and a variety of left-wing politicians fled across the Congo to Brazzaville to set up revolutionary committees with the avowed purpose of overthrowing the government, it was obvious to everyone that more trouble was just about to start.

By June 1964 as the last of the disillusioned U.N. troops left the country, half a dozen of these politicians were successfully filling the vacuum they left behind by fomenting rebellion in many parts of Congo.

Stanleyville fell to the self-styled General Olenge and his

Simbas with scarcely a shot fired. He was aided by his chief of witchcraft, Mama Orena, an ancient crone four-and-a-half-feet tall, who wore a leopard skin wrap and waved her magic amulets as she pranced into towns such as Bunia, Paulis and Wamba which offered only token resistance before surrendering. This introduced a new dimension into modern warfare – the use of drugs, fetishes, magic incantations, witchcraft and cannibalism – and it was so successful it terrified whole battalions of the National Congolese Army; in Stanleyville seven thousand soldiers deserted to Olenge's ranks. Communist guns, ammunition, provisions and advisers were ferried in from Brazzaville, and across the borders from Southern Sudan and Uganda, and within weeks four-fifths of Congo were in Simba hands. The coup looked complete.

Its hold, however, was tenuous. By a political sleight of hand as mysterious as one of Mama Orena's magic formulae, Moise Tshombe, discredited after the failure of Katanganese secession, was now recalled to become Prime Minister of Congo with Kasavubu as his President. His first move was to recruit a force of three hundred white mercenaries under an ex-British officer Major Mike Hoare, and another force of six hundred, mainly French-speaking, under Major 'Black Jack' Schramme, and there is no doubt whatsoever that this comparatively small force of mercenaries preserved Congo from the rebels. They stiffened the morale of the National Congolese Army to such an extent that slowly through 1964 and 1965 all the major towns were recaptured, even though the much more formidable task of flushing the rebels out of the endless rain forests still remained.

Tshombe did not survive much of this action. In 1965 General Mobutu, a sergeant in the Belgian Army at the time of independence, instigated a military coup which deposed him, and Tshombe retreated to the warm padding of his Swiss bank-account existence in Europe. Eventually he was lured to his death in North Africa in 'mysterious circumstances'. Deaths in mysterious circumstances were commonplace during Congo's years of violence.

Doctor Swertz's arrival at her front door in August 1964 was therefore not totally surprising to Helen, even though her answer was delivered with utter finality. 'I'm not leaving, Dr Swertz.

Thank you very much for your offer to drive me to the airport at Paulis. But what are you going to do?'

Suddenly he smiled and Helen realised that it was the first and only time in her life she had seen this happen.

'Go back to Pawa and kick my patients about.'

It was also the very first time she had ever heard him make a joke. She presumed that the story of John Mangadima's departure from his hospital and John's reasons for joining Helen must have reached him sooner or later.

'Gently, I hope,' said Helen. He stared at her. 'Yes, gently.'

'What about the danger for you?'

He shrugged. 'I'll be all right. They'll need doctors in the future; they'll need them very badly.'

He said goodbye, turned on his heel and left, this abrupt, enigmatic yet peculiarly gentle and inevitably professional Dr Swertz, who had made his Congo bed and was, for good or evil, going to lie on it. She never saw him again. Certainly she could not have foreseen the bitter finale life held for him. While Helen was held in the convent at Wamba, he had travelled from Pawa to Ibambi to see a patient. Seeing him, a white man, in the street, a twelve-year-old 'cub' opened fire with his machine-pistol killing him instantly.

When the Simbas first over-ran their district they made reassuring noises and insisted to the missionaries that now they were in power everything would be bigger, better and brighter. Their intentions were good, their sense of economics childlike. Their ruling that all prices in the shops should be cut by three-quarters meant that goods disappeared overnight. Quite quickly no one had any money and no one was paid any wages. Helen was told to make a list of all the drugs she needed, that this would be sent to Stanleyville and that the drugs would arrive within a few hours. As Helen already knew that Stanleyville was as short of drugs as she was, the incredible stupidity of their actions was almost beyond her comprehension; she realised that in their minds they had decided that if they *said* it would happen, it *must* happen. After all they had been given magic powers by the witch-doctors.

But what was appallingly real was the barbarism of their

[167]

power. Legal courts, tribunals and juries were things of the past. If the Simbas *thought* you were guilty you were executed. And from every town and village in their vicinity, bestial stories of hundreds of innocent people tortured and killed became sickening reality.

Her first medical involvement with the Simbas was frightening. A truck full of soldiers roared into the compound at Nebobongo. A sergeant grabbed her arm and gabbled away in a peculiar French of which she understood about half. Even as he spoke they were lugging a wounded civilian out of the truck.

'He's been shot in action. Bullets in the chest. His life is in danger. You must attend to him at once.'

Helen had a worrying vision of smashed ribs, pumping arteries and massive internal injuries for which from an emotional, surgical, or any other viewpoint she was completely unequipped to deal. The man would almost certainly be dying from his wounds; there was little she would be able to do except pray.

But she couldn't run away; they hemmed her in. There was no alternative but to examine him. In the operating room she was at once relieved and puzzled to find that his wound had already been bandaged quite professionally.

'Yes, yes,' the sergeant concurred impatiently, 'the nurses at Wamba did it. But they are not *real* doctors. That is why we have brought him to you.'

The man was conscious and she was aware of his dark anxious eyes examining her face. She undid the bandages and saw at once that the wound was not serious: a single bullet had struck him high up in the chest, ricocheted along his clavicle and emerged at the point of his shoulder. She cleansed and rebandaged it and reassured them all. But when they had gone she sat down and contemplated the future with dread: she knew she would never be able to cope with bullet or shrapnel wounds in the stomach or chest; the very thought of such injuries unnerved her.

The house inspections soon started, in effect looting 'liberations' of radio sets, tape-recorders, typewriters and any other piece of equipment they fancied. On Friday, October 23rd a gang of young hooligans invaded Nebobongo armed with spears and knives. They rushed into her house demanding the keys to Helen's car and the chauffeur to drive it. 'I'm the chauffeur,' declared Helen, and then stalling for time, 'Who is in command?'

It was utterly and unbelievably ridiculous. The leader was twelve years old, a swaggering little boy whose feet wouldn't even reach the clutch pedal of her car. Yet he intended to drive it away. Vainly Helen protested that it had no lights, needed its plugs cleaned every ten miles or so, that its tyres were likely to blow apart at any minute; the car was commandeered.

To save her house from destruction by a boy who could not drive forward let alone reverse, Helen backed out of the garage and gave him a short course of instruction. It was quite hopeless; every time he tried to accelerate he stalled the engine, and it became obvious that unless she drove, they were never going to move in any direction now or in the future. The scene ended when without lights she drove the car to the palm-oil factory beyond Ibambi, and the local mechanic accepted responsibility and took them to Wamba.

But the real terror which culminated in their arrest commenced during those first four weeks of November 1964. During this period they knew from radio reports that fighting between Simbas, the National Congolese Army and white mercenaries was taking place at various points within a hundred or so mile radius, but they had no way of confirming these broadcasts and absolutely no means of communication with anybody.

Two days after her rape and their move to Ibambi on November 1st, a gang of Simbas arrived to arrest Bill McChesney. In the course of the confused argument they wanted to know why, as doctor, she was not at Nebobongo.

Helen tried to avoid the issue by being polite, by making formal application for permission to stay at Ibambi. This did not please them at all.

'But your hospital is at Nebobongo. It is your duty to be at your hospital.'

'At this moment I request permission to stay here.'

'Why don't you want to go back?' Helen's face was swollen and bruised, the traumatic effects of that night still haunted her, 'Because I'm frightened.'

'Frightened. What is there to be frightened about?' Exasperatedly Helen exclaimed, 'Two nights ago I was struck in the face.'

She didn't want to say any more but they would not leave her alone. Who had struck her? A Simba officer. This was beyond belief. Was she not aware that a Simba would never molest a white woman. They were blessed by magic powers and cleansed of such improprieties. A statement would have to be made about this whole affair and forwarded to the proper authorities. Paper and pens were produced, questions and answers duly noted, the whole melancholy story revealed. At the end of it she had to sign a document. Because of it Lieutenant George was arrested and spent a short period in prison. And she earned the continuing enmity of the Simbas.

So the series of dangerous incidents continued until the Stanleyville massacre brought everything to a head. On Thursday, 26th November, two days after the well-advertised Belgian parachute drop on that town precipitated the murder of white civilians, Brian hurried in with alarming news. Contingents of angry Simbas fleeing from Stanleyville and other battle fronts were driving through Ibambi in stolen cars and trucks some of them pausing to loot and wreck. It was rumoured that the Greek traders were being beaten up and possibly murdered.

In the past the missionaries had discussed what seemed like obvious common sense, the idea of hiding deep in the forest until the danger had passed. On this occasion the senior African mission workers thought it an excellent idea. Mama Anakesi, one of the most respected Ibambi midwives, was deputised to lead them to such a hiding place, and reluctantly five bewildered grown-up white people carrying raincoats, sandwiches and thermos flasks trooped in single file into the rain forest. Possibly many of those middle-class Europeans clutching handbags and children as they journeyed towards concentration camps and gas chambers had experienced the same bewildering disbelief.

Mama Anakesi led them along muddy paths, across streams and into the deep silent forests. 'You settle down here,' she said, 'I will come back tonight when the Simbas have left.'

Helen looked around, her eyes appraising the beauty of the forest. Enormous, smooth black tree trunks soared upwards to support a thick canopy of branches and leaves. Sunshine filtered downwards in a golden haze. Little pools reflected light and were occasionally fragmented by the plop of a raindrop from high overhead. Insects hummed and buzzed but were not troublesome, and Jessie Scholes, lessening the tension, said cheerfully:

'Well, I never expected to be one of the Babes in the Wood.'

Brian was more practical. 'We'd better not stay in one group. Much better if we split into pairs and find hiding places about a hundred yards apart, make ourselves comfortable, read our books. I'll bring sandwiches and coffee round at lunchtime.'

The forest floor was wet and slushy but Amy and Helen found a small island of dry ground amongst the gnarled roots of an enormous mahogany tree and sat down.

No more than an hour had passed when suddenly they heard the roar of planes overhead.

'It could be the mercenaries,' exclaimed Amy excitedly. 'Supposing they did manage to capture Ibambi!'

The thought was so intoxicating that it actually increased their tension, and it wasn't until Brian brought round the coffee and sandwiches at midday that they calmed down again.

'No sign of Mama Anakesi yet,' he reported, as a new thought occurred to Helen. 'I hope we're not supposed to stay here all night,' she said glancing uneasily at Amy. It was one thing sitting around happily in the daylight, but the idea of staying there after dark was intimidating. For perhaps half an hour after Brian had gone they sat in silence. There had been no sound, not even a whisper, a twig snapping, a rustling in the undergrowth, but suddenly – enveloping them – the yelling war chant, 'Simba! ... Simba! ... Simba! ...' The men, and there must have been about twenty of them armed with crowbars, spears and clubs, herded them back through the forest, jostling them out on to the red gravel road which linked the mission station with Ibambi village.

Their delight at their own cleverness alternated with rage. The missionaries would be taught a lesson this time. 'All shoes off! All hats off!' As Amy began to wipe her muddy feet on the grass one of the Simbas yelled, 'Do people wipe their feet when they're going to be executed?'

Barefooted and bareheaded they were prodded in the direction of the village.

'Run!' their tormentors shouted, 'Run.' Pointed sticks and iron bars were shoved into their backs. 'Run, run!'

Each victim was pushed by at least two men, and Helen quickly understood this method of torture. The stones and gravel cut into her feet, the sun on her head and neck was blisteringly hot. Two hundred yards and it was unbearable; three hundred and she knew she could go no farther. Her chest constricted, she could not get her breath, she staggered, and suddenly the red gravel road came up to meet her face. But there was no respite. They yelled and kicked her to her feet again. Gasping, Helen looked round for Mrs Scholes. She too had fallen to the ground. One of her tormentors hit her, urging her up on her knees then jerking her upright. Helen had no time to see more. She was prodded and pushed onwards. Pouring sweat, their feet bloody, staggering from exhaustion the seven of them were chased and jeered through Ibambi village and up the hill to the factory which the Simbas were using as headquarters and gaol.

The five women were herded into one room, the two men taken elsewhere. There was a bed in the centre. The Simbas crowded in after them ready for the fun to start. The leader shouted the orders. 'Sit on the bed. Now stand up. Now sit on the floor again. Now stand up. Sit on the bed.'

It was childish and petty, but beneath it ran a current of viciousness and anger quite unmistakably evil. You did what you were told. Death or brutal punishment was a threat as close as the fists waving in their faces. Their captors were drinking spirits and beer now; half of them already had the glassy look in their eyes which indicated native drugs.

'Wait till tonight,' they threatened. 'We'll show you what women are for.'

Two men lurched into the room and began to fight, striking and screaming at each other and cannoning into the women. Then suddenly they stopped, roaring with laughter; it was a mock fight to disturb and upset them.

At this moment some local bully recognised Helen. 'That's the woman who accused Lieutenant George of raping her,' he shouted and now they had discovered a specific point of hatred on which to concentrate. She was separated from the others and pushed outside.

'Give her the same sort of justice that Lieutenant George got,' they cried.

They demonstrated a schoolboy delight in mock tribunals as if by choosing a judge and jury and calling upon a variety of hostile witnesses they were fulfilling some democratic process of exemplary virtue. Helen was thrust into the centre of the ring.

'You accused Lieutenant George of raping you?' Helen knew that unless she answered their questions she would certainly be beaten up.

'I did not accuse him of anything.'

'You accused him of raping you.'

'When I was forced to by your examiners.'

'There was no reason for you to open your mouth. Why did you open your mouth to accuse an African?' Helen did not reply. 'Did he beat you? Tell us that.'

'No.'

'Did he hurt you? Tell us that.' Helen thought of the smashed teeth, the cuts and bruises.

'No.'

'He used you as a woman, that was all?'

'Yes.'

'Aren't you a woman?'

'Yes.'

'Well, what are women for? Answer me that.' She did not try and argue with the fatuous male logic of the self-appointed inquisitor. But he could not leave the point alone.

'You are a woman and what are women for? You were used as a woman, weren't you?'

'Yes.'

'Yet you have accused our comrade of a dreadful crime, when any normal human being knows that such things are no more than the natural order of events. Tonight we'll show all of you what the natural order of events can be.'

And so it went on, an endless repetition of the 'Well, you're a woman aren't you?' routine. But eventually they could squeeze no more out of it. She was pushed back into the other room with her friends. The immediate future seemed to hold little peace for any of them now.

A little later they heard a truck roar into the factory compound, the noise of a dozen drunken soldiers reeling into the room to communicate the latest rumours. There were great battles going on at Paulis and Wamba, they said; the National Congolese Army was attacking with planes and guns. There were air raids and slaughter everywhere. Noisily they barged around until someone remembered the five women again. Weren't they responsible for all this trouble? Yes, another run would do them good, wouldn't it?

They were jostled out of the room and into the sunshine again. Shoes off! A lot of exercise was necessary for white women. The soldiers jeered and applauded the spectacle. But only three guards could bother to run behind and prod them along now; the beer drinking and the heat of the afternoon had diminished their interest. After two hundred yards only one guard remained.

Round the corner and out of sight of the soldiers Jessie Scholes collapsed.

'We'll have to carry her,' said Helen. 'Can you get on my back, Mrs Scholes?'

'I'm all right,' said Jessie faintly. 'I'll get up.'

But she could not get up, even with help. 'Helen, let's make a chair with our hands,' suggested Elaine. 'We'll carry her between us.'

They linked hands and carried Jessie, but before they had completed twenty paces Helen knew it was hopeless. Even without Jessie's additional weight the pain caused by the sharp gravel cutting into their feet was excruciating; the extra weight made it intolerable. Helen caught a glimpse of Elaine's face, and knew they had to stop.

The remaining guard came up behind them.

'All right,' he shouted. 'Put her down. Put her down.'

For an instant Helen thought he was going to strike them but his next move was far more mystifying. He turned and stooped, offering his back. 'Go on, help her up. I'll carry her.'

In silent, incredulous amazement, Helen and Elaine watched him jog-trot off down the road carrying Jessie. Half convinced that he planned some fresh outrage they hurried after him. But he was sincere; he gave Jessie a piggy-back to within a hundred yards of the factory gates before lowering her to the ground.

'Now, go on all of you,' he ordered. 'Run, so it looks as if I'm chasing you.' Neither Helen or Elaine understood until later that to Jessie Scholes the episode made perfect sense; she had recognised the man as an ex-mission worker from Ibambi.

There was still no respite for them as they stumbled into the factory compound. The soldiers were drunk and ready for another opportunity to humiliate the foreign white women.

'Get into line. Quick march!' They were pushed across the compound and lined-up in front of the temporary Simba headquarters. A large crowd of jeering Africans quickly gathered.

The Simbas began to taunt them. Were they tired? Didn't the poor missionary women look tired? Were they thirsty? Would they like a glass of beer each? Bring beer from the store and give it to the ladies.

The crowd applauded. This offered new excitement. Everyone knew that the Christians adamantly refused to drink beer; several African Christians had been badly beaten up, a few killed, for sticking unwaveringly to principle.

Helen, first in line and standing next to Jessie Scholes, sensed her determination to resist. 'I'll not touch a single drop. I'd sooner die.'

The frightening truth about her statement was that most certainly she would not drink it and would most certainly die. Fortunately, in her agitation she forgot her Swahili and shouted her refusal in English.

The first glass of beer was thrust into Helen's hand. She had occasionally wondered what she would do in such a situation. She knew that the idea of strong drink of any sort was frowned upon in her missionary circle. Generally she thoroughly approved of the principle, but whether she approved strongly enough to sacrifice her life for such a cause she was not sure about at all. Could she make a Joan of Arc stand on this point or was she merely being absurd? She knew there was no scriptural necessity for such a stand. God, in Helen's terms knew of their present situation. Would He wish any of His hard-working and hard-pressed followers to die as part of an anti-drink campaign? In Helen's mind it was now a clear choice of being thrown to the crowd to be raped, mutilated and probably killed – the soldiers' threats made this quite clear – or of drinking the glass of beer.

She was conscious that Jessie Scholes was eyeing it as she might a black mamba poised to strike. Helen raised her glass high in the air. 'I am drinking this liquid in the name of the Lord Jesus,' she said loudly and swallowed it to the accompaniment of loud cheers and laughter. To her slight surprise, it made her feel better almost immediately. And she had certainly deflated the beer-drinking joke; if they were all going to behave in this way, there was no fun in this sort of missionary baiting. Accordingly they were all herded into the store and not long afterwards Jack Scholes and Brian were thrust back in to join them. They had also had an unpleasant time but for the moment they were left alone. The soldiers were bored with them, and in any case another truckload had just arrived with more stories to tell.

Helen was therefore a little surprised when one of the younger Simbas, a sergeant and one of the local leaders, approached her. He wanted a word with her outside.

It was pitch dark as she followed him out on to the veranda. Obviously, in his unworldly opinion the fact that she had been raped and now drank beer gave her a certain glamour in his eyes. It was all very simple, he explained. All she had to do was agree to make love to him, act as his wife, and the other missionary women would not be molested. He came closer and put his arm round her. He tried to kiss her and she turned her face away.

There was no doubt, however, that *he* believed her silence meant acquiescence; she realised this by his change of manner. He adopted the same possessive attitude that Lieutenant George had shown after that terror-filled night at Nebobongo. He took her back inside, gave her a chair, offered her a glass of water. The other missionaries, he announced to the room generally, would be taken across to a nearby European household. They were not to be harmed; no one was to touch them.

When they had gone she felt very isolated and vulnerable. The arrivals and departures of the Simbas were still very confusing, and a noisy lieutenant who had just arrived seemed to carry authority. He began to talk and harangue the others at the top of his voice, and Helen with a chilled feeling in her stomach understood the gist of his message quite clearly.

'All Simba units are falling back,' he shouted. 'There must be no mercy shown to any of the whites in this area. None of them must survive. Civilians, missionaries, Catholic or Protestant, are to be executed at once.'

He paused and there was silence. The Simbas realising they

Jack Scholes, Helen and Jessie
Scholes at Ibambi with a young
man who once saved Jessie's
life

Pope Paul receiving several nuns
rescued, like Dr Roseveare, from
Wamba
photo: AP

Helen, Dr Herb Atkinson,
Dr Carl Becker and Dr Ruth
Dix at Nyankunde: Helen
and Carl planned this medical
centre, connected by a flying
doctor service with remote
jungle villages

Helen and John Mangadima
winning the three-legged
race at School Sports Day

Helen with two pupils

Nyankunde: Helen built her medical school here in
the grasslands above the rain forest to complement
the hospital pioneered by Dr Becker and other
American doctors

Helen welcomed on a visit to
Nyankunde by Florence
Stebbing, nurse-midwife

Dr Helen Roseveare and the
author, Alan Burgess, in Africa

had a victim already in their midst drew back with dramatic slowness to reveal Helen sitting on her chair.

Their withdrawal brought her to the lieutenant's attention. He went across and stared at her. Helen was now almost too exhausted to care what they did to her. The lieutenant's actions however, were very strange; he bent down and touched her shoulder.

'You are the lady doctor?' he said in surprise.

'Yes.'

'Well, don't you remember me, doctor?'

Helen glanced up. It was quite dark outside, and the lamps in the store were dim and smoky. She couldn't see him very well. She certainly didn't recognise him. When he said, 'You saved my life,' it didn't make any sense and her eyes widened in bewilderment. 'Did I?'

He turned back to the others his arms stretched wide. 'This woman is good. She saved my life. No one will touch or harm her. D'you hear me?'

And then she understood. He was the first wounded civilian the soldiers had brought in for attention during those first days of the rebellion; she had been terrified that he might be suffering from massive internal injuries.

'She's good, this woman. No one is to hurt her.' He was making his point very clear and now Helen understood his authority. He was one of the 'magic' ones. A bullet had struck him. It should have killed him; instead he had survived; he had demonstrated that the witch-doctor's powers were potent and real; bullets would not, and could not, kill those who followed their doctrine. It was an up-to-date and improved version of the fanatical Muslim belief of the Middle Ages that death in battle delivered the true believers straight to Paradise and the bountiful bosoms of beautiful houris. Small wonder he had risen to his present military rank.

'Where are your friends?' he demanded, his solicitude overwhelming. 'They must not be harmed either. And you must be with them. What are you doing here by yourself?' Helen, quite content to be taken across to the European house to rejoin the others, did not waste time explaining.

As the hours passed the situation became completely confused. Local and fleeing Simbas argued. There was no focal point of authority to issue orders; the missionaries became an embarrassment. During the night they were marched in various directions and then marched back again. Eventually some temporary authority decided that the best way of solving the problem was to send them all home.

At 6.30 a.m. they were loaded into a truck and driven back to Ibambi. Two days later they were re-arrested and taken to the convent in Wamba.

Part Five

I

All through that long hot December of 1964, imprisoned in the convent, a spring of tension inside each woman slowly tightened towards breaking point. The nights were agony: a footstep in the corridor, the sound of a voice raised somewhere outside in the darkness, enough to grip the mind in terror.

There was growing evidence that the Simba revolt had failed; that slowly and inexorably they were being ejected from town and village, but it seemed also inevitable that they would continue to fight as a guerrilla organisation in the forest for years to come. And this news did not reassure Helen or any of the others at all; the preservation of their lives as front line hostages depended entirely upon the National Congolese Army and the mercenaries keeping their distance; the closer the fighting crept to Wamba, the greater the threat to their safety. Each day brought some new crisis.

One Saturday, Helen, Amy and Elaine were clearing tables in the dining-room when they heard a shouted commotion outside. There was only one place to hide – behind the refrigerator – quite absurd if a proper search was made. They crouched there for more than two hours listening to Simbas storming up and down the corridors, and racing across to the dormitories of the black nuns. Occasionally they heard the Mother Superior's voice trying to bring some sense into the total and horrifying confusion.

When the noise subsided they crept out of their hiding place. Apparently the colonel had come for Sister Clothilde; he wished to declare his love and continuing determination that she should become one of his wives. She had pleaded illness and he had

had to leave without her; dragging her away by her wrists would hardly match his loving words.

Early next morning the guards rushed in, herded them all back to their rooms and locked them in. They were let out in the early afternoon. Apparently another convoy of fleeing Simba troops had passed through Wamba looting and hooting, and driven to the convent looking for trouble. Eventually the guards had persuaded them to leave, and they had departed stealing bread from the kitchen and nuns' underwear hanging on the clothes line.

That afternoon the Commandant from Wamba arrived, accompanied by his second-in-command, who travelled everywhere with a small transistor radio blaring jazz dangling from a shoulder strap, plus a twelve-year-old 'cub', in charge of local 'magic'. Helen had met the cub before. He boasted he had fought in the war at Beni and killed a white man. Bullets fired by the National Army he asserted had passed harmlessly over his head. He was, therefore, one of the élite and the other Simbas, many much older, treated him with the greatest respect. Helen also discovered that he had managed to reach sixth grade in a primary school and had passed his scholarship examination to secondary school, but that now he had reached his present eminence 'childish ambitions' no longer interested him.

The purpose of the Commandant's visit was to assure the Mother Superior that he was wholly on her side, and when the delivering troops arrived, should it be in his power, he would certainly hand over the women unharmed.

'I seem to be the only one in authority left,' he admitted sadly. He had obviously decided that in the very near future the moment to stand up and be counted would arrive, and he had no wish to be counted on the wrong side. 'Everyone else has run away. However, I must warn you that hundreds of Simba soldiers are passing through Wamba, and the next few weeks will be very dangerous. The safest place is definitely the convent, and my guards will do their best to keep you safe.'

The prospect did not sound alluring and the fact that their safety should now depend upon the very guards who had used them so brutally was hardly conducive to a feeling of confidence.

The Mother Superior gathered them all together. 'We must all sleep in the dormitory,' she ordered. 'We are plainly safer if we stay as one group. Your windows,' she indicated the Protestants, 'are much lower, and open on to the outside. If shooting started you would be very vulnerable.'

Helen and Jessie obtained permission from the guards to move their bedding and settled down in one corner of the big dormitory. That night the Mother Superior went round arranging the 'watches'. Watches of prayer rather than of lookout. Each pair of nuns were to intone two chaplets – five repetitions of ten Ave Marias repeated twice; then they would wake the next pair of nuns who would continue the prayers until eventually they would reach the Protestant corner where Helen and Jessie would continue the prayers until morning.

They wedged a large wooden cupboard against the most vulnerable point, the French window, and settled down to sleep. But all of them were uneasy. The Commandant had not made a special journey to warn them without good reason, and anticipation of attack was almost as unnerving as the real thing.

It was not long in coming. Still on edge, the children fretful, the mattresses creaking, the heavy robes of the nuns rustling, for no one had undressed, suddenly they heard the screaming war cries outside. 'Simba! Simba! Simba!' Then a great battering and banging at the French window.

The Spanish nuns who were nearest leapt for the shifting cupboard and braced their backs against it, all of them holding and pushing back in a frenzy of desperation. A second hammering started on the shuttered windows so that the whole room echoed to an enormous drum roll of sound. The children yelled, Sister Marie Frances' big Alsatian began to bark. Helen, Jessie and the others were shocked with fear, too much at first even to run to the Spanish sisters to aid their delaying action at the door. Ten minutes of pandemonium, which ceased as abruptly as it started. They heard the voices of their own guards expostulating as the jeering, laughing Simba invaders went away. There was little sleep for any of them after that. Helen abandoned the idea altogether. She sat with her back against the wall her arms curled round her knees, and dozed fitfully and uneasily.

She was still tired next morning when a summons arrived for her to proceed into Wamba town. An armed guard and driver with van appeared at the front door, bringing orders from the Commandant. She was needed to give medical attention to the

Greeks, several of whom were sick. The message was vague, the dangers obvious, and Helen was reluctant. She distrusted all directives coming from Simba authority, and how was she to know this one was actually from the Commandant? Danger was always magnified when one was alone and this might be a trap.

Her reluctance did not bother the Simba guard. He patted his rifle; he had his own methods of dealing with resistance.

It was then that Sister Ignacio, an Italian nursing sister, who had served for five years at Wamba hospital and whom Helen knew quite well from her work there, offered to help.

'We will go together, Doctor Roseveare,' she said, giving the Simba the bleak look she reserved for patients about to be injected with a blunt needle.

Sister Ignacio was thin and virtuous; her long Italian face, patrician nose and hooded eyes could have been inherited from generations of Borgias, and from personal experience Helen knew that her sense of humour was as curiously contorted as that of an Inquisitorial Jesuit. But she trusted God, did her duty with scolding severity, and at a moment of trial like this she was as reassuring as a dozen paratroopers.

They were met in Wamba by Mr Preostos, one of the leaders of the Greek community. He came from Cyprus, and usually his seamed brown features broke into a white-toothed smile at the sight of them. But the façade of his face seemed to have weathered overnight; it was grey with strain. The Greeks in Wamba had managed to float on the flood of Simba violence for one simple reason: they maintained – not so much strict neutrality – but a tacit support which they sweetened with bribes, gifts of food, clothes and commodities. Their reasoning was one of self-interest. By reality of conquest the Simbas were now sole authority in the area. To oppose them meant imprisonment or death. So how else could they behave? It was the only way they could protect their stores, livelihoods and families.

This bubble of expediency had burst twenty-four hours earlier. An Army Commander arriving from Paulis brought a most unlikely but damaging rumour: the Greeks there had taken up arms against the Simbas and were fighting with the National Congolese Army. Revenge against *all* Greeks now acquired immediate priority.

'They came for us yesterday,' explained Preostos in a low voice. 'They arrested all the men, tied us up, beat us, marched us off to prison threatening they were going to kill us . . .'

He paused, the memory of the outrage returning. 'It was worse for the women and children. They stripped them of their clothes and beat them when they resisted. All night they abused them telling them that the men had been murdered.'

He looked at Helen with dark sombre eyes. 'We are kept under guard in three houses, and we have little hope.' As he led her across to the first, Helen realised that emotionally he was defeated. Thirty women and children were packed inside, and immediately Helen was struck by the children; they sat absolutely still, cowed and silent; even their eyes did not move.

Preostos took her round. 'This woman,' he said, indicating a young girl lying on a bed, 'is seven months pregnant. They knocked her down and kicked her again and again. We think the baby is dead. She cannot move her left side . . .'

The dark desparing eyes of the girl flickered up to Helen's as she bent to examine her. She placed her stethoscope against the woman's body and listened to the heart beats. The baby's heart was beating normally. Further examination revealed that the girl was bruised but not seriously hurt.

Shock had helped to contribute to her breakdown and it was the same with all of them. They were in a state of intense emotional shock, and their morale was at its lowest ebb. Helen now realised that they had taken refuge in a euphoric world confident that the magic lubrication of their very existence – money – would secure their salvation. It had always worked before; everything, and everyone had a price. Now dramatically, it had failed and they had nothing of spiritual value, no inner strength to fall back upon; they were bankrupt and defenceless.

She had to start from this point. Somehow she had to restore their value as human beings, and with an instinct and inspiration which was half medical and half missionary Helen began to talk.

She spoke in English. 'Now there's a guard here who will be suspicious of what I'm saying. He'll understand Swahili but he won't understand English. Some of you are from Cyprus so you'll understand English and you can translate what I say

[185]

into your own language. Don't translate the Swahili – translate the English.'

To the woman she said in Swahili. 'Now tell me what happened to you? Where does it hurt?'

Then as if translating these words, and without taking her eyes off the patient, she began in English.

'I know you are all desperate. I know you are all lost. But don't despair. Don't lose hope. We are Christians. God will protect us. Believe me, God is on our side.'

She told them of the situation at the convent, of the plight of the nuns and of the handful of Protestant missionaries amongst them. She told them of the strength of her faith and how, because of that faith, she – and they – could and must stand the strain of the terrible times they were undergoing. God did know what was going on, God had not deserted them, God did love. They must put their faith in God.

During this speech she alternated in Swahili, making polite noises of concern to the patient. She told them – and this seemed to relieve them enormously – that the girl was not badly injured, that the baby was unharmed, that they would all be secure if only they had enough faith and strength to pick themselves up off the ground.

'Many of you must belong to a church,' she said. 'But it's not the church that matters, it's you. A belief in God is a personal and individual thing. An individual can touch God. I have this faith. It supports me. It supports me in times like this when I most desperately need it. It can support you now. *Now* you need it.'

The Simba guards were suspicious but didn't interfere. She was, after all, only talking in normal tones. It was quite strange, almost electric, how the atmosphere changed. She gripped her audience, inspired and charged them with her oratory.

Towards the end she said, 'I'm going to pray for you. And I want you to pray with me . . .' She bowed her head. 'Father, will you pass to these in need the love you've given me for you? Will you reach out to them with that same love that kept us sane and whole through all the wickedness and evil? Give us your peace in our hearts. Keep us sane and fill us with hope. Make these here believe this Lord.'

They gripped her hand when she stood up. Their faces were

relaxed, there were tears in many eyes. The children were moving and smiling. In a place which had been without hope now there *was* hope.

Helen did not think of this episode as a personal triumph for herself, but she sensed that through her actions she had accomplished God's work, and it filled her with an intense feeling of spiritual joy. So rarely in our modern world do we face the fundamental issues of life and death; so seldom is a therapeutic stronger than a large whisky necessary to quieten our undertones of despair. Once again she had witnessed the consolation her faith brought to people so deeply in need. It had lightened their hearts and given them strength and hope to journey through another day and another night.

Sister Ignacio had been unable, in terms of language, to understand much of what was going on, but spiritually she was quite aware, and did her best to help by smiling and whispering encouragingly to the Greeks.

When they left to be escorted back to the van and driven to the convent, Helen was so full of elation she could not prevent herself from telling the Simba guard, in Swahili, what she had done.

'I was preaching the Gospel to those people,' she said bluntly. 'Did you know that? Did you know that woman might have lost her baby? Her suffering is mental as well as physical, and it's my responsibility as a doctor to help her find a mental balance in a situation like this. Explaining the Christian faith helped them greatly. Do you understand that?'

The Simba driver and the guard with the rifle stared at her with serious eyes. They did not say anything. The one with the rifle scratched himself. But Helen, now full of her work for the Lord, was not stopping now.

'Do you understand how Christianity can help you also? Support you and give you strength at terrible moments like this? Do you know what joy it gives you to have somebody bigger, all-powerful, all-loving – God in fact – to call on in agonising moments of stress?'

The driver looked straight through his windscreen, muttered a threat as a cat ran across the road. The guard scratched the other armpit.

'Do you understand that if you had this faith, this belief in

[187]

Christ it would give you a sanity and a joy to fill every day?'

Even in Swahili Helen was not quite sure if they understood it all. But they understood enough, and Sister Ignacio, who in another age might have been extracting penitence from Helen as the only way of avoiding the stake, nodded approvingly. The guards, whether they liked it or not, were cooped in a small lorry with a militant Helen, and no alternative but to listen to the sermon. And she was determined they should listen.

When they decanted Sister Ignacio and herself outside the convent door, Helen had a feeling they were not really sorry to say goodbye. Fighting a war against good saintly women is always a trial even for the most determined fighting men.

The feeling of triumph ended abruptly. At eight o'clock that night the door bell rang and Helen sensed trouble: in those days she often felt as if she had grown an extra-sensory waveband in her head; a sort of radar scanner which blipped when trouble approached. As usual eyes met, hands were tightened into nervous fists, the sickness churning in their stomachs.

A little later a sister came to fetch Helen. Her eyes were grave. 'The Mother Superior wonders if she could have a word with the doctor?'

Helen followed her back along the verandah. At the entrance to the large dormitory she could hear voices, sobbing confusion. She looked through the door and decided that the five distraught, dirty European women must be Belgian civilians, probably brought up from the hotel in Wamba. They had five children with them.

The Mother Superior saw her and came out to confirm Helen's guess.

'Five wives of Belgian planters. They've been kept down in the hotel for three weeks. Every night the soldiers have used them – threatened them that their husbands would be murdered unless they accepted a succession of men.'

'But I thought,' Helen began.

'Yes, the husbands are all dead,' said the Mother Superior finishing the sentence for her.

'Then they must know?'

'Like the others they refuse to believe it. They have suffered all this time believing they were helping to keep their husbands alive. They have been brutalised beyond belief. Every night hour after hour with the children there. But they will not believe their husbands are dead.'

'How can we help?' whispered Helen. It was impossible to know where to start.

'We can comfort them.'

Helen watched her as she turned to go back. Sister Ignacio was good, virtuous, holy and academic. The Mother Superior was driven totally by God, as she fussed around them: 'You're all going to have a nice hot bath. Then you'll feel better. Yes, the children too. Then clean clothes and a hot meal. You can share a room between two of you. There's no need to worry.' She put her arm round a young woman in her early thirties, 'You're all right now. You're safe here with us.'

Observing this scene as a spectator Helen suddenly realised one sad little figure was looking in her direction. She turned to focus on the solemn blue eyes and pigtails. The little girl, she guessed, was about nine years old.

'Hallo,' Helen said, 'What's your name?'

'Godeliefe.'

'That's a pretty name. Are you glad to be here?'

'Yes, but it was better at home. My daddy had a plantation.'

'Yes, but this is nice. It's quiet, and there's lots to eat. And other children to play with.'

Godeliefe was hardly listening. 'I expect my daddy will come and fetch us soon.'

Helen, stung to the heart, put her arms round her. She lied as any good Christian would. 'Yes, darling. I expect he will.'

They waited for Christmas with an almost desperate expectancy as if the arrival of the holy festival might in some way mitigate the tension and solve some part of their dilemma, for almost every day brought some sort of crisis. Half way through the month Amy approached Helen bursting with her news.

'Have you heard? They've captured Paulis. The Greeks picked it up on the radio. The Mother Superior knows! Helen, d'you think . . . ?'

'Who's captured Paulis?' Helen refused to be excited. Rumour blew through the convent every time the front door opened.

'The National Congolese Army. And the mercenaries. It's only a hundred miles away. They could be here tomorrow . . .'

'Wapi,' retorted Helen using her favourite Swahili expression which signified collectively 'Stuff and nonsense!' 'I'll believe it when I see it,' 'Tell me another!'

'It's true,' Amy insisted. 'It really is true.' They had captured Paulis but neither the National Congolese Army nor the mercenaries arrived 'tomorrow', or the next day, or at the end of the week. Nevertheless, no matter how firmly they tried to close their minds to this dream of freedom, no matter how hard they tried to forget that they were 'front line hostages' under threat of immediate execution, it was impossible not to hope, impossible not to be filled with the most desperate longings.

The days leading to Christmas inevitably made it worse. Bucolic and childlike memories of church bells echoing across the snow, the lights on Christmas trees, red-breasted robins, log fires, packages tied with Christmas ribbon, smiling aunts and uncles, tinsel, crackers, carol singers and the laughter of friends haunted their minds.

Outside the sunshine was brazen: flowers – roses, lilies, irises, poinsettias – in full bloom. The cloudless blue sky was an affront to the season.

Somehow Christmas would make things better. It must.

Helen chopped wood and fetched water. Jessie Scholes made cakes and jellies. Amy, in collusion with her pretty Italian friend, made miles of spaghetti. Two turkeys, bred by the nuns and kept inviolate and out of Simba hands by all manner of subterfuge, came to their predestined end; and one stroke of good fortune: the three Protestant missionaries in Wamba, Daisy Kingdon and the two girls were allowed to join them.

Every morning the convent rang with clear explicit joy as the nuns rehearsed the great Mass they were going to sing on Christmas morning. Helen with a fine sense of international sisterhood typed out dozens of song sheets of 'Silent Night' in Swahili and 'Oh Come All Ye Faithful', in French, writing a Christmas greeting on every sheet so that Catholic and Protestant could share and unite in the festival. For all of them it became more than a repetitive religious occasion; it took on a symbolism which gave it new dimensions; it renewed belief that in their cruel, unjust and frightening situation God existed and protected them; it revived that most vital ingredient to their survival – hope.

On Christmas Eve that hope suddenly became a dilemma.

The Commandant came to deliver a message to the Mother Superior, and she summoned an immediate assembly.

The Protestant women gathered round with grave faces, realising from the Mother Superior's seriousness that something important had happened.

'The Commandant has received orders that one priest and one sister are to go by truck to Mungbere immediately. From there they will go to Aba three hundred and fifty miles northwards and then be flown to safety to Juba in the Sudan. If the journey is successful we shall all follow in due course.'

There was a long silence. The Sudan meant freedom but there was no excitement, only a meeting of eyes, and lips tightening in distrust. 'Only *one* sister and *one* priest?' exclaimed Helen.

'*That* is too dangerous, I agree,' said the Mother Superior. 'I have decided therefore to go myself, accompanied by four other sisters. I have asked that five priests join us. If we get through safely then all the rest of you will follow in similar groups.'

'And if we don't hear from you, we shall still all be ordered to leave?'

The Mother Superior nodded. 'We must put our trust in God. There is no other way. This area is likely to become a battleground and if we can move we must.'

Helen reserved a doubt about this course of action.

'When is this going to happen?' she asked.

'Tonight. We have to pack at once and be ready to leave.'

She looked around at their glum faces. 'We have no alternative. If we don't go voluntarily, we shall be moved by force and we all know what that might mean.'

Amy caught Helen's eye. 'The General is at Mungbere,' she whispered.

Helen nodded. 'Knowing that, I don't fancy anyone's chances much.'

They turned aside to discuss their doubts. 'You think we should stay here?' said Amy.

'As long as we can, yes.'

General Nicholas Olenge was an officer not given to humane or civilising motives: he was the man who had issued the order for the slaughter of Stanleyville's white civilians. Another large group of white hostages collected at Mungbere might suit his purpose very well. To be delivered to his authority sounded to Helen rather like cattle being collected for the abattoir; she wanted no part of such an arrangement.

While the Mother Superior went to prepare for her journey the Protestants discussed the future. Jessie, Daisy Kingdon, both Elaines and Stebby all felt the same way as Helen. They had survived one nightmare journey from Ibambi to Wamba; they did not want to face another. They decided to postpone leaving as long as possible and be the very last to leave if they could.

The Mother Superior's party left within the hour, many of the sisters excited and emotional; they believed this was the great moment, the answer to all their prayers. Helen wished she could share their feelings as she gave her raincoat to one of the nuns to keep out the chilly night air.

The departure meant that Christmas was inevitably dampened, they could not concentrate on either celebration or devotion, knowing that the Mother Superior and four other nuns were somewhere out there defenceless in the darkness.

Christmas morning arrived and there was still no news. The nuns sang their Mass, the children opened their little presents, the kitchen was busy, but somehow the sparkle of excitement and anticipation had gone, replaced by uncertainty, fear and anxiety.

The Commandant returned to wish them if not a happy Christmas then at least good fortune, and Helen seized the opportunity to ask if she could take the children across to the men's quarters to see the Christmas tree and crib the priest had built. He agreed. Holding Marie Frances's adopted pygmy daughter by the hand and followed by a bobbing delighted train of children and one puzzled Simba guard, Helen led them across and managed to talk briefly to Jack and Brian.

They had already heard rumours of the impending move but did not really know what was going to happen. It was only when she returned to the convent and they were sitting down to lunch that the real news arrived. Trucks were driving in from Mungbere to take them back there in small batches. The first group were to leave immediately.

Without Mother Superior's sense of discipline no one knew quite what to do, but eventually two Belgian women and their

[192]

children, five Spanish sisters and four Italians piled aboard the truck. They heard also that a second vehicle had arrived to transport Brian, Jack and eleven priests to the same destination. Each person was allowed to take one suitcase, money, and as much food as they could carry.

It meant the end of Christmas celebrations: they sat down to the evening meal hardly able to touch the jellies and cakes prepared so lovingly by Jessie Scholes. Next day, when Helen was escorted into Wamba to see a sick Greek, Mr Preostos advised them to leave.

'The National Army has advanced thirty miles out of Paulis,' he told her. 'They're also at a village only sixty miles south of here. If they can cut the road between Mungbere and Wamba they'll have driven a wedge between the main Simba forces.'

This kind of military rumour did not make much sense to Helen. 'But if they make us all leave the convent shan't we be more isolated, more vulnerable?'

'You must go,' he urged. 'You'll be safer at Mungbere.'

She had no more time to discuss the situation; in any case their freedom of action was limited: they did what they were told.

Rumour and counter rumours increased during the next three days. On Sunday night the final, irrevocable order arrived. 'The entire convent will be evacuated. All women must prepare to leave immediately.'

Helen clambered aboard the open truck filled with an overwhelming presentiment of evil. Eight Protestant women missionaries and five nuns huddled together trying to cover themselves with blankets more to hide the whiteness of their skins than to keep out the cold. Wamba was dark and empty. Patches of mist seeped over the forest road, and their white headlights threw blurred reflections back in their faces. They halted at two deserted road barriers; at the third a surly guard glimpsing a white face struck out angrily with a stick, a blow which caught Elaine on the head and dazed her. Fortunately the truck was moving and they had accelerated out of range before he could do more damage.

Helen peered out from her blanket at the stars high in the night sky. Usually this brilliant blaze of constellations would have filled her with wonder. Now she felt sick with apprehension. Why had they been moved so late at night? Practically everyone else had left in daylight. Everyone knew that danger and death skulked in the darkness, that Simba law and order – if it existed at all – certainly did not function then. In the darkness ultimate barbarity took over.

They passed through several more road blocks and all were deserted. They reached Betongwe at half an hour past midnight and stopped. A guard came round to the back of the truck.

Helen knew Betongwe as a minute village where very little happened. 'Why have we halted?' she asked. The guard was bored. 'We spend the night here. Get out all of you. Come on move.'

Helen clambered down. 'But it's only twenty-five miles to Mungbere. Why can't we drive there?' she protested.

She received a prod in the back for her impertinence and saw then that they were being taken towards a large dark bungalow set back from the roadside.

One of the nuns whispered, 'It belonged to the Belgian planter. He was murdered weeks ago.'

Jostled up the veranda steps they were pushed into a big room with huge picture windows, furnished with two armchairs and a sofa. Everything else seemed to have been looted. They were ordered to sit on the cement floor, their backs to the wall, and a few seconds later a Simba lieutenant marched in to issue instructions. 'We're taking the truck back to Wamba to pick up another batch of prisoners,' he snapped. 'You'll spend the night here and be moved to Mungbere tomorrow.' He banged out and they heard him shouting orders to the local Simbas.

Helen sat against the wall her hands clenched, her mouth dry. The room was lit by one hurricane lantern. Other lanterns flickered outside. There was movement but not the normal, rowdy, drunken noises the Simbas usually made. This was more sinister, this set her teeth on edge. There seemed an almost physical atmosphere of evil and hate in that dark house.

Instinctively she knew that they had been deposited here either for Simba violence or sexual attack; that the entire episode had been pre-arranged. It could not be a coincidence that thirteen defenceless women were bustled into a lonely deserted house by the roadside, when in forty-five minutes easy driving they could have reached Mungbere.

She was right. The attack was systematic and ruthless: its objective, rape. The door opened. Two Simba guards – those who had brought them from Wamba – came in. They grabbed the first girl sitting by the door, hauled her to her feet, pulled her out into the corridor. She began to scream. They heard the screams choke into sobs in a nearby room. Helen closed her eyes in sick despair, then almost without conscious reflection moved across to take her place. She had lectured Sister Dominique on the principle that by accepting ravishment she saved others from the same humiliation. Helen did not dread rape any more; she knew she could endure the shame and humiliation and survive. The act would not destroy her. She had made peace with God and her own heart. She knew what to expect; perhaps she could save others. Above all she was frightened of intense physical pain. She was not afraid of death. A quick death would be a merciful release. But the thought of torture, of prolonged physical agony was a continued nightmare in her mind.

The door opened again. A figure loomed above Helen. A hand grabbed her shoulder to pull her up. She did not resist being pushed along the corridor and into the bedroom.

Through the next two hours the rapists brutalised them. To resist meant a vicious beating up, possibly death, but certainly no avoidance of the humiliation. There were acts of protest. When the rapists came to take out the young girl sitting next to Jessie Scholes, Jessie cried out angrily, 'You'll leave her alone. D'you hear me? You'll not touch this girl!'

The guard did not argue. He reversed his rifle and lifted the butt end high into the air, to smash it down on Jessie's skull.

The young girl scrambled to her knees, to her feet throwing herself forward to protect Mrs Scholes. 'Please don't hit her. Please don't. I'll come with you. I'll come with you.'

She was led out and Jessie Scholes wept. When Elaine de Rusett's turn came and she was taken into the bedroom she slid gracefully to the floor and sat there, saying in Swahili delivered with a forceful Australian accent that she did not then, or ever, intend to accede to their demands. She was not violent, tearful or hysterical; only firm and resolute. And her tactic worked.

They had satiated themselves and could not be bothered with anyone so adamant. Hearing Elaine's story afterwards Helen felt a great sense of guilt. Perhaps she should have reacted violently, screamed, kicked, scratched and defended herself until knocked unconscious. But that night there was no time for civilised reflection. It was an occasion devoid of humanity and mercy; without doubt a situation with many precedents in the Congo of that period, but such knowledge did not lessen or diminish the sickening outrage.

By 2 a.m. the Wamba guards were finished. Before they left to go back to town they brought in half a small deer they had killed with the truck on the journey from the convent, and contemptuously left it for their captives as a gift. The women now lay in a tight square against the wall hemmed in by the flimsy defences of the sofa, an armchair at either end. They heard the cab door slam, the engine rev up, the vehicle grind away into the night. Then all was silent except for stifled sobbing.

Helen lay there holding one of the girls who had been raped. She sobbed in an agony of pain and shock, and Helen could do little to assuage her bitter grief except to hold her tightly in her arms and wait for the dawn. She scarcely knew what to pray for now, except that the daylight and the indifferent sunshine might come soon.

But morning brought only another menace. The news had gone round the village that white women prisoners were held in the house, no doubt that some had been raped, and a mob of Africans gathered outside the windows shaking spears and sticks and yelling obscenities. It was like being trapped in a huge fishbowl with predatory creatures threatening them through the glass walls.

Fortunately the sergeant major in charge of the local garrison did not appear to be hostile. Food? There wasn't much food but he would try and find some rice and peanuts for them. Water? He would get a couple of old men to draw some. Meanwhile they had better cook the half deer left by the Wamba guards before it putrefied.

At lunch time another truck arrived from Wamba carrying seven Belgian women and nine children. They were to be left at Betongwe while the driver returned to Wamba for another load. While the unloading and arguments were taking place another overloaded truck arrived carrying eighteen nuns and five men, and when it moved off for Mungbere by some trick of persuasion it took as extras five nuns from Helen's party and two Belgian women and their children.

The driver of the first truck insisted that his orders compelled him to return to the convent to pick up the last of the prisoners; he promised, however, that he would be back before nightfall to take them all to Mungbere.

This news left them silent with apprehension. The thought of another night in the bungalow contending with the Africans howling outside their windows and the uncertain tempers and designs of the local Simba guards was sickening to contemplate. 'Please,' they appealed, 'please come back and take us to Mungbere.'

They were deeply depressed when he left and someone pointed out that there was practically no chance of him returning that night because he had no lights. Fearfully those remaining: eight Protestant missionaries, five Belgian women and six children watched the coming of darkness and made their pitiful attempts at defence. Throughout the late afternoon and early evening the young Simbas and local hooligans continued to shout threats outside the windows, while Helen tried to console little Godeliefe. Only one thing seemed to be in their favour. This time the local sergeant major and his men appeared actually prepared to take their guard duties seriously. Although the water situation was grim – they tried without much success to filter the scummy liquid carried in by two old men – the sergeant major produced more rice and peanuts and even a chicken, so they were not hungry.

That evening they arranged their tiny fortress of sofa and two chairs in a square against the wall. They covered themselves with blankets so that it was not possible to distinguish between old and young, woman or child. They made a pact to cling to each other and refuse to let go, a strategy used by the nuns who formed human circles when attacked, clinging desperately one to the other.

They lay motionless under their blankets, each tiny noise causing breath to be held, muscles to contract.

An hour later the attack seemed certain to come. They heard shouts and threats outside; fists and sticks banged against their door, feet thumped across the veranda. Two of their guards were forced back into their room, levelling their rifles at the intruders while the third guard scampered off to fetch the sergeant major. The sergeant returned with his second in command. The invaders, three Simbas of his own garrison demanded the right to be assigned to guard duty over the women.

The shouting and argument went on in a Bangala dialect which Helen could barely understand. But one thing was clear: the intruders' demands were simple, rape the women and then destroy them.

As the argument continued, a further farcical aspect emerged: the intruders charged that the guards who had levelled their rifles and tried to protect the women were traitors; they had refused them their 'rights', and therefore blatantly offended against the Simba code. They demanded an immediate tribunal to judge their guilt. To Helen the limit of frightening absurdity had now been reached. She heard the sergeant major agree to their preposterous demand, and other Simbas, who had drifted into the room, alerted by the shouting match, were all in favour of the trial.

In the room, literally over their heads, the tribunal started its idiot proceedings, argument, accusation and counter-accusation flying through the air. With first one and then another taking the part of defence counsel, prosecution counsel, judge and jury, it may have seemed ridiculous but to the cowering women its impact was terrifying. The three newcomers maintained that the other guards should be relieved of their duties; they, as loyal upholders of the Simba creed, should be granted responsibility for the prisoners.

Helen clung to Amy and prayed. There was nothing else to do, no other action of which she was capable. So often in those weeks of continuing suspense their lives had seemed to hang on a mood, a whim, a turn of argument, but this situation had reached the limits of human credibility.

Fortunately the weight of the sergeant major's authority and argument carried conviction; the three loyal guards were, if not acquitted, at least given the right of appeal and dismissed to the adjoining room while the altercation continued. Suddenly the debate which had been going on, for what to Helen seemed like hours, was interrupted. Abruptly argument and prayer were cut off in mid-sentence as a strange wailing sound emerged from the next room. Was it tortured human being or animal? Was it human at all or some horrific creature out of the jungle? The sergeant major and his interrogators rushed for the door, as at the same moment the whine of sound was obliterated by roars of laughter.

One of the guards appeared. In his hands he carried a piano accordion. With enormous pantomime producing a great bellow-ing squelch of music, he pumped the bellows backwards and for-wards. The murdered Belgian owner could never have known such an appreciative audience; they howled and capered around the player. Rape had flown from their minds. A concert was the thing! Music to delight the heart! They all wanted to try it out.

Helen and Amy, clasped in each other's arms felt their facial muscles relax, their screwed up eyes open, their giggles become compulsive as they dissolved into helpless suppressed laughter. Tears poured down their cheeks, the temporary relief from ten-sion so overwhelming that their mirth, choking them, bordered on hysteria. The Simbas happily carried their instrument outside into the night, chuckling children who had forgotten murder now they had a new toy with which to play.

During the last few weeks Helen and Amy had promised themselves that if ever they survived they would write a book about their experiences called *Alice in Simbaland*. There was no doubt that this scene would be described in its pages.

A little later their own loyal guards crept back into the house and closed the door. The women huddled closer together under the blankets. The children slept easily and quietly, the women dozed and moved fitfully.

None of them dreamt that the first light would lift the curtain on the last act in this desperate and bloody arena.

II

At 1.30 a.m. on 31st December, 54 Commando, under Lieutenant Joe Wepener, left their headquarters at Paulis. Their objective: to rescue a group of white civilians thought to be held prisoner at Mungbere. They were also in radio communication with two Sikorsky helicopters which would rendezvous with them in Mungbere and land to help in any evacuation should it prove possible.

It was pitch dark. The headlights of the leading Ferret Scout car followed by three armoured jeeps and four big trucks cut white swathes through the darkness. They had not been going for more than an hour when their big, ex-United Nations truck broke down, and as speed and surprise were essential to their enterprise – they expected to encounter a well-defended machine-gun post a few miles farther on – they immediately abandoned the U.N. vehicle and transferred its ammunition and armament to the other vehicles.

Every vehicle was fully armed: fixed mountings for the Browning machine-guns and Ericksons, plus a variety of weapons from captured Russian Kalashnikov AD 47 automatic rifles to Lee Enfields which had seen service since the First World War. A variety of young men recruited mainly in South Africa: Rhodesians, British, Germans, Belgians, French, Australians, South Africans, New Zealanders, Poles and Danes manned the vehicles; toughies all of them, practically every man with army experience, recruited on a six months contract at around fifteen pounds a day. In action they earned every penny of it; they were to earn every penny in the Mungbere operation.

They had picked up one new and useful volunteer in Kurt

Van Wilde, a Swiss planter rescued the day before in their foray into Wamba. He had been one of the few remaining prisoners in the convent and was able to tell them that most of the civilians had been evacuated to Mungbere. Knowing both the road between Paulis and Mungbere and the surrounding district, he offered his services as guide. Lieutenant Wepener accepted his offer gratefully and drove with him in the leading scout car. He had also introduced one colourful tactic into their strategy. The flying column of jeeps and lorries were to operate without lights in darkness, and for much of the journey, with dust swirling up from the wheels. In such conditions it was easy for one of the vehicles to lose the car in front and turn the wrong way. Van Wilde owned a trumpet. One blast meant that the leading scout car was proceeding straight ahead, two blasts that it was swinging right, three and the turn was to the left.

Their speed slowed as they moved out on to the rough dirt road and headlights were switched off; there was no point in alerting the Simbas to the fact that an enemy convoy was penetrating their positions. They had to cover the one hundred and twenty kilometers along a road held by one of the strongest Simba concentrations in Congo, thousands of armed black warriors, lying – hopefully they might be sleeping – between them and their objective. The jungle on either side was dark and silent, its very blackness giving definition and direction to the road ahead.

After driving for about an hour Van Wilde said, 'The village where the first machine-gun post is sited lies about a mile from here.'

'Okay,' replied Joe Wepener. 'We'll close to about three hundred yards and then blast through with headlights blazing and all guns firing.'

'They'll hear us before we get there.'

'I like to think they'll believe it's a Simba convoy approaching.'

'We shall wake them all up,' said Van Wilde cheerfully.

'Something like that.' Wepener was a tall, tough, laconic Rhodesian, one of the few mercenaries driven by a deep sense of mission. He believed, rightly or wrongly, that Congo in particular and Africa in general, should not be allowed to fall under either Russian or Chinese domination. His thin lips and jutting chin, the steady eyes which seemed to look straight through you and out the other side, gave him an air of resolute dependability.

During those Congo hostilities the Geneva Convention played about as important a part in military operations as the Congress of Vienna. You killed or were killed. Prisoners on either side were tortured and then murdered. Simbas and National Congolese Army committed bestial atrocities against each other's forces as a normal concomitant of warfare.

Van Wilde reacted to some passing landmark. 'The village is ahead now.'

'Right,' snapped Joe Wepener to his gunner. 'Prepare to open fire.'

The action on the road to Mungbere will never be written up like the 'Gunfight at the Okay Corral', never considered as even a minor skirmish by any military historian, but to those engaged the hectic dash through the darkness and into the village took on some of the same breathless delirium that Winston Churchill recorded about the last cavalry charge at Omdurman. The noise of their approach in low gear had obviously been heard by the Simba defence. As headlights were switched on, gears thrust into fast speed and machine-guns opened up, they were met by return fire from half a dozen positions in the village.

Like a weird naval action, jeeps and trucks rolling and swaying in line astern, as if butting into a choppy sea, wheels lifting and bumping over rutted surfaces, machine-guns, rifles and revolvers pouring broadsides from port and starboard sides, they roared into the village knocking the flimsy barricades of boxes high into the air and cannoning off elderly cars set up as road blocks. Incendiary tracer shells sliced through the darkness in brilliant scarlet arcs, their speed and parabola beautiful to watch. They struck thatch, and fire broke out. Dark figures scurrying between the houses and across the road were suddenly silhouetted by flame and toppled to the ground as they were caught in the concentrated stream of bullets.

Someone in the last truck was tossing out hand grenades which burst in a series of spectacular orange-cored explosions.

A truck without lights lumbered down the road towards Wepener's Ferret car. Its windscreen disintegrated under a blast of bullets from Wepener's Browning and, slowly, like some enormous and surprised Neanderthal creature, it fell sideways into a ditch. Headlights were switched on and off to confuse defences. Horns blared. Engines raced. Dust churned from spinning wheels, the loud chatter of machine-guns was constant, and Van Wilde blew long single blasts on his bugle. Although the scenario was confused and bewildering, the action could not have lasted for more than two or three minutes even though it felt like an hour. They roared on through the village leaving carnage behind them and suffering no more than a few holes in each vehicle's superstructure.

In the next few miles, as the first pale greyness began to filter into the sky a few sporadic rifle shots were directed at them from the edges of the road. They replied with bursts from the Brownings and usually there was no return fire.

At the next village with darkness now steadily fading, Africans raced towards them shouting loudly and Van Wilde translated their cries as, 'We are Simbas like you. Don't shoot.'

Joe Wepener at the magazine of his Browning fired a short burst. The figures fell.

Dawn arrived in its usual luridly tropical manner; the first flush of rose pink changing to a wash of scarlets, golds and purples, and then the sun, brazen and strident as a brass alarm clock, flared in their faces.

It was broad daylight and they were acutely vulnerable when they reached the outskirts of Mungbere. Like Wamba it is a small Belgian colonial settlement with wide earth streets, single-storey bungalows, a few administrative buildings and a line of wooden stores. That they represented an attacking mercenary force had probably been telephoned in from somewhere along their route, for the defences appeared to be alert and shots were directed at them as they passed the first buildings. They charged down the main street returning the fire, swirling round corners, blasting out windows, with Van Wilde trumpeting loudly to indicate changes of direction.

Any well-organised defence force faced with this vulnerable column of jeeps and lorries would have blown them apart within minutes. As it was, the noise and surprise of the attack scared the Simbas into immediate flight; and the column glimpsed them scuttling to safety through the gardens at the back of the bungalows. The resistance did not crumble completely however, and progress was constantly punctuated by the sound of bullets ricocheting off armour plate. Above the racket Joe Wepener yelled, 'Where the hell are these prisoners supposed to be?'

Van Wilde scarlet from his exertions with the trumpet shouted back, 'How do I know?'

'We can't go on driving round and round these streets under fire for ever.'

'They're here somewhere.'

'Well we'd better find them quick.'

They accelerated down another side street and Wepener's driver shouted, 'I saw a white face at a window back there, Lieutenant.'

'Good,' returned Wepener directing a burst in the general direction of a tall building. 'Get back. First right and right again.'

Their circular route seemed to have cleared a complete section of Simba resistance. They braked to a halt outside a number of large bungalows set back on green lawns. The well drilled mercenaries slid out of their vehicles, Brownings loosing off regular intimidatory bursts, and with machine pistols ready for action, they raced forward to kick down doors. Within seconds they were submerged, embraced, hugged, kissed and wept over by what seemed a whole convent full of crying, laughing, joyous nuns.

(2)

When Jack Scholes and Brian Cripps were despatched to Mungbere three days before Helen, the journey proved uneventful. Eighty male prisoners, priests and civilians, an assortment of nationalities, were locked into three bungalows; the women and children were imprisoned in other bungalows nearby. By this time, with one exception, every Belgian or American male had been murdered; the single Belgian left alive owed his life to the fact that the others insisted he was Walloon and the Simbas, unable to distinguish between Belgian, Flemish and Walloon, imagined he came from some far-off country unknown to them.

One can understand the reasoning behind the Simba command decision to concentrate its white civilian prisoners at the railhead of Mungbere on the pretext that they would then be taken three hundred and fifty miles north-east to Aba, on the Sudan border, and then flown to safety. Simba forces were running out of territory. The National Congolese Army with its supporting units of white mercenaries had already captured Paulis. At Stanleyville the Simbas had proved wantonly that they regarded the deliberate slaughter of civilians a legitimate arm of warfare; a similar concentration of hostages at Mungbere might provide a useful bargaining counter.

They were outside the bungalow sitting around on the lawn when they first heard the firing. But this time the noise was different. The Simbas were always banging off shots to amuse themselves or impress their friends at odd hours of the day or night, but this gunfire sounded like automatic weapons and it was accompained by a peculiar and repetitive trumpet blast.

'Better get back inside the house!' shouted Jack. But they could not get back inside the house. The Simba guards had suddenly become menacing. Rifles were levelled. Bolts snapped into breeches. Fingers curled round triggers. For three heart-stopping seconds Brian was certain that this was going to be another Stanleyville; a single order by a wide-awake officer would have started a fusillade which would have killed him and all his white-faced fellow prisoners outside in the sunshine. But it was seven o'clock in the morning and there were no wide-awake officers, only confusion amongst all ranks which eventually resolved into shouted orders.

'Back into the house, everybody. All prisoners inside at once!'

Brian and Jack flattened themselves on the floor beneath the eighteen-inch window-sill. Above the huge window a burst of machine-gun bullets stitched a neat row of pock-marks in the concrete lintel but left the glass unharmed.

An enthusiastic Dutch voice from one of the back rooms shouted, 'The Simbas are running for their lives back into the forest.' A few moments later they heard the noise of lorries, jeeps and English voices shouting incomprehensible orders. The door was kicked open; young men in camouflaged jackets and black berets poured through and Lieutenant Joe Wepener stared down at them. He was abrupt and decisive. 'Get moving,' he snapped. 'My orders are to get you back to Paulis with the speed of light. We shot our way through various Simba encampments on the way here. We'll have to do the same going back. So into the trucks – quick!'

They clustered round him. 'The women and children?' someone called.

'They're all right. We're calling down our two Sikorsky helicopters on to the football pitch now. They'll take as many as possible. The rest in the trucks!'

A voice called 'One of the priests is wounded; a bullet in the thigh.'

'Right! Load him in the helicopter too.'

It was Jack's turn to protest. White-faced he protested 'But my wife? All our Protestant women. They're held in a house at Betongwe. We can't leave without them. We can't.'

Joe Wepener was at once alert. 'How d'you know they're still there?'

'We had a truck come through from Wamba only yesterday afternoon. They must be still there.'

Wepener glanced up at the huge Sikorsky helicopters clattering overhead.

He said, 'The Simbas will have heard all this racket.'

He didn't have time to spell it out for them. When the Simbas had time to reflect on vengeance they killed their prisoners.

'But we *must* try to save them,' pleaded Jack. 'There are other women and children with them too.'

Joe Wepener frowned. 'How many?'

'At least eight British. Probably half a dozen Belgian women and children.'

'You're certain they're there?'

'Yes, people on the last truck which came through from Wamba saw them.'

'You know they're alive?'

No one wanted to answer that question.

'They must be alive,' said Jack. 'They must be. After all this they must be.'

Joe Wepener intoned as if trying to reassure himself, 'I've got strict orders to rescue all civilians in Mungbere and get straight back to Paulis. Those are my orders.' He looked at Jack again. 'British you said? British?' That seemed to make a difference.

'Yes, British missionaries.'

The Sikorsky helicopters coming into land were now drowning the sporadic rattle of gunfire. A civilian, short, wiry and thin-faced whom Jack remembered from Wamba, came up.

'Mr Van Wilde, d'you know this Betongwe place?' asked Wepener.

'Of course. I've lived in the district for years.'

'How far?'

'At our speed about an hour from here.'

'Do we have to retrace our steps; come back this way to get back to Paulis?'

'No, about twenty miles past Betongwe we can take a right fork and another road to Paulis.'

Wepener turned back to Jack Scholes. 'Okay. As soon as we've got everybody aboard we'll try for the ladies.'

Within an hour most of the women and children had been crammed into the Sikorsky helicopters leaving eighty men and twenty-five women and children to be carried by the three trucks which were incredibly overloaded. No luggage could be taken. The tail-boards had to be let down to find room for the last few and Brian and Jack Scholes hung on there.

Joe Wepener's tactics continued to be simple and direct. He let the Simbas know they were coming and hoped, by so doing, to terrify the life out of them. He kept engines roaring and machine-guns firing, spraying patches of grass or jungle at the side of the road where Simbas might be lurking, relentlessly bashing forward.

Ten miles from Mungbere they were waved to a halt by a group of pathetic Greeks, who stood at the roadside outside their store surrounded by enough suitcases, boxes and bales to fill the three trucks twice over. They had heard the helicopters and prayed the rescuers would come their way.

'No luggage,' ordered Wepener sternly. 'Not a single suitcase. Just get aboard quickly.'

The Greeks pleaded but even they realised that there was no room. Their possessions were left behind in a cloud of dust.

Van Wilde said, 'I pray to God we'll be in time.'

Brian glanced at Jack's tense face. His prayers were concentrated on the same hope.

*   *   *

For Helen and the others the night passed peacefully enough. As usual daylight woke them, and almost immediately they were aware of more trouble ahead. They heard the guards quarrelling amongst themselves again; last night's arguments renewed even more violently outside on the verandah. It ended in a fight, blows being struck, and in a few minutes they knew the worst. Their old guards had lost; the new contingent marched in to take over and their truculent aggressiveness presaged immediate danger. Almost coinciding with their entry, from somewhere above the roof, from somewhere high in the sky above the forest, the sound of aircraft engines.

They did not know that they were hearing the Sikorsky helicopters loaded with refugees flying them to safety in Paulis. They did not know that Lieutenant Joe Wepener and his convoy of lorries and armoured jeeps were already on the way to try and rescue them. They only knew that the Simbas went mad with rage.

They were pushed, pummelled and kicked back into the big room. Doors and windows were slammed shut.

One of the new guards harangued them. 'If the planes begin to bomb us, we'll kill you. If the bombs don't do it, then we shall. D'you understand? If necessary we shall all die together, but you will die first.'

Helen glanced round at the hunted faces of the other twelve women and six children. Little Godeliefe sat huddled in her mother's arms her eyes bleak.

Helen knew this was the climax and that they were expendable. Their use as prisoners, as hostages or simply as women available for rape had ended. Their only remaining value was as human objects on which the Simbas could vent their anger, hatred and barbarism.

The distant sound of explosions in Mungbere – how were they to know that the mercenaries were blowing up Simba ammunition dumps? It sounded exactly like bombing and enraged their guards. The door banged open. The sergeant major, as angry and savage as the other Simbas now, headed this party. They struck out with rifle butts and boots driving them this time out from the big room into the smaller one.

And now the guards had a new inspiration. Some military genius, unable to fathom that the helicopters were following the

Mungbere-Wamba road as a reliable geographical guide line, had decided that they must have been summoned by radio signal. Therefore one of the women must have a radio transmitting apparatus with her.

The new guard commander, his eyes bulging with self-induced authority, the thick cords of his neck straining, screamed, 'We know how you brought the planes here to bomb us! One of you has a radio which transmits signals. Who sent this signal? We demand to know and she will be punished.'

Daisy Kingdon, oldest by far of all the ladies, spoke up, 'It's ridiculous to think . . . .' she began, but was unable to complete her protest because the nearest guard lifted his rifle butt and smashed it down against her head. Blood streamed from the wound. The brutal act of violence triggered off another vicious wave of hysterical anger against all the women and children. They were attacked indiscriminately. If you talked you were struck; if you kept silent you were hit just the same. And above the angry shouts the guard commander's hysterical voice continued: 'Where is the radio transmitter? Who has the instrument? We shall find it, understand that. You will be searched.'

They were driven, because there was nowhere else to go, into the farthest corner of the room. Helen shouted, 'We've been searched before. Dozens of times. Our clothes, baggage, everything. We've nothing to hide.'

'You're lying. We know you're lying. You will be searched in couples. Everyone will be searched.' He prodded two terrified Belgian women. 'You two first.' The weeping women were jostled back into the big room and ordered to point out their baggage. It was torn open, the contents scattered. And here was justification for further humiliation; their clothes were torn off in this ludicrous excuse of a search. Practically naked, the two Belgians were bundled back into the inner room. The next two were selected for the same brutal process.

To move, speak or make any gesture now invited a torrent of abuse and a series of vicious blows. Daisy Kingdon sat bowed, her hands clasped over her head, blood welling between her fingers.

Helen sensed rather than saw Stebby's sudden terrible apprehension. From a corner of her eye she saw the look on Florence's face.

'Stebby, what's the matter?' she whispered.

'My hearing aid,' mumbled Stebby in confused agony. 'My hearing aid.'

'What about it?'

'It's in my suitcase, here.' With a slight nod of her head she indicated her feet.

'But?'

'They'll think it's a radio transmitter.'

'Oh Stebby!' But even as Helen opened her mouth to say 'Of course they won't,' she realised that Stebby was right. *They* would think it was a radio transmitter. Explanations that it had been shown to the Commandant at Wamba who understood perfectly what it was, would not suffice here. These were Simbas out of the forest; they were unsophisticated and suspicious. They would not know what it was, but they would see in it absolute proof of their outraged accusations.

'They can't think it's a transmitter,' whispered Helen, 'Someone will know what it is.' She did not believe what she was saying, and she knew that Stebby did not believe it either.

'I'll take it in and show it to them,' Stebby whispered bravely. 'I'll try and explain, convince them what it really is . . . .'

Helen began to say, 'No, you mustn't do that,' and stopped. Stebby was right; it was the only sensible thing to do. If the rebels found it when they searched her baggage probably all their lives would be forfeited. If Stebby owned up then they might have a chance.

She watched Stebby fumble in the small suitcase and produce the small box-like amplifier with its length of wire and ear piece. As she went towards the door the second pair of Belgian women clutching the torn remnants of their clothing and weeping hysterically were pushed back past her. The guard shouted at her angrily. Then he saw what she was holding and he shouted excitedly to his comrades.

Helen heard the triumphant screech of anger as soon as they saw what Stebby carried in her hand. They struck her across the face repeatedly; the hearing aid was snatched from her.

So this was the apparatus she had used to signal the enemy planes. Right, she would be executed. At once the firing squad would be arranged to attend to her. The others who were obviously part of the plot would also be executed. The guard commander struck her across the head and face again and again.

'You will go before a firing squad, but first you'll confess. How did you signal the National Army with this machine?'

'I didn't signal,' cried Stebby. 'It's for my deafness. It's a medical device.'

'You're a liar. We shall shoot you. But there are worse things for you before that happens. Explain how you signal with this machine.'

The crude brainwashing continued. The bullying, searching and stripping went on. Now the entire house was full of maddened Simbas shouting and haranguing in noisy hysteria. Dresses were torn off. Women pushed and kicked. The message had gone round: the Protestant women had signalled the enemy planes. They were going to be executed. A blood lust that was almost tangible filled the air.

Children huddled against mothers crying. Women clung together. Stebby was jerked to her feet to be led off the verandah to be shot. Then she was pushed down again. A quick death was too good for such a crime. The scene was lunatic, full of noise, confusion and violence.

It seemed plain now to Helen that their prayers had gone unanswered. This was the end God had obviously chosen for them. They must face this conclusion with whatever reserves of courage they could find. But how difficult it was. Terror caught at the heart, stopped the blood.

Then another sound! In the distance a strange staccato stuttering . . . a quick, repetitive tattoo that seemed to freeze the screams, threats and expostulations.

Somebody gasped. 'A machine-gun! It's a machine-gun.' The guards' reactions were maniacal. Those being searched and interrogated in the big room were driven back into the smaller one with curses and violent blows. But it was the last Simba outbreak of frenzy. Now self-preservation took over. They fled in noisy panic, falling over each other to leave the house.

Abandoned and bewildered, the women could hear the gunfire getting closer. In their inner room there was only one small window set high up in the wall. But the walls were made of thin match-boarding. Bullets would slice through as if they were muslin.

'Down on the floor,' shouted Helen. 'Quick! Down on the

floor.' A volley of bullets, one long burst from a machine-gun might kill them all.

The noise outside was chaotic. Simbas yelling contradictory orders. Running feet. Rifles firing. And droning closer all the time the sound of powerful engines.

Helen's mind was confused. Lorry engines? Jeep engines? Surely it couldn't – at long last – be rescuers? It was not possible. No, it couldn't be possible ... Then black despairing reason hit her with the force of a physical blow. Of course it must be rescuers. Why else would the Simbas run for their lives? But if that was the case the rescuers *wouldn't know* they were here. They would think this was only a Simba road block. This inconspicuous bungalow near the roadside would mean nothing to them. They would crash past and as soon as they were gone the Simbas would be back to murder them all.

The thought, with help so close, sent her into a blaze of hysteria.

'They'll miss us,' she screamed. 'They won't know we're here.' Ignoring her own entreaty to lie flat on the floor she leapt for the window. It was too high for her. She couldn't see out.

'Amy,' she cried desperately. 'Lift me. Lift me. Oh, lift me so they can see a white face. Quick, quick!'

Amy scrambled to her feet. She grabbed Helen round the waist trying to push her upwards. Desperately Helen scrabbled at the window-sill, tried to push her face against the glass. Her spectacles fell off. She could feel the glass but she couldn't see through it. Oh God, somehow they had to see a white face!

Then the noise of heavy boots outside. Their door was kicked in. And the kickers had white legs.

Helen slid down from Amy's hands, slumped to a sitting position on the edge of a chair. It was beyond belief. This couldn't be rescue. Not at this last minute ... not like this ... it couldn't happen that way. She felt the tears running down her face. She heard as a loud, confused background, women and children screaming, crying, laughing in an overwhelming hysteria of relief.

It was so absurd. She was adult, a grown-up woman, a doctor, and yet she was weeping as if her heart would break. The relief was as unbearable as the agony.

Through blurred eyes she saw the young soldiers throwing in

their shirts so that some of the Belgian girls could cover their nakedness. But the young men were being dragged in, kissed and hugged so frantically they could scarcely move. It must have been more than two minutes before one put his hand on Helen's shoulder. He said 'We're glad, Miss. We really are so glad. You're the first British women we've managed to save. We've saved Italian and Dutch, Belgian and Spanish, all sorts, but we've always been too late to save the English girls. We've always found them murdered. Sometimes we've been only a few minutes – seconds almost – too late. We're so glad.'

Helen could not speak at all. She just went on crying, not even trying to pull herself together. There seemed to be a young Lieutenant in charge and he was urging speed. They all seemed very young. Helen had never seen a mercenary before. The word summoned a harsh distasteful connotation to her mind, but it never would again. In the future whenever she heard the word 'mercenary' she would remember Joe Wepener and his twenty-four brave young soldiers who came to their rescue in such story-book fashion.

Wepener's words started her moving. 'Ladies, you can't take any luggage. You can't take anything except yourselves.'

'Not even a briefcase?' somebody asked.

'Yes, a briefcase, okay, but no luggage. We haven't got room and we must hurry.'

Helen went out into the sunlight. Outside it was not all joy. Little Godeliefe was walking back towards the house crying bitterly and Helen stopped to pick her up.

'Godeliefe? What's the matter? We're rescued. We're all going home.'

But Godeliefe's mother had been first to race out of the house and along to the trucks.

'Daddy's not there. Mummy's been to look for him but he's not there.'

Helen's feeling of intoxicated euphoria was instantly dispelled. Discordantly into this lyrical moment of stunning and startling happiness thrust this bitter note of truth. Of course there were no daddies for any of the Belgian children; they had been murdered long ago. Helen knew that; everyone knew that; she had forgotten that the Belgian girls had refused to know it. Now they had to acknowledge this certain finality; to accept, live with and surmount that most agonising heartache of the human condition: grief.

Helen's heart went out to the despairing child. For a small girl, her life made bearable by the promise that 'Daddy will be back, Daddy will take care of us, Mummy will be better when she sees Daddy,' there was now no refuge but tears. Helen gathered her up and wept with her and tried to comfort her.

'There, darling, there. It'll be all right. You're going home. It'll be all right.'

She knew it wouldn't be all right. But what else could she say?

The scene around the three trucks was also chaotic. Godeliefe's mother – a lonely inconsolable figure – was standing at the side of one, her forehead pressed against the wooden side, weeping with bitter and silent intensity. She had endured it all ... those endless terrible nights at the Wamba hotel, supported by one flimsy hope, and she had accepted that she could endure almost anything if the tenuous possibility or the grain of hope was real. They had promised they would let her husband stay alive, they would not murder him; if she allowed them to use her body they would save him. Perhaps the fact that he was already dead gave the rapists some sort of pleasure; perhaps they thought of their actions as an extension of vengeance; perhaps they did not think at all. They would probably have raped her anyway, but the promise made her more compliant.

As she hurried towards the trucks carrying Godeliefe in her arms, Helen realised that for the time being, at least, Godeliefe's mother could offer no comfort to her small daughter. All around similar scenes of rejoicing and anguish were taking place. Everywhere people were crying. Jack Scholes had leapt down from the lorry to gather Jessie into his arms. The two 'grey-hairs' who had done so much to help Helen in all her troubles wept unashamedly together.

Joe Wepener and his men were equally as moved as the women they had saved, but a trained military sense of self-preservation re-asserted itself.

'We must get back to Paulis before nightfall,' insisted Joe Wepener. 'It's a hundred miles. We must get back before it's dark. All aboard, please. Quickly!'

A mercenary helped Helen to hand little Godeliefe back into the interior of one of the trucks. A woman took her on her knee and made a fuss of her. Helen scrambled up and found a place on Brian's knee. He grinned and said, 'Hallo, Helen.'

She was light-headed. The physical emptiness of relief was still inside her. She hardly knew whether she was laughing or crying, but the tears were almost all used up now. It was so good to feel the lorry move off, so wonderful to be amongst friends, warm, human friends. She could not feel safe yet; at that moment she doubted if she would ever feel safe again. But to be moving away from that dreadful bungalow and those terrible memories was to start life anew.

The armoured jeeps raced ahead of the convoy their wheels churning the red dust. It covered their faces and clothes – such clothes as they had. Helen wore a blue and white spotted dress, a pair of sandals, one with a broken strap, a pair of spectacles, no underclothes. Some of the Belgian girls wore the long khaki-coloured shirts tossed in to them by the mercenaries: they had nothing else.

The leading jeeps kept up a constant pattern of firing. A two- or three-second burst into any patch of jungle which might provide cover for an ambush. They met no resistance and drove into Paulis at six o'clock just before dark. The little town Helen remembered as a gay and bustling place was derelict, its very silence sinister and sad. The streets were deserted, windows were smashed or boarded up. The war had left Paulis a ghost town.

The mercenaries, with a keen Anglo-Saxon discrimination, had set up their headquarters in the modern brewery, but it speedily became clear that this happy coincidence did not conflict with their sense of discipline.

When Helen and the other women were off-loaded and led into the building crowded with a number of young and high-spirited soldiers, the sight of the female missionaries in various stage of undress precipitated an echoing chorus of wolf-whistles. God-fearing and steely-eyed Joe Wepener, their deliverer, who knew of the emotional state of his charges, was having none of this. He halted the procession. With arms folded across his chest he turned to glare with dramatic disapproval at his younger subordinates.

There was immediate silence, an embarrassed shuffling of feet, a few hesitant coughs; the procession moved on to the rooms allotted to them without further comment. Nevertheless a quick, genuine and warmhearted friendship grew swiftly between Helen, her colleagues and the young mercenaries.

Their main task had been to stiffen and bolster the morale of the National Congolese Army, but during the past few weeks this duty, now mainly accomplished, had altered and they had taken on the role of a swift and dramatic rescue force. And this in itself had worked a philosophical change in the men.

They had joined for a number of reasons: they were young and wanted adventure; they could not stand their wives; they thought that the simple experience of danger and violence against a strange tropical background equipped them to write best-sellers; they needed the money. Few of their motives had had anything to do with philosophical or Christian values though some were probably mixed with 'saving civilisation in Africa'. They were mercenaries, impure and unsimple.

But this work as a rescue force – this saving of many selfless people who had laboured for a lifetime under the hot Congo sun – had given them a new and unexpected experience.

Their quite extraordinary courage – to hurl themselves, a puny force of twenty-five through a territory occupied by literally thousands of armed black Simba warriors demanded an inordinate amount of that quality – had moved them into a new dimension of feeling. It had given their profession – a profession almost as old as the one which has occupied a small proportion of the female gender since the beginning of history – both dignity and purpose. Helen recognised this fact and wrote 'They were deeply touched by our gratefulness and also by our obvious overflowing joy . . . our hearts are too full for words.'

That night they all collected in the great brewery hall flanked by its stacked tiers of sugar sacks, at a long table formed by pushing a series of trestle tables together. Young soldiers and rescued missionaries sat down to a simple meal and joined in a community thanksgiving, which was very moving.

They had come through the fire. They had survived. And they gave thanks. The soldiers sang their songs suitably bowdlerized for the occasion. A New Zealander performed a Maori war-dance.

Helen and the others sang the doxology:
'Praise God from whom all blessings flow. . . .'

They spent the next morning scrubbing their clothes and having the first real wash, for as Helen blithely admitted: 'Some of us hadn't really washed for weeks and I have an idea we must have smelt and looked like it.'

Suitably cleansed and smelling sweetly, she posed for a picture with Lieutenant Joe Wepener, and waving the still wet, polaroid picture, she dashed for the entrance to the huge open-ended C.130 U.S. transport plane. Joe Wepener stood on the tarmac waving. It was to be very many more months before Helen heard that he had been killed only a few weeks after this leave-taking.

The plane roared through the night to Léopoldville. The American ambassador and a group of missionaries stationed there met them at the airport. For the first time they heard of the murders of many of their close friends and colleagues. Helen wept when she heard the name of Muriel Harmon amongst them. Muriel had been such a good friend to her. A skilful senior nurse, in the early days she had earned Helen's undying, if unspoken gratitude, by always calling her *Doctor* Roseveare, a little courtesy which meant so much when you were young and uncertain of yourself.

Perhaps because it was New Year's Eve there were only two newspaper men to meet them: a man from Reuters and another from the *Daily Telegraph*. Both were kind and considerate.

But even next day on the plane taking them first to Brussels and then on to London they could not really orientate themselves. It was not so much the transportation from the blinding sunshine of Congo to the frost-rimed airport buildings and tarpaulin skies of Heathrow which kept Helen silent, it was the physiological fact that she simply could not forget or diminish her overwhelming sense of fear. It had grown inside her like a cancer; it lurked in the recesses of her mind; it stayed on the periphery of sight like some dreadful apparition always there, never tangible. Oh yes, she opened her mouth and words came out; she moved her lips and formed laughter; they giggled helplessly at the sight of each other wearing the old army greatcoats and woollen balaclava helmets issued to them in Brussels. When a reporter asked Helen if she would ever go back to Congo, she laughed and answered glibly, 'When you've just escaped from the lion's cage at dinnertime you don't go back to offer yourself as dessert.'

She was frozen up. Perhaps the spring thaw would come eventually and bring back sanity and awareness into her life, but she could not believe this. When she arrived at her mother's home she did not cry, she was quite controlled, she just wanted to sleep. A little later she wrote, with a certain dry academic detachment, as an epilogue to a slender published edition of letters she had written to her mother. 'The situation in Congo is so disturbed and fraught with danger from inside and outside, that it is almost impossible to predict at all what the future may hold.'

Many other people felt the same way. A team of *Reader's Digest* editors doing a blanket coverage of the Congo disaster reached the conclusion that '... the Europeans won't go back for a long time, if ever.'

Helen agreed with that sentiment. She was never going back. Nothing in the whole wide world would ever make her go back.

For Lady Roseveare, who not only loved her eldest daughter very dearly but also admired her, the reappearance of Helen was little short of a miracle.

She had read weeks previously the report of Helen's death: a picture on the front page of a newspaper and the headline, 'Doctor Killed In Ibambi.' Lady Roseveare, unaware that another doctor, Dr Swertz had been the real victim, had closed her eyes, prayed silently and tried to keep a tiny flicker of hope alive in her mind. The local minister had also visited her and said in troubled fashion that he supposed they should hold a memorial service for Helen, but he was uneasy about the whole matter and hoped that Lady Roseveare felt the same way.

On December 31st she received an invitation to a New Year's Eve party from a close friend, but declined it because she knew she could make no pretence of enjoying herself at a time like this. Later that evening an acquaintance rang her to tell her that the B.B.C. six o'clock bulletins had reported the rescue of a group of missionaries from the north-eastern province of Congo.

Her sister who had been a missionary in China for twenty years was staying with her over the holidays and both of them waited up anxiously for the B.B.C's late night news. At last it came and with it the most joyous anticipation: a list of names of missionary survivors all of whom were colleagues of Helen's: Jack and Jessie Scholes, Florence Stebbing, Amy Grant, Elaine de Rusett, Brian Cripps . . . eight names in all. Then the announcer stopped. But where was Helen's name? He must have made a mistake and left her out. He'd correct himself at once, apologise and say, 'And Dr Helen Roseveare.'

But he did not do this. He paused and turning to a different subject went on reading the news.

The two sisters sat silently in their living-room. They did not speak for they knew this was the end; they were old and wise enough not to buoy themselves with vain hopes any longer; the news of the doctor killed in Ibambi must have referred to Helen after all. It was certain that if she was not with this final group of dear and personal friends then she must be lost.

At last Lady Roseveare said quietly, 'I think I'll go to bed.'

A she climbed the stairs the bells of thousands of suburban Victorian churches and the ancient chimes of many more hundreds of tiny village churches throughout the English shires began to peal out the message that it was midnight. 1965 had arrived with goodwill to all men; God was in His Heaven, all well with the world.

She lay back against the pillow and stared into the darkness. Helen, her first-born daughter was dead. She had to live with that fact; she had to bear it. When the sudden strident ringing of the telephone beside her bed startled her she wondered how she could possibly answer some kind friend's greeting at this moment. Hesitantly she lifted the receiver. She managed a muffled 'Hallo.'

A tiny voice from the other end of the world said: 'Lady Roseveare. This is Leopoldville. We have news for you.'

She couldn't answer. What was there to say?

'This is the *Daily Telegraph* representative. It is good news. Your daughter Helen is alive and well. She will fly home tomorrow.'

Lady Roseveare began to cry. She was so overcome she replaced the receiver in its cradle without even thanking or even saying a word to the *Daily Telegraph* representative for his kind thoughtfulness, an occurrence she regrets to this very day.

Tears on her cheeks she slipped out of bed and hurried along

[219]

to her sister's bedroom. As soon as she opened the door she knew from her sister's look that she too had heard the phone, and supposed that this was confirmation of the very worst. Lady Roseveare's face did not reassure her And all Lady Roseveare was able to get out was a choked, 'She's safe, she's safe.'

In a second her sister was by her side and she was crying too. Two elderly ladies on New Year's Eve 1965 weeping as if their world had come to an end when actually it had just started again. Then because they were two well-brought-up and gallant English ladies they dried their eyes and Lady Roseveare said she just couldn't keep this news to herself, she was going to ring up her friend who was giving the party because she was bound to be up.

A male voice backed by the sound of a very jolly party indeed answered the phone. Lady Roseveare suddenly a little confused and nervous said, 'Oh, I wonder if you'd mind passing a message to your hostess saying that Helen is safe.'

The male voice at the other end of the phone had obviously heard of Helen. He paused as if taking in the news and then burst out: 'Why, that's marvellous. That's great!' She heard him turn from the phone and shout, 'Listen everybody. Helen's safe. Helen Roseveare's safe.'

Lady Roseveare heard the message passed around the room, the sudden cheers, the marvellous clamour of people at a gathering who loved her daughter and whose hearts had lifted at the news. And she didn't even wonder – when tears were pouring down her cheeks – how she could be so happy.

Part Six

Part Six

I

Palm Sunday morning a week before Easter and the tiny stone-built Cornish church was crowded. Bunches of yellow daffodils filled the vases near the altar, pale spring sunlight filtered through the thin Gothic windows. In the deep lanes which led to the church, primroses blossomed along the sheltered banks, and below the lanes and out to the horizon stretched the dark blue sea, restless and flecked with foam.

To Helen, the voices of the children in the front rows, trilling clearly and with incandescent innocence, was most moving. Upsetting too, for they sang the same hymns that the children would be singing back in the church at Nebobongo. She was hardly aware of the first tear to run down her cheek and splash on her prayer book. She looked at it with some surprise, never guessing that this was the breakdown point, the release of all the pent-up emotion. Suddenly tears were flowing and her sobs must have been audible to everyone, not least of all to her poor mother standing next to her in the pew.

She tried to stop, tried to control herself, but every time a hymn started she was off again and the entire service seemed designed to batter her emotions; it brought back so many memories. The vicar was good at his job; he brought all the children seated in the front rows into the service, he made them aware of their part in the ancient, loving Christian ritual. A small girl read shyly a story about Christ's entry into Jerusalem seated on a donkey. The vicar took up this theme extending the thought and saying that all of them should be little donkeys willing to be led by the Lord. And Helen wept, clearly, openly and eventually unashamedly through it all. No matter how she tried to staunch the tears they kept coming. She wept in the car driving back through the lanes to the cottage; she wept as she prepared the lunch; she went on crying for the next two days and her wise mother did not interfere except to say, 'There, there dear. You'll be all right soon.' She had no idea why this bottled-up emotion should expend itself at this particular moment so long after all danger was past. Perhaps it had something to do with the fact that she was never going back to Congo; she had to consider a new sort of life for she had not made up her mind what she was going to do in the future: probably a three year training course, another degree, perhaps: then some sort of post at a university if she was lucky?

She found herself very popular as a speaker in the next three months travelling all over the country and often speaking twice a day. That August she went to a youth camp near Anglesey run by the British leader of W.E.C., Len Moules, a man she much admired. She did not care much for camps, 'youth' or otherwise, and this one seemed to be inhabited exclusively by dozens of noisy, unruly, girls and Helen could not understand them. It poured with rain practically the whole time, and what with squelching mud and rosy-cheeked, high-spirited young ladies – Helen could barely repress a shudder as she realised she must have been exactly the same at their age – she felt depressed.

No news of Ibambi or Nebobongo had reached Helen or the Scholes since they left, though the newspapers served up daily reports of fighting and general unrest.

When Helen found the letter in her tent bearing a Congo stamp and addressed in John Mangadima's handwriting, she tore it open eagerly. They were free; that was the first miraculous news she grasped. Ibambi and Nebobongo had been liberated by mercenaries only a week before he'd written this letter. But that was not the important point. John was filled with joy to learn that she and all the others were still alive. He had heard – and later reports had confirmed – that they had been murdered. Then the mercenaries had brought him this stupendous news of their preservation and he was so overwhelmed that he found it hard even to fashion the words to write. They had no stationery or pencils at Nebobongo, but a mercenary soldier had given him this piece of paper he wrote on, and an envelope, and promised to post the letter for him.

[224]

And more important still, he wanted from the bottom of his heart to apologise for all the dreadful things she had gone through in Congo. As a Congolese he was ashamed that country-men of his could act in such a manner. She had given her-self entirely and unselfishly to his people; given all her love and affection, all her skills, all her hard work, only to be re-paid by brutality and imprisonment. He hoped that she would find it in her heart to forgive him personally and Congo in general.

He knew she would never return after such treatment; he took that for granted; there was no point in even mentioning the subject. But would she try and remember that so many people there still loved her? Things were very bad at Nebo. They had nothing left; no food, clothes, money, utensils, drugs, medicines – nothing. It was, he supposed, like Congo before the first missionaries arrived. They would have to start again from the beginning. But with God's help they would persevere and succeed.

There was no self pity in his words, only a deep affection and understanding.

Helen carefully folded the letter and returned it to its en-velope. Then she squelched across the muddy grass to the tent occupied by Len Moules. He had been a pioneer missionary on the Tibetan border; it was his film about that experience, en-titled *Three Miles High* which had thrilled Helen in her uni-versity days and turned her spirit towards W.E.C.

She pushed back the flap, walked in and said quietly, 'Have you got the group arranged yet for the return to Congo?'

Len Moules, tall, good-humoured and greying, looked up from the table where he was writing. His face creased into a smile. He began to laugh. Len had a very infectious laugh and he obviously expected Helen to laugh with him. When she didn't laugh and he saw the look on her face he stopped, 'Sorry. I thought it was a joke!'

'No joke.' she said firmly.

He rose from the table pushed forward another chair so she could sit down. 'Helen,' he said. 'You had a very hard time. D'you know what you're saying?'

'Yes. I want to go back to Congo.'

Len sat down again and tapped the table with his pencil.

'There's still fighting in the north-east province. The Simbas still hold huge territories there. The mercenaries and National Congolese Army are having a rough time.'

'I know.'

'Winnie Davies is still held by the Simbas. We haven't given up hope for her, but . . .' he lifted his eyes and shoulders in an eloquent gesture.

Winnie had been abducted by Simbas and was still a prisoner, dragged from forest camp to forest hideout.

'I know,' Helen repeated.

Len Moules stared at her solemnly. He knew Helen well enough.

'All right,' he said after a pause. 'I know Jack Scholes has something similar in his mind. I'll write to him.'

The return letter indicated exactly what 'something similar' Jack and Jessie Scholes had in mind. They wanted to go home. Their lives, their hopes, their work, their dreams – even their eventual graves – waited out there in that clearing in the tropical rain forest for their return. They were too old to change now; too young to retire but too old to change. They knew that missionary work in north-east Congo was back at its beginnings. They wished to help in that second beginning. There were no teachers or doctors. As John had pointed out there was no food, clothes, medicines nor equipment, no grain even to plant for the next harvest. They *had* to go back and they agreed with Len's suggestion that Helen could return – if not with them – then as soon as possible afterwards. Jack Scholes and Frank Cripps would go out first and push up through territory occupied by the military and see if they could reach Nebo and Ibambi; they would cable back as soon as it was possible for Helen and the two wives to join them.

Jack and Frank flew to Léopoldville in January and began to hitch-hike their way northwards in army planes and army convoys. Their letters described the misery and destruction. They reiterated that when the women came out they must bring everything with them: food, clothes, supplies, medicines; the shops were empty; there was nothing left. And eventually the clinching letter arrived; although there were huge areas where fighting was still going on, they had the necessary permits for the three women to enter Congo.

With hindsight Helen realised that she had simplified and at the same time dramatised her return to Congo. For better or worse the rebellion had altered her; physically, mentally, philosophically and spiritually she had changed, and she expected everyone else who had been through that rebellion to have changed also. They had not.

In the lectures she delivered during the months they waited for Jack and Frank to give them the all-clear, she tried to define her new feelings. She reasoned that the first period of her life in Congo had coincided with the end of the colonial era in which the Europeans had treated the Congolese as small children. Independence had ushered in adolescence; but now she would be returning to a new black and white relationship: an adult friendship would exist between the two races. The blacks would need the finance, teaching, training and intellectual skills of the whites; they would work as partners side by side. Later, of course, she realised that she had made far too glib a generalisation. Life was never as simple as that. Friction and frustration, disappointment and heartache were the normal companions of the human condition, commoner by far than the joys of friendship, understanding, tolerance or love.

In March – fifteen months after leaving – Helen arrived back on the Ugandan border of Congo. With Jessie Scholes and Mrs Cripps as passengers she drove her brand new Land-Rover, bought by subscriptions from a thousand well-wishers, with a self-satisfied feeling of having, at last, a vehicle to do the hundred jobs she required of it.

She began the long climb from the level of the Nile up the steep escarpment which separates Uganda from Congo.

On a particularly bad bit of road with no room for two vehicles to pass they met a descending bus. The bus driver shouted impolitely at Helen, instructing her to reverse. In barbed Swahili she pointed out she had never in her life reversed a Land-Rover hauling a trailer and she did not intend to start risking her precious vehicle now. The bus driver was offensive. Did he have to insist that it was the duty of the smaller vehicle to give way? He could insist as much as he liked, retorted Helen, she had not brought her beautiful Land-Rover all the way from England to lose both it and herself over a precipice. The argument reached boiling point. Her Swahili was as good if not better than the bus driver's, her shrug of the shoulders equally disdainful. How to be offensive without actually becoming obscene was the keynote of their exchange. Mrs Cripps and Mrs Scholes got out and pretended to admire the scenery. All the passengers got out and listened enthralled to the slanging match. Helen put her hands on her hips and reiterated her position. As far as she was concerned she would, if necessary, stay put for the rest of the week; she would not, repeat 'not' in all declensions of Swahili, reverse her Land-Rover and trailer one inch down the mountainside.

Her dramatic if slightly un-Christian confrontation won the argument. The bus driver reversed. They continued and reached the point in the escarpment at the Congolese border where Customs Officers took over. Soldiers looked them over suspiciously. The Customs Officers were away getting drunk; they had to be fetched. In general everyone was surly and unhelpful, but they were allowed through. Helen engaged the gear lever and accelerated away knowing that her throat was dry, her nerves on edge. The bus driver episode had nothing to do with it; that was no more than an occupational hazard for Congo drivers. But those soldiers! That road block! Simba road blocks had been exactly the same. Here she was imagining things were going to be different and now in her heart she had to accept the fact that nothing had changed, and with a terrible, sinking awareness, understand that she had probably made the biggest mistake in her life by even *thinking* she could come back to Congo.

They spent the night at the mission station at Rethy. Jack Scholes and Frank Cripps were there to meet them. It lay eight thousand feet up in wide sprawling grasslands. That night the stars were high and clear and it was cold enough for a fire. It was also eminently suitable for a nightmare. Tall, spear-carrying African watchmen patrol in the darkness; the cadence of the wind in the eaves is sometimes a soft whistle and occasionally a shriek, and Helen passed a dreadful night. She tossed and turned, she talked in her sleep and screamed aloud as she relived the rebellion. How did she begin to tell all of them that it was no good ... she had overplayed her hand ... she was a silly frightened woman and she could not go through with it? The fear ... the past terrible fear had seeped into the marrow of her bones; she was like a shell-shock victim and this return to the battle field was unendurable.

Next day, in the pouring rain, with windscreen wipers that didn't work, they reached Nyankunde, a place which was to occupy much of her time in the future, but then only a comparatively small mission station. Helen made the usual noises of 'Hallo' and 'How are you?' and 'How wonderful to see you again,' and tried to push back into the dark undergrowth of her subconsciousness the cringing realisation that she wasn't going to be able to cope any more.

The physical crunch came the following day with the rain still driving down. As they toiled up a steep hill over a track which even the most sanguine estate agent might have hesitated to describe as a road, a track cut into deep gullies by the pouring torrents so that Helen had to make instant decisions where to put which wheel to maintain momentum, the trailer dropped into a gully, skidded out again, slid sideways, jack-knifed and jammed across the road.

Fortunately the leading vehicle had been stopped by a road block at the top of the hill. Hearing their yells Frank Cripps and a group of Congolese soldiers came down to use manpower to get them moving again. Back on the road and pointing in the right direction Helen felt a little better; certainly immensely relieved as she reversed and manipulated the Land-Rover – a different machine altogether without its tethering trailer – out of muck in which any other vehicle would have been helplessly bogged down.

But the endless road blocks – about one every thirty miles – revived all her old fears. She sometimes wondered afterwards what Jack and Jessie Scholes thought of those stops? They might have seen everything as normal; the National Congolese Army glad to see them back? In Helen's terms they were frightening; the soldiers were invariably drunk, they were rude, she was never quite certain which one was going to hit her, and this added the final certainty to her decision that she knew she was not going to be able to stick it. The farther she got into Congo, the more she wanted to leave; she had not realised she was quite so mentally unprepared; she was bewildered by the extent of her unpreparedness.

After another night on the road, next day they drove along

the straight, red-gravel road between palms which led to Ibambi. Again by a strange coincidence it was Easter Sunday morning, just over a year since she had wept through the service in the tiny Cornish church.

The noise of their arrival penetrated the open windows of the great brick church where the three-thousand-strong congregation were singing a hymn. The hymn stopped, or rather it half stopped, and then the congregation came pouring out – a great stream of people laughing, crying, singing and clapping. Helen, Jessie, Mrs Cripps were hugged, kissed and swept back into the church in a scene of enormous emotional exaltation. Helen had her tape recorder all prepared to record their welcome home but she never even managed to free a hand to press the button. The patients in the leprosy camp heard the news and came carrying flowers, and bowls of eggs and fruit. It was a scene totally impossible to visualize in Western society because of the depths of its emotionalism, the ecstasy of reunion. They sang and they sang and they sang in joyful cadences of harmony.

They were allowed out of the church for sandwiches and coffee, then they went back again and, after the initial emotionalism, Helen saw things she had not observed at first because they had made no impact but which now dismayed and grieved her. Before the rebellion the congregation had had clothes; now their only clothes were a few rags and cloth made from beaten tree bark. They sang the hymns by heart because they had no hymn books. They were older, they were scarred and she could see the suffering in their faces. And they were so poor. Of course they had always been poor, but now they were indescribably poor.

One thing, however, remained. As they sang the hymns over and over again with soaring voices, they were uplifted; whatever the rebels had taken from them – and they had stolen or destroyed practically everything they possessed – they had not taken their faith.

At Nebobongo a thinner, older but equally overjoyed John Mangadima clasped her in his arms. He explained how the Simbas had occupied Nebobongo using it as a military centre.

He told her with pride how he had saved the drugs. 'I divided them up into ten parcels, each containing aspirins, antibiotics, anti-malarials. Then one at a time I called in each male nurse and said, 'Take this parcel away and hide it in the forest where no one can find it. Don't tell anybody. But when I ask, you must bring it back.'

'And it worked?'

'The Simbas never got a thing.'

On reflection Helen realised that John *had* replaced her during the year and a half she had been away; there *had* been a doctor at Nebobongo.

The whole place was badly damaged: there were bullet holes in roofs, walls and doors. Her own house had also suffered but attempts had been made to repair the damage; one wall had been completely rebuilt and even though the office, bedroom and bathroom were stripped, her friends had one secret to reveal. The guest room was locked, and the women made great play, giggling delightedly, as they turned the key. Within stood a bed with an interior sprung mattress neatly spread with sheets and blankets; there were curtains at the window, a jam-jar of flowers on the table. Poverty stricken beyond belief, they had managed this for her!

That night she lay in bed and looked up at the ceiling. She was thrilled by their welcome; boundlessly touched by their joy at her return. But the inner doubt still remained. Was she a fool to come back? Would she summon enough strength to continue? Anxiety oppressed her. If she was honest with herself she knew she would not be able to stand it.

There were at once so many things to assess, repair and restart – even to forget. First of all she had to look at her own capabilities: to admit to *herself* that the rebellion had altered her. Reluctantly she accepted that working eighteen hours a day was too much; she would have to settle for sixteen.

As usual the problems at Nebobongo were constantly frustrating. Where and how did she start? Nobody had any money; she was faced with a refugee problem, a housing problem, a clothing problem, a feeding problem. In the primary school the teachers hadn't even a blackboard, a piece of chalk, a sheet of paper, or a pencil. Her heart was torn in a dozen different ways. Whom did she help first?

But her main consideration was survival: how to stay in Congo? It was all very well to wear herself out in an internal conflict of indecision, when it could be only a useless emotional luxury; the authorities might throw her out anyway!

All five of them had come in on visitor's visas which allowed three months residence; the days were running out quickly. When she journeyed to Paulis to make inquiries about new passports the authorities were totally unsympathetic. They made it clear that whites were not welcome. Without whites there would have been no rebellion, would there? Why, therefore had they chosen to come back?

Helen did not bother to point out that the whites in the shape of the Belgian colonial regime had been ousted some four years before, and the rebellion had concerned one black, so-called People's Liberation Army fighting a legally constituted black republican Government. The tensions and suspicions in the town made her feel nervous every time she went in; obviously nothing could be accomplished there. Permits were needed for nearly every activity: road permits, identification permits; each form to be approved and stamped by at least three government departments. When she went to Léopoldville to make a serious effort to get their passports renewed and talk about having her medical school recognised by the Government she made her feelings quite clear. 'You don't know what's been happening up in our north-eastern province. You've had it all right down here in the seat of Government, no great battles, no scorched earth; you've been comparatively comfortable. And now you're making all sorts of unreasonable laws. It's no use telling us that children over the age of fourteen can't go to secondary schools, because where I come from all the children over the age of fourteen are dead. They were collected by the Simbas in lorry loads and taken off to the battle front near Bunia where National Congolese Army mowed them down with machine-gun fire.'

But she could not really find the correct Government department to confront with this statement. She could only walk from office to office for hour after hour and wait in queues and end up talking to some bored and indifferent civil servant.

She did manage to get her own passport extended; the other four had to attend in person before theirs could be issued.

She also managed to get fourteen tons of goods; blankets and food, pencils and paper, clothes and utensils to distribute back at Ibambi and Nebo.

(3)

Long before Independence, Helen's fundamental objective had been government accreditation of her medical school. This gave her the right to train students to sit examinations and issue diplomas with which they could get jobs in government hospitals or in any branch of medical work, and little did she realise when, inspired by the appearance of John Mangadima, she began her work, the years of trial which lay ahead.

Vividly she remembered a certain traumatic day back in 1963. Wearing an old, dirty dress she was busy cleaning the carburettor of her car and hardly noticed a second car draw up alongside. She did, however, recognise one of the three white men getting out of it as Dr DeGott, the local government doctor at Paulis.

Wiping oily hands on a bit of rag, she walked across for him to introduce her to the others.

'This is Dr Trieste, a government doctor from Léopoldville, and this is Mr Jenkins from the World Health Organisation.'

Helen shook hands and invited them into the house. All the time a nagging little worry disturbed her. What did they want? Surely this couldn't be the inspection? No, it wasn't possible. After all she'd been waiting nine years for the important event and they were bound to give her notice about such a matter.

Inside the house she brushed aside all discussion with, 'Of course you'll have coffee? Of course you will . . .'

Dr DeGott glanced at his watch. 'We don't like to sound impatient, but we haven't got much time if we're going to inspect the entire hospital,' he announced, thereby shattering her equanimity.

Helen passed her hand across her brow to reassure herself that her head was still there.

'Inspect the entire hospital? Oh yes,' she said. Three learned gentlemen – one who had flown specially from Léopoldville – wanted to inspect the entire hospital? The idea was preposterous, the time inconvenient and the outcome too hideous to envisage. This was undoubtedly the government group who would decide

[233]

on her qualification and right to run a medical training school and who would recommend or destroy any hope she had of recognition. But why had they not warned her they were coming? Why? Why? Why? She had been waiting so long for this visit. A surprise call like this might have its merits as far as they were concerned, but it was totally unfair to her. She did not know what to say. She did not know how to react. Should she protest and say this went beyond a joke, that really gentlemen didn't behave in such a manner?

She said instead, 'But of course there's time for coffee.'

It was not until the *next day* that the telegram they had despatched a week earlier arrived; they had thought she was quite prepared for their visit.

Helen knew she had only one move left to her. Somehow, she had to delay them. Twenty minutes were vital; half an hour would be better, but twenty minutes were an absolute necessity.

'You must have coffee,' she insisted again. 'It won't take a second.'

Dr DeGott was philosophical.

'All right then, as long as it's quick, but remember we have to make several other calls.'

Benjamin was already at the door waiting instructions. 'Coffee, Benjamin, please,' said Helen in a voice she hardly recognised. Then as he turned to leave she followed him for a few steps. 'Tell John Mangadima at once,' she ordered. 'At once! Tell him Plan X. Plan X.'

Benjamin stared at her with wide uncomprehending eyes, then nodded. He was used to his mistress's perpetual madness.

Five minutes later she poured the coffee with a hand she hoped was not visibly trembling and began the series of ridiculous delaying questions.

'How was the weather in Léopoldville? Were the plane services between the capital and Paulis functioning all right? Now Independence had brought Congolese Government supervision to all medical services did Dr Trieste think they could train sufficient staff?'

She ploughed on, each time-wasted minute passing like an hour, her guests becoming increasingly impatient.

'We're really only allowed one hour for the inspection,' said Dr DeGott, 'I really do think we ought to be starting.'

'You've plenty of time,' insisted Helen busily refilling another coffee cup. 'After all it's only fifty yards from here. Another biscuit, Dr Trieste?'

But Dr Trieste was already on his feet. 'Thank you very much, Dr Roseveare, but no. I agree with Dr DeGott, we must start the inspection at once.'

Helen plodded across the hospital compound her heart making the same sort of anxious creakings as her feet on the gravel. Slowly they passed through the women's ward, the men's ward, the bureau, the out-patients, the operating theatre.

The beds were superb, their bedspreads spotless. Every patient was either lying in bed or sitting up, neatly tucked-in, washed, combed, immaculate. None hopped about on one foot, smoking or sprawled on each other's beds as was usually the case. All had up-to-date charts hanging at the foot of their beds. Every nurse or student nurse wore his very best uniform; John Mangadima in his white overall coat and trousers would have done credit to the Mayo Clinic.

Across then to maternity and Helen's heart was full. She had never seen a hospital like it. She had certainly never seen *her* hospital like it. All the female staff were drawn up in two lines outside the door as if waiting for an inspection by royalty. Their faces shone, their uniforms were impeccable. All the mothers were in bed; all the babies in their cots. The ward was spotless. Helen began to glow like an electric bulb so deep was her pride in her team.

For precisely for such an emergency Plan X had been devised. John and Helen had worked it out and rehearsed it with the regularity of a fire drill. The bedspreads and uniforms had been laundered and re-laundered for so long that several sets might have been worn out. The staff had been trained with military efficiency. And nothing had gone wrong.

After the inspection party had left John grinned at her. 'What kept you so long?' he joked. 'We were ready for you in eighteen minutes and thirty seconds flat!'

Helen could have kissed him. 'It was the longest twenty minutes I've ever wasted in my life,' she admitted.

But it did not do them any good. The report commended them for uniforms, general turn-out, presentation of facts and high morale, but unfortunately their hospital buildings were not up to the standard required by the Government, which was hardly surprising since Helen had employed local labour to construct them from mud and thatch. The number of students under training was also criticised; there were not sufficient patients to warrant such a number.

Helen had expected this reaction. Every other mission hospital in the north-eastern provinces had also failed to qualify. It did not mean they would have to shut down or stop training medical students – although in the long run this was the Government's objective. It did mean, however, that their students would not receive the much sought-after accreditation which would qualify them for jobs anywhere in Congo.

Some two hundred miles away from Nebobongo the Africa Inland Mission at Oicha ran a hospital and training school on the same lines as her own. In charge was Dr Carl Becker, a much respected veteran American surgeon whose mission hospital had also failed to qualify. Dr Becker, a tall, spare, greying, scholarly man whom Helen knew and admired had spent forty years toiling patiently and tirelessly. He was a first-class surgeon and physician who would have graced the top echelon of any major American hospital, but he sought neither notoriety nor personal advancement. Helen was certain that in his quietly effective manner he had done more to promote the essentially humane conception of his nation than a dozen 'big wheels' operating in the various international agencies. She understood his motives completely. He was a godly man, and they were friends.

Behind his glasses his eyes twinkled with benevolence as Helen repeated the story of Plan X. Both of them were knowledgeable enough to know that Independence spelt the end of the small mission hospital and one doctor trying to cope with all the problems it entailed.

All the mission hospitals had in their time and way performed miracles. They had provided medical services where none existed before. But the newly independent and ambitious Congolese Government wanted better things, higher standards, a twentieth-century medical service, not something out of Dr Livingstone's handbook.

Dr Becker and Helen agreed emphatically with that ambition, but both wanted to preserve in their medical service the Christian ethic and ideal. So their plans began to take shape.

For many years the enormous north-eastern territories of Congo had been divided into spheres of influence by the five Protestant missionary organisations working there. No one organisation had enough money, equipment, or medical staff to fulfil Government requirements. Alone they were powerless. Together they might succeed. It was from this starting point that Dr Becker and Helen were exploring when the rebellion broke out.

They envisaged one all-embracing medical centre, with a large hospital, maternity and out-patients wards staffed by European and American doctors and highly qualified nurses. The medical teaching school would be directed by Helen; Dr Becker would run the hospital and be overall Director; no one else possessed the seniority, experience and qualifications necessary for the job. They drew up plans for a flying doctor service. Small airstrips would be hacked out of the rain forest at places like Nebobongo where the flying doctors would spend a week on rota duty. They had even chosen their site; Nyankunde four thousand feet up in the grasslands above the rain forest. To the west lay the great mountain ranges bordering Uganda. It was remote. But it was healthy.

It was an ambitious plan and in June, as soon as Helen had solved most of the problems she found at Nebobongo, she went up to the border station at Rethy where Dr Becker was working. It was the first time they had met for more than two years. He had not altered at all, Helen decided, although she knew that now he was over seventy; he was still the lean, kindly, fatherly figure, intensely dedicated to his task of advancing Congo's medical history. Work did not stop because of Helen's visit; he simply co-opted her to act as his assistant surgeon and she found it an enlightening experience. Indeed, as she stood beside him at the operating table, she couldn't help reflecting a little regretfully how much better it would have been for her if she could have spent a year under Carl Becker's guidance when she had first arrived in Congo. He was so much more experienced and skilful than she was; under his tuition she would certainly have lost much of the fear which inhibited her surgery for so many years.

He was far advanced with plans for Nyankunde. 'We've got the site for your medical school arranged,' he explained. 'I'll drive you down there tomorrow and you can see it. Nice piece of ground about two hundred yards square. My hospital foundations are already under way.'

Helen cleared up one thing she had on her mind. 'You've abandoned the possibility of taking over a Government hospital now that most of the Belgians have left?'

'Absolutely. The Government is adamant – and who can blame them? – that in their own hospitals they'll be responsible for the recruitment, training, advancement and dismissal of staff.'

'Which means Christian influence and teaching will play no part at all in that training?'

'None at all. It's their country; they can call the tune. So as arranged we're going ahead with our own Evangelical Medical Centre at Nyankunde.'

He smiled at her, 'What about your students? Where are you going to get them from? When will you be ready to start?'

Helen had considered her plans, even though she was surprised to find Dr Becker so far advanced in his. 'I'll obviously bring some of my own from Nebobongo. I've sent details by radio and letter and word of mouth to all the secondary schools in the north-east asking for students to sit our examination and be ready to start in August.'

Dr Becker's eyebrows lifted. 'I hate to mention it, but what about the school buildings?'

She said cheerfully, 'I hope they won't run back home when I confront them with the fact that they've got to build their own classrooms before I can start to teach them.'

'Knowing you,' said Dr Becker, 'I expect you'll manage.'

Helen deeply regretted having to leave Nebobongo after so many years, but the Government's decision made it inevitable and she would, of course, as W.E.C.'s medical director, still be in charge. Nebo would still continue as a small hospital and medical centre, and with luck and understanding co-operation from W.E.C., John Mangadima would eventually be ready to take over as medical director there.

(2)

During these first weeks after her return to Congo two other dramatic needs deeply concerned Helen. Winnie Davies, her friend and colleague, whom she had visited so many times at Opienge, deep in the Ituri forest was still a captive. Winnie had lived in Congo for twenty years; she had worked at Nebobongo when it was only a small leprosy settlement and maternity centre before Helen took over.

When the Simbas captured Opienge it was thought at first that Winnie had been killed, and many months of confusion passed before news was received that she was a captive of the Simbas in the rain forest. Rumours that she was still alive reached British authorities; it was Helen who received the first letter from an African pastor at Opienge giving accurate information. With a Dutch priest named Father Strijbosch Winnie had been marched through the forest, always a few miles ahead of the approaching National Congolese troops and obviously in continual danger.

Helen felt strongly that an attempt to rescue her must be made. Accordingly she visited the lieutenant in charge of the Nationalist Army in Bunia, explaining that she knew the treacherous road through the forest to Opienge very well; after all, she had had experience of gorillas and night stops there. To her it was obvious that a full-scale army attack through this sort of territory would never succeed, but she had another idea.

'The Simbas must be by now lulled into a false sense of security. They know that you can't mount an attack along such a road, so why not surprise them? A small, resolute force could take them unawares. Just a small force ... I know the district very well.'

The lieutenant listened politely. Plainly the idea of a commando raid led by Dr Helen Roseveare did not appeal to him at all.

'Dr Roseveare,' he replied, 'The colonel in charge of the operation is in Stanleyville. He has given orders that the Bafwasende–Stanleyville road is to be opened within a month and the area cleared of rebels. I believe that a ...' he fumbled for words, obviously discarding 'foolhardy', 'idiotic', 'insane' and 'suicidal' ... 'expedition such as you suggest would clash with these plans and not meet with his approval.'

'But if you wait it'll be too late,' Helen protested. After more argument she departed thoroughly depressed. She had an overwhelming presentiment that unless some dramatic action similar to the mercenary dash which had rescued their party was undertaken, Winnie's life was desperately at risk.

Within weeks the news she dreaded was confirmed. Father Strijbosch had been rescued and he told their story. For thirty-four months Winnie had been held captive by the Simbas, driven to stumble on long exhausting escape marches as the National Congolese Army closed in. But even weakened and ill from lack of food and living in the soaking jungle, she had nursed the sick Simba women and continued to preach to the Christians amongst them.

With the final National Army encirclement, flight became a chaotic rush for safety with neither Winnie nor Father Strijbosch able to do more than stagger along. Father Strijbosch, forced on ahead of Winnie by his Simba guard, realised when he saw Winnie resting by the side of the path ahead of him that in the general panic they must have circled on their tracks.

He limped closer. 'I thought she was resting,' he wrote, 'but as I approached I realised she was dead, lying there in her faded green dress. She must have been dead for about fifteen minutes. There were knife wounds on her head and throat, with blood on her mouth.'

Staggering on for another few hundred yards Father Strijbosch was confronted by three armed men. Thinking it was his turn to die he crossed himself and waited for the bullets. Then a voice shouted, 'We are the National Congolese Army. We are here to rescue you.' Father Strijbosch broke down. As the young mercenary had once reported to Helen with such sadness, this time, as so many times in the past, the rescuers had arrived a few minutes too late.

Helen grieved deeply for Winnie. To have gone through so much and then succumbed was such a bitter irony. But she knew that Winnie would have made her peace with God and would have wished them all to go on working to save the living.

When Colonel Yossa appealed to Helen for help it was no surprise at all.

(3)

He expected that his forces would flush the enemy out of Wamba within the next two to three weeks. They would then press on in pursuit. But the news that Wamba was free would reach those hiding in the rain forest. The exodus would begin. Refugees who had been hiding there for as long as two years would drag themselves out into the sunlight again. He expected there would be thousands; he knew that they would be in a pitiable state. Could she help? Could she mount an immediate relief operation and give the Army and the Congolese authorities a breathing space?

Helen knew she had no alternative. The school at Nyankunde, affairs at Nebobongo, everything would have to wait. There was no one else equipped medically but herself to do the job and this was an emergency.

Above all else she would need two things: supplies and willing helpers. Obviously she could recruit church workers when she arrived in Wamba, but she wanted two or three experienced Europeans to help supervise the operation. She decided she would rope in Colin and Ina Buckley, two W.E.C. missionaries recently returned to Paulis, and then with great joy, she realised that one of her two favourite 'aunties' had also just arrived back in Congo. Agnes Chansler her lovely American 'auntie' who had worked in W.E.C. for thirty years had just returned for more.

In all her time in Congo Helen admired no one more than her two 'aunties', Agnes Chansler and Margery Cheverton. She had known and loved them since her first arrival in Africa. Two spinster missionary ladies with hearts of purest gold, their Christianity was compounded of its essential virtues, compassion, love and pity, and Helen always realised instinctively that to be with them, for even a short time, was to renew one's hope in humanity.

In 1961 after that first year of Independence Helen's health had broken down completely. A solid twelve months with no other doctor within a hundred miles, and an eighteen hour day her normal working span, meant that when she collapsed with acute malaria and hepatitis and physical and mental exhaustion if the 'aunties' had not carried her off to their mission station away from the wards and responsibilities at Nebo she would probably have died. Without a moment's hesitation they had taken her to Egbita some sixty kilometers away and for ten weeks nursed her back to health and sanity. The pale, skinny and very depressed Helen received their mutual and undivided attention; they fussed, mothered and spoon-fed her to such a degree that the very act of nursing took on a new dimension of healing. In that time she learnt much about them. They were happiest when they were out 'visiting'. 'Visiting' meant loading up their old car – in the old days it was either a journey on foot or on bicycle – and driving off into the rain forest. They would seek out the loneliest paths and the poorest villages and there they would carry out the mission which brought them to Africa in the first place: they would tell the story of the Christian miracle.

For thirty years they had ventured into places in the dark, mysterious rain forest full of snakes, pygmies, wild animals – places which would frighten ten years off the lives of most maiden ladies; they had gone about it with a comprehensive cheerfulness, oblivious to all but the job in hand, as unperturbed as if they were setting out to catch a bus in Peckham High Street.

In the villages they would introduce themselves to the head-man or chief, admire the babies, chat to the mothers, make notes of the more obvious illnesses which later they would bring to Helen's attention. In the evenings they sat by the fire and discussed the crops and the trials of mankind generally. Grad-ually they moved towards the purpose of their visit, to tell stories; to tell the most important story of the man called Jesus Christ who promised forgiveness of our sins and life everlasting. Sometimes in Swahili, often in the local Bangala dialect, the tall elegant Englishwoman and the shorter but not less indomitable American – a million light years removed from what their mothers envisaged for them – went about their business with a quality of humour and laughter, a capacity for friendship, a belief and that inner serenity which is irretrievably linked with the very roots of their faith.

There was no hesitation about Agnes's acceptance of the re-lief expedition to Wamba. When did they start?

By now Helen was beset with logistic headaches. She worked out that the Wamba operation could only last one week; by the end of that period their supplies would be exhausted; if she could get any supplies at all, that is. She could not steal back her hard-won drugs from Nebo; they were so scanty that they would be used up in two or three hours anyway. Better to leave them for the needy at Nebo and Ibambi and endeavour to get new supplies from somewhere else. That meant a journey to Stanleyville to harass and harangue, plead and cajole from every source she could find.

She arrived at Stanleyville on the morning of July 5th. Two hours later she met Big Bill, the American in charge of air transport in that area. He was huge, cheerful and he listened carefully to her appeal. Certainly he would do all he could to help.

At once radio messages began to flash backwards and forwards between Stanleyville and Léopoldville and from them to Army H.Q. in Bunia and Wamba. In the war-torn city of Stanleyville Helen began her search and in her own words ransacked every medical source she could find. 'I raided everybody. I showed no mercy to anybody. Greeks in their shops, relief organisations ... I went to the big hospital at Stanleyville and saw the marvellous Spanish doctor who ran it and said, 'If you've got two hundred flacons of penicillin I want one hundred!' Everybody who'd got any drugs I confronted and said 'I want half of them.'

The Protestant and Roman Catholic relief missions reacted generously. They delivered corn, oats, wheat, milk, soya-bean flour, clothing and blankets.

In Paulis a few days later she received a wonderful donation from Dr de Ville, the Belgian doctor in charge of the hospital there; he handed over sufficient penicillin for at least five thousand injections, and later Helen realised she could hardly have started her relief work in Wamba without this generous gift.

Meanwhile Big Bill pulled out all stops and jerked all strings. The sound of his naturally nasal and normally indolent voice, cajoling, suggesting, intimidating, and occasionally threatening if his demands were not met, buzzed across the Congolese radio waves.

On Helen's behalf he demanded air transport, lorries, government permits; all drugs and supplies to be flown to Paulis and then trucked in to Wamba. He reported cheerfully that when talking to Government medical supply officers in Léopoldville they appeared to lose the use of speech for several seconds when confronted by the size of Helen's demands. Distressed radio replies confirmed that the matter had been taken directly up to General Mobutu himself, and over a crackling radio line

Helen had a slightly incoherent conversation with the great man now military dictator of the land engaged in bringing law and order back to his troubled country. The interview was inconclusive, but she understood everything was being done to help though as usual red tape and inefficiency were responsible for many disappointments. One huge transport plane arrived from Léopoldville reportedly filled with foodstuffs and supplies. As it droned to a halt at its dispersal point the great doors were winched open. Big Bill and Helen hurried forward – to find the holds completely empty.

Towards the end of her hurried search for supplies she had to break off and return to Nyankunde for a task which by comparison seemed tame, but which was vital to her first school year. She had to mark examination papers.

To travel from Stanleyville to Nyankunde and back to Nebobongo at a time when any form of transport was in a chaotic condition was an ordeal in itself. She wasted day after day at various small airports trying to hitch a lift by military aircraft, hoping that when she landed she could get another lift by road.

At Bunia Dr Becker met her and drove her to Nyankunde. She spent eight consecutive hours selecting forty-eight students from several hundred applicants, and returned to Nebo hoping that those she had selected were strong, willing lads who would not object to a pre-course three-months chore as building labourers.

She left almost immediately for Paulis. The road between Ibambi and Paulis had survived Simba destruction fairly well. Every hundred yards or so an elephant trap, a huge hole dug in the road, mined and covered with palm fronds, had been roughly filled in. On one steep muddy hill with a deep water gully on either side, two lorries were stuck, apparently permanently. Helen viewed the possibility of manoeuvring the Land-Rover through the narrow gap with a decidedly glum expression. Fortunately one truck driver, an Egyptian of much character and determination volunteered to pilot the Land-Rover through.

This he accomplished with great skill and then gallantly insisted on driving them all the way into Paulis.

Next day the expedition, reinforced by Colin and Ina Buckley with Agnes, elegant and charming as ever, resolutely determined to play her part in any emergency, transferred to a large lorry and headed for Wamba. As they neared the town they saw the devastation caused by the fighting: deserted villages, burnt-out houses, schools overgrown and derelict. In one village they found the first group of refugees building flimsy leaf huts against the impending torrential monsoon rains. There was mud everywhere. The refugees had no clothes. They were living on leaves and grubs, tiny animals, anything they could scavenge.

Helen regarded them with a sense of overwhelming pity and explained the object of her journey. 'We've come to help you,' she announced, 'We're setting up at the Protestant mission in Wamba and in forty-eight hours time we'll be ready to start our distribution. Tell anybody you meet the missionaries are back. Tell them to come to Wamba.'

II

Driving into Wamba was like visiting a graveyard. The centre, government offices, post office and shops were gutted; only the prison – of such sordid and brutal memory – remained untouched. They observed that in one main street some repairs had been made and at the first store which showed signs of occupation they stopped. Inside Mr Mitsingas, her old Greek friend, was chatting to two mercenary officers.

Mitsingas saw her and stopped in mid-sentence. His mouth stayed open like that of a fish gasping for air. Then, recovering, he rushed to embrace her.

Hugging her, he said excitedly, 'Doctor Roseveare! It can't be true. You're in England! You're not in Congo! You're in England . . .'

'In Wamba at present,' Helen contradicted, her eye already expertly appraising the selection of goods he had on display; items she was going to need very badly in the next few days.

'But why come back to Congo? You must be . . .' With difficulty he swallowed the word 'mad' and hardly pausing he babbled on. 'And Wamba of all places! You were in prison here. All those dreadful things happened here.' He stopped, quite unable to comprehend her actions or motives.

'*You're* back, Mr Mitsingas?' she said pointedly. He released her from his embrace so that he could use both hands to make his point clear. 'But we've got nowhere else to go. Everything we have is tied up here. Shops, houses, money . . .'

She interrupted his catalogue of interests. 'I've heard that there are thousands of refugees all around Wamba.'

Mitsingas spread his hands. He was not greatly interested in that problem.

'We've still got trouble,' he admitted, indicating the smiling mercenary officers. 'You can see we've still got trouble. There's fighting less than fifty miles from here. This place is not far behind the front lines.'

'But it will soon be ended,' she insisted. 'And we must start to get things organised.' It was plain, however, that Mitsingas was not really concerned with this part of the conversation; he turned back to the two mercenary officers lifting his shoulders in the inimitable gesture that the Greeks have made their own. It expressed admiration, doubt, love, friendship and perplexity. Above all, perplexity.

'She didn't have to come back,' he murmured wonderingly. 'She didn't have to come back at all.'

'Oh, yes, I did,' replied Helen promptly directing the conversation back into its proper path. 'We shall need buckets, tables, cups, axes, soap, matches, all sorts of things.'

But even the thought of these sales did not really excite Mr Mitsingas. 'Your mission station's in a terrible mess,' he confided. 'The Simbas used it as their headquarters. A dozen homeless families are squatting in it now.'

'We shall clear it up,' Helen countered briskly. 'We shall enlist every church worker we can find as a volunteer. We understand there's a great need.'

'Ah yes,' echoed Mitsingas, 'a great need.' It seemed to be his cue to return to his natural role as a practical trader. 'All these things you want, I can supply them for you.' The shrewd glance and the tone of his voice took her straight back to the old days of percentage discounts for cash, short supply, a cousin who might use a little influence, and to whom should he charge the account?

She stared straight back into his eyes and said nothing. Like Mitsingas's shrug it was a mannerism absolutely typical of her. Usually it meant that she was considering the implications of the question and the shape of her answer. On this occasion, however, it meant nothing of the kind. She already knew her answer. She was aware that no African in that district had smoked a cigarette for nearly two years; that the newly arrived traders had rushed in supplies and were prepared to sell a single cigarette at the price – which she thought outrageous – of one shilling *each*! The traders had arrived behind the advancing troops, stocking their shops with every conceivable item which made life a little easier. They were now overcharging with the certain assurance that their goods were unobtainable elsewhere.

Helen, with her finely tuned sense of fair play, thought this sharp practice against which she had a sure defence. She had been, after all, the Greek's family doctor. For years she had made no fortune out of their births, deaths or illnesses and she intended to have a say in this matter.

She had already made up her mind that this was going to be Mr Mitsingas's day of brotherly love and Christian charity. She was not going to pay him one single cent. Donating the utensils she intended to pry out of him for the benefit of the starving children, hungry, desperate and sick at heart, was the gesture she had decided he would make for the good of his soul and the benefit of the community. On reflection, in the years to come, he might even thank her for it.

As they left she said, 'Thank you, Mr Mitsingas. We'll send round tomorrow to collect all the things we need.'

Helen had anticipated that the mission centre would be damaged and filthy. As their deadline to begin distribution was only forty-eight hours away they had to move quickly, cleaning, scrubbing and collecting volunteers.

On Saturday night the sound of the talking drums went rolling across the countryside. When they stopped you could hear far away their message taken up by other distant drums. Over an area some eighty miles in circumference the news was relayed. 'The missionaries have come back . . . it is safe to come out . . . they have brought things to help us . . . they will be giving these things away in two days' time . . . 'Come to Wamba . . . Come to Wamba!'

In the darkness of the rain forest the Africans came out of leaf shelters they had erected, out of holes they had dug between jutting, angular roots of trees. They came out and stood in the darkness listening to the muted throb of the hollowed tree trunks competing with the sharp chirp-chirp-chirp of the night birds, the shrill cicadas, the grunt of the leopards, the occasional distant squeal of elephant. For two years they had managed to survive, not knowing if they would ever return to

[248]

their villages or if they were destined to die in the forest. Now they went back into their hiding places, took up the tiny bundles of possessions, the children, the sick, the old – even the dying – and began to walk through the night towards Wamba.

That evening Helen faced her audience of fifty-six church workers; they had assembled as soon as they heard she needed them. Many had only recently come out of the forest and were thin and undernourished too. But they wanted to work, they wanted to help; it was the therapy of which they were most in need.

'The church will be the distribution centre,' she explained. 'And we must keep a numbered record card of every single case. We must know what we've done and what we've got to do. There must be a continuity of treatment, especially with the penicillin injections and any special feeding that is necessary, and there will be much that is necessary.'

Most churches in the north-eastern provinces of Congo are immense. Materials and labour are cheap, congregations are large. The church at Wamba was built of grey cement blocks; of simple but cathedral-like proportions, with wide open spaces for windows which admitted both air and light. It held fifteen hundred worshippers. All the benches had been stolen or burnt by the Simbas. The floor had never been finished – money had run out. There was an area of raised concrete around the baptistry which Helen knew would be useful as a platform.

'We'll admit them through the big doors at the end of the church,' she went on. 'We'll erect four lines of bamboo stakes so that we can get them into four queues and control the flow.'

One of the senior church workers gave his information. 'The Army Commander has said he will send us soldiers to keep order. The Army is afraid of riots when the food distribution starts.'

Helen pulled a face. 'We may need soldiers. I hope not. Tell him to have a couple standing by just in case.' She returned to her briefing. 'Now we're not going to issue the clothing until later in the week. If we start issuing *that* straight away there might well be a riot. We all know that most of them would probably sooner be clothed than fed. It's status. If you've got a shirt on your back to cover your nakedness you're respectable again. No one can see an empty stomach therefore you can put up with it.' With similar blunt and elementary philosophy she told her co-workers what she expected of them.

That Sunday* evening they laboured into the night to get things ready. Switching the headlights of the lorry into the church made it possible to continue after nightfall. They divided the length of the building as Helen intended, into four aisles separated by rows of bamboo stakes. They placed tables and chairs near the main doors; they arranged piles of differently coloured cards ready for their identification processes; they prepared syringes and medicines, great bowls of oatmeal, gallons of milk.

They went to bed late and very tired unaware that the next day would start an experience of near biblical intensity, a day Helen would remember for the rest of her life.

She woke conscious of a faint, almost inaudible noise, a persistent sound which she had never heard before, and went to the door to peer out. The pre-dawn mist was thick and drenching; she could barely make out the outlines of the church. As the light grew the noise increased, a sort of rustling, like trees shaken in the wind, but a deeper, more bass sound, closer to soft surf rolling on a distant reef. Then she realised that it was a human sound: the murmur of thousands of human beings moving, gathering and assembling together.

For the first time Helen began to understand the pathetic harvest which the genocidal war had brought to an Africa of bewildered primitive people. Their tribal systems had been destroyed, their faith distorted, their value as human beings proved superfluous. The fury of men driven by alien faiths and foreign dialectic had destroyed them. Now the black child with the swollen belly, the emaciated mother with the starving eyes and the outstretched skeletal hand were the pitiful residue of that anger.

Helen went out into the half-light and watched them straggling in towards the church. She began to form them into lines, to push them gently into place, to tell them that they had to be patient. At 8 a.m. the church doors were opened and the lines pressed forward. At that precise moment a Congolese lieutenant and three soldiers drove up in a jeep and perfect order was restored.

They queued in silence and misery and poverty. All of them

were as near naked as made no difference. They were all physically bent with suffering and sorrow and near starvation.

Helen took the cards for the medical cases. She wrote out every card herself as she went slowly down the line; each card indicated what treatment that individual should receive when he reached the front of the queue. As the light grew she saw that the line of people stretched from the church, across the football field, past the mission station, past the sentry boxes and away into Wamba itself. As the sun rose almost all stood with a hand shielding their eyes. They had been hidden in the forest for two years and the light was too much for them. Very quickly she found that most were suffering from eye disease.

The condition of some of those who had emerged from the forest was unbelievable; many were in the final, irreversible stages of malnutrition: skin stretched over bone, hair cream-coloured, even the irises of their eyes depigmented. Some had flesh which was bloated and rotting, peeling off their bodies. Helen separated the very sick into a small compound near the church giving them special cards and immediate attention. Many of the children were in a desperate state and Agnes took charge of them. Helen showed her how to feed them by making up the milk powder into a thick cream and feeding each child with half a teaspoonful every half hour. Many of the children died there at the church. Even small corpses were brought in by desperate mothers who thought that somehow, perhaps, the breath of life could be blown back into the child. Agnes was quite undone by it all. She did not stop working and she hardly ever stopped weeping, for the plight of some of the children was heart-breaking. But as long as there was a child to feed, her tears and her work continued.

Helen discovered two of her old students waiting in the queue for attention. Immediately she hauled them out and made them part of the medical team. 'You're trained and you know what to do,' she told them. Within hours their recovery was remarkable.

Young men with limited medical knowledge gave the penicillin injections in two teams: one did nothing but clean and boil syringes, a second drew the penicillin from the phials, a third handed the syringe to the boy who injected, one checked cards, one prepared the patient. Others put ointment in eyes, others treated ulcers, others issued food. The cycle went on endlessly from sun-up until late in the day.

By the end of that first day two thousand six hundred people had been treated and fed.

Late that afternoon Helen received a message that she was urgently needed at Wamba hospital. There she found one African head nurse gravely concerned over the condition of a pregnant woman. A quick examination revealed that an immediate Caesarian operation was needed. Tired, but now working with an automatic determination, without gown, mask, general anaesthetic, uterine or delivery forceps using a blunt scalpel – the only one she could find – Helen delivered the baby. Mother and child did well. Helen's mind flew back momentarily to that first traumatic Caesarian on the pygmy mother . . . so long ago.

On Tuesday, five thousand one hundred and seventy-six people passed through the church for attention. Wednesday's total was six thousand eight hundred and sixty-eight, and now word had gone round the district that the missionaries really meant what they said, and the queues stretched out of sight.

Every night with lorry headlights flooding into the church they worked until every patient had received attention. Helen ate very little; the starving condition of so many of the refugees completely shattered her. She had never bothered much about food; now she could not eat knowing that so many outside were hungry. On Friday morning Ina Buckley carried two sandwiches and a cup of coffee out to where Helen stood attending to the patients. 'Now come on Helen,' she urged, 'drink this, and get these down, else you'll be no use to anybody.'

Obediently Helen took a bite of her sandwich. A second later it was snatched from her hand. A small boy aged perhaps five stood below her in his place in the queue. He had crammed the whole sandwich into his mouth and gulped it down like a starving animal. His eyes were huge and sick with hunger. With a terrible inner despair he looked up at the second half of the sandwich on the plate beyond his reach. Helen stared back at him. Then quietly she handed it over. It vanished instantly. She went on working.

They distributed the porridge, multi-vitamin tablets, iron tablets and milk. The soya-bean flour, the corn, everything they had, and they made it a rule that the milk and tablets had to be swallowed as soon as the recipient received them. Most of the mothers they entrusted with a supply of milk to last a fortnight, teaching them how to make the mixture and what dosage to give the children. By eleven o'clock on Friday morning they had used up everything; every flake of oats, every tablet, every drop of milk, the penicillin and ointment. The difference in their patients was spectacular; some of their 'cures' bordered on the miraculous.

By Friday they had clothed ten thousand people and Helen had photographs to prove what an astounding difference to morale and simple happiness a garment made. Every one of the ten thousand was also given a piece of soap. They had also issued half a ton of grain for planting and a hundred hoes to till the soil. The horde had been fed and they'd been doctored, and they no longer shaded their eyes from the sun. It was only a beginning, Helen knew that, but at least it was a beginning.

The sufferers would not go back to the forest, that was the main thing. The Army would take over now and feed them a small ration. They would be put to work clearing the debris, rebuilding the broken houses, starting again. Helen knew it would be a year before they were really back on their feet, and in that time their subsistence would inevitably be border-line. They could harvest a crop of ground nuts within three months of planting; but sweet potatoes took ten months to swell, so in between times they would have to forage. But they would survive.

Helen lectured her church workers on the importance of continuity. They must lead. Morale must be maintained. There must be no backsliding. The white missionaries would be back as soon as it was possible; but the African church workers must see that the patches of land were dug and hoed and planted with seed. Everyone must throw off despondency and despair. The schools had to start again; Helen personally would see there were exercise books, blackboards, chalk and pencils. They had recovered some of their self-respect. That was plain, said Helen, for everyone to see. Now they must keep going forward and she would send them all the help she could. Her last call was on Mr Mitsingas. She explained that unfortunately she was not in a position to pay anything at all for the goods he had so kindly provided. He smiled and nodded and said no doubt she would do *him* a favour some time. And as she drove away Helen had a strange feeling that the old rascal had known from the very beginning that she had no intention of paying.

Helen looked round at her flock, the 22 eighteen-year-olds gathered around her in the wilderness.

'Now,' she said authoritatively, 'This is our first meeting. You've all been found a place to sleep. You've each been given a blanket, plate, mug, spoon, and last night you had an evening meal.'

She felt she was sounding like a Girl Guide mistress appointing her charges to their places in the tent, but the sooner they realised that they were not starting an academic career at Cambridge, Heidelberg, Harvard or the Sorbonne, so much the better. This was Congo after years of bitter civil war.

One of the better dressed students stepped forward, a look of slight perplexity clouding his face. He came, Helen knew, from Blukwa, was certainly better educated than some of the others and probably already saw himself, white-coated and benign, discovering a cure for cancer like the Curies he had read about in some popular magazine.

'Madam,' he began politely, 'we have passed our entrance examinations and come here to study at a medical school. Where is the medical school?'

Helen nodded understandingly. 'Ah,' she said, 'now you have put your finger on the problem. As a matter of fact you are standing in the medical school.'

Twenty-two pairs of mystified eyes rolled round to observe the waist-high grass, the brambles, the thick bushes; their eyes moved upwards to the distant green mountains, passed over the foundations of Dr Becker's new hospital, the brick walls now three feet high, standing some three hundred yards away, and came back to rest on Helen. No doubt this small white lady in the spectacles was playing a joke on them and at the proper moment would surprise them all with an enormously diverting denouement.

She did. She said, 'I have to tell you that before I can start to teach you about medicine we have to build the school.' Ignoring the startled reaction she continued rapidly, 'But for the Simba rebellion the school would certainly be completed and functioning properly by this time. Because of the troubles, the vast damage to property, the lack of money and building materials, as you can see for yourselves there is, as yet, no school.'

The look of mystification on their faces had now changed to one of utter and total disbelief. 'But, madam . . .' began the bright student from Blukwa.

Helen decided her point of view demanded both priority and bluntness. She brushed him aside. 'We have to build the entire school: lecture rooms and laboratories; we have to build the student village, dormitories, kitchens, married quarters and all the things that go with them.'

'But, madam . . .'

'We'll need cement and bricks, doors and windows eventually, but to start with we have to cut timbers from the forest, build the walls, thatch the roofs. In fact I'd say getting ourselves basically started will take about three months.'

The voice of the young student from Blukwa was a long wail of protest. 'But, madam, we do not know how to build. We are students who have just passed our entrance examinations.'

'Very creditable,' she retorted firmly. 'But don't worry. I shall teach you. First we shall build and when we have completed the first classrooms we shall open the medical school and your real studies will begin.'

The young man from Blukwa, silent and defeated, withdrew from the unequal confrontation.

Helen looked boldly into as many pairs of eyes as she could manage. 'No doubt you will want time to consider this proposal of mine and discuss it amongst yourselves. Therefore I suggest we all meet again tomorrow at the same time in the same place and you will then tell me of your decision.'

She felt it necessary to add a note of encouragement. 'But please remember we are building this medical school for Congo. Not only will you benefit yourselves, but generations of students who will follow after you.' She paused and smiled at them. 'So that's my offer. You work. I'll teach.'

They went away, a stunned and silent group, and that afternoon Helen found it difficult to concentrate. After the rioting and mutiny which followed Independence in 1960 and intervention by the armed force of the United Nations, huge problems were left. The Simba rebellion in 1964 – pockets of Simba resistance still continued even in the seventies – added to these problems. The net result of these civil wars plus the enormous size of the country, its bad roads, poor communications, and a civil service and local government organisation which scarcely existed meant that 1966 when Helen was planning her medical school, was an inauspicious time to start anything in Congo. Every day on the radio came news of riots and mutinies. Apparently the latest concerned a mutiny by Katanganese and mercenary soldiers stationed near Stanleyville against the Central Government in Léopoldville for a reason valid since military history began: they had not been paid. Rumour suggested that they were proposing to march back to Katanga and it seemed likely that the whole dreary process of coup and counter-coup would start all over again. There were other disturbing reports of hundreds of Simba prisoners released from gaol. It was all terribly depressing. What was most certainly true was that Greek, Cypriot, Portuguese and Indian traders in their area had had their shops looted by Katanganese deserters and that no plane services had operated for weeks. Due to this un-certainty and lack of travel facilities half her students had failed to reach Nyankunde by the start of term, and the best she could expect was that the rest of them would dribble in, by ones and twos, during the months to come.

Next morning, therefore, with some uncertainty she faced the students on the same bramble patch. The thought that she might have to confront Dr Becker with the news that the medical school had no students had already kept her awake for most of the night.

'Well, have you made up your minds?' she asked.

There was something uncomfortably reminiscent of a jury about the earnest faces staring solemnly towards her. The boy from Blukwa stepped forward. 'Yes, we have talked it over madam,' he said and smiled. With that smile Helen knew she had won. 'All of us have decided to accept your offer.'

'Good,' said Helen. 'Very good indeed. Now we shall start work immediately.'

Her first preoccupation was to find lodgings for her students Nyankunde, chosen as the site of the new medical centre, ha functioned for many years as a simple mission station, and a the primary school children were on holiday, temporarily, she obtained permission to bed her boys down in their classrooms. Three girl students, with dreams of romantic medical careers, were immediately demoted to supervise the cookery and shopping, although in those first few weeks their meals were Spartan: morning coffee, midday coffee and a large dinner in the evening. They ate in the open air, using planks set up on bricks as benches, while Helen expounded some intricacy of the builder's craft. Her own knowledge had been acquired from field courses supervised by Jack Scholes at Ibambi plus years of trial and error at Nebobongo.

Very quickly she discovered that seventy per cent of her students knew nothing whatsoever about the art or craft of building or indeed about the hard labour such work entailed. To ask the average student to wield an axe to cut down a young sapling was to risk amputation of a limb. Nevertheless she persevered, and slowly their skills improved. At a reasonable price, she had obtained permission from a local chief to cut support poles for roofs and walls from his re-afforestation plantation, and each morning at dawn she set off in a lorry with a party of chosen students to cut the essential timber.

She went out with them felling and hauling young trees; clearing the site; measuring out buildings for the student village; erecting suitable poles; fixing roofing saplings; thatching; in short the dozen and one skills needed for African house building.

It was not all work. From her earliest days in Congo she decided with true British athleticism that games should play a large part in any school curriculum. She had discovered that as far as she was concerned there was very little difference between the rules of hockey and soccer, and she refereed the football matches from the playing position of either left-back, or, if she was very tired, goalkeeper. Inevitably everyone was healthily exhausted when they went to bed.

Nevertheless there were many frustrations. The Belgian colonial administration – in the manner of all administrations – had bequeathed to the new regime a heritage of red tape complicated enough to strangle it at birth. The Congolese *fonctionnaires* followed the same pattern with zeal and determination. As Helen's upbringing and dedication made it absolutely impossible for her to dispense the normal Congolese lubrication

– the bribe – she found that on numerous occasions they would be progressing rapidly when suddenly there would be no timber for the roofing, or no nails for the timber when the timber appeared, or no window frames available when the wall supports were in. Petrol was scarce, and there was frustration in even trying to change money at the bank in Bunia. The bank never knew what the exchange rates were supposed to be and inevitably had to refer to the bank in Léopoldville a thousand miles away.

Sixteen extra students from Paulis and six from Stanleyville eventually turned up. Two from Stanleyville took one look at the building work in which they were expected to involve themselves and immediately departed for home.

Although Dr Becker's hospital was not finished, with his small team of medical workers he was already attending to fifteen hundred out-patients, one hundred bed patients, and a long list of operative cases was steadily building up. Association with other doctors also meant that for the first time in Congo a new factor had entered Helen's life. There had usually been two or three white co-workers at Nebo but nevertheless it had been a lonely life. Now she lived in a small community, mainly American, and although there were occasions of petty irritation, trials and jealousies, there was a great deal of friendship and genuine help.

Richard Dix for example, who was in overall charge of design and building at Nyankunde. His wife Ruth was a doctor working with Dr Becker's team. Almost immediately he fixed a tap in Helen's school compound giving a constant supply of pure water from a high mountain spring. Helen wrote to her mother: 'We've never been so spoiled in our whole lives.'

Later, when she built her own thatched-roof bungalow on a hill overlooking the school compound and Richard installed a toilet which actually flushed, a phenomenon unknown in the rain forest, she could scarcely credit her good fortune.

Good-natured leg-pulling and teasing was a natural hazard of conversation between British and Americans, and one incident took Helen a long time to live down. One morning she cut her thumb while opening a tin of sardines. Deciding it was rather silly to get the wound full of mud on the building site, she decided to drop in at the hospital to have a strip of plaster stuck round it, and, bending her fingers back to stem the blood she arrived at the operating room. The young male nurse on duty was eager to help. As she was the lady doctor he obviously felt it not quite the thing merely to stick a bit of plaster over the wound. He procured a sterile towel, a bowl, disinfectant and bandages and sat her down to perform an expert job. He took her hand, opened the fingers gently, and blood gushed out. Helen took one look at the crimson flood and swooned clean away in a full blown syncopal attack which left her prostrate on the floor.

The horrified male nurse tried to take her pulse but could not feel a pulse; he tried to take her blood pressure but there wasn't any blood pressure. Horror turned to terror. In his care the lady doctor had died! Deborah, a girl student assisting in the theatre, came in at that moment and he screamed his panic at her. 'The lady doctor has died! Go fetch help! The lady doctor has died!'

There were two wards in use at that time: Dr Becker was working in one, Dr Herb Atkinson, a young American, in the other. To make certain of maximum publicity, Deborah rushed through both of them screaming the news that the lady doctor had died in the operating room. Herb Atkinson, being the younger man, beat Dr Becker to Helen's side by a few seconds, realised at once what was happening and brought her back to life by the undignified but necessary procedure of pushing her head between her knees.

By October 30th the school village of three dormitories and homes for twenty-one married students was ready for occupation. The mud walls hadn't properly dried out, it wasn't completely whitewashed, but the walls were up, the roof was on and they could move in. And the Mission lent them a hall as a classroom for the time being.

Helen knew very well that a building programme lasting many years still stretched ahead of her, but she was satisfied merely to stick to her first promise. 'You work, I'll teach,' she had said, and three months from the commencement of that work she faced them in her classroom ready to begin to impart the fantastic story of the blood rivers that run from the heart, the great winds which course through the lungs, the miracle of livers and spleens, bowels and bladders, and the enormous and unfathomable mystery of that mighty work of creation, the brain.

In Congo nothing was ever easy and nothing ever stood still. Besides the constant conflict with the educational authorities in Léopoldville to get them to accredit her medical school, besides the ceaseless job of attempting to educate, inform, coerce and discipline some forty boisterous, noisy eighteen-year-olds, bursting with pride at their secondary school achievements, and separated by coming from fourteen different tribal areas and speaking fourteen different languages – their *lingua franca* was Swahili and the official school language was French – she was busy with many other tasks. Primarily, she was a member of the Christian brotherhood of doctors dedicated to moving medicine in that great province of Congo into the twentieth century. Although providing Dr Becker's wards with a succession of willing trainees was an important part of her task, it was only one of many duties.

Nebobongo had to benefit from Nyankunde, but to do so a landing strip had to be built so that the light planes flown by the Missionary Aviation Fellowship could ferry patients, drugs and doctors in and out. Helen encouraged the Nebo team into haranguing the local chiefs into providing labour for a runway eight hundred and fifty yards long and not less than fifty yards wide on terrain which had to be cleared of vast ironwoods and mahogany with roots driven deep in the earth and tangled undergrowth. Five local chiefs were supposed each to provide two hundred workmen, and for three months this somewhat unwilling labour force worked intermittently between rainstorms and holidays. Fortunately the soil proved to be gravel and when the site was finally cleared a Land-Rover dragging a large tree trunk behind it harrowed the ground fairly level. In the tropical atmosphere grass immediately sprouted, and keeping this down below the height of a field of flourishing wheat was the constant job of workers from the nearby leprosy settlement.

When the first light, five-seater plane droned in over the high trees and bumped along the runway to settle like a contented queen bee amongst a swarm of delighted Africans, Helen realised that a new medical future had been established for the whole region.

Indeed all through the late sixties and early seventies their ability to cope with medical problems in the area improved enormously.

Five medical centres, of which Nebobongo was one, each with an airstrip were established in a huge circle around Nyankunde. Each centre also supported between ten and fifteen smaller rural hospitals.

Every Monday on a weekly rota a doctor from Nyankunde flew in to one of the centres carrying a supply of drugs sufficient to last the centre and its ancillary hospitals for a month. The plane then returned to Nyankunde ready for any emergency work. The flying doctor commenced operations immediately; there were usually thirty to forty surgical cases to cope with in those five days, and at Nebobongo the surgeons were most ably assisted by John Mangadima whose skill – as Helen was to discover later – improved beyond belief.

In his week's duty the doctor operated and examined all medical cases. He assisted the centre with their book-keeping, drug orders, and generally boosted the morale of the European and Congolese workers. On Saturday the plane flew in from Nyankunde to pick him up and ferry him back for a week's stint there, before flying another doctor to another medical centre for the next week. Radio links kept Nyankunde in touch with every centre, and every day a local roundup of news, requirements and emergencies was relayed between all stations.

Helen's twenty-year-old dream of clinics scattered throughout the territory had become reality. More than that, allied to Dr Becker's identical vision they had provided a network of medical facilities beyond all her hopes.

Part Seven

I

March 19th, 1971, and as they circled above the dirt airstrip Helen glimpsed the corrugated-iron roof of her old house at Nebobongo, almost hidden amongst the trees, and the thatched huts of the leprosy village directly below. They levelled out and dropped down towards the narrow corridor cut between the trees their wheels bouncing on the sunbaked earth, the propeller of the light aircraft shrieking in reverse pitch. On either side the rain forest towered to what seemed an enormous height. It was on these trips back to Nebo that Helen first began to understand how the forest isolated you from the rest of the world, and magnified both your problems and your loneliness. It was only when you soared off the ground again, saw the trees and branches whipping past at incredible speed and emerged high up, in the sunlight and the wide blue sky, with a view of the mountains and a distant horizon, that you realised any other world existed.

Nevertheless, as they swirled round in a cloud of dust at the end of the runway and the young American pilot from the Missionary Aviation Fellowship switched off the engine, she knew she was home. She unfastened her seat belt as he opened the door, and there waiting were all her friends.

At once the atmosphere was different. The sun was hotter, the shade deeper, the colours brighter, the earth baked as hard as ancient terracotta, the welcome torrential as a flood, drowning her in a sea of laughter, kisses and hugs. It had been so many months since she had been to see them. They had heard she had been back to England on holiday since her last visit. They were so pleased when they heard she was back and working at Nyankunde once more. Was everything at the school all right?

Yes, said Helen, everything at the school was all right. She could have told them about her feelings of depression during that holiday in Britain over the fact that no one in authority seemed to think that accreditation was important, about her growing determination not to quit but to return and start again. Her battle with the educational authorities was not finished yet.

She had come to Nebobongo for two reasons: a visitor had arrived who wanted to see Nebobongo, Ibambi and Wamba; and she had received a message through the usual jungle grapevine that all was not well at Nebobongo and as medical director of W.E.C. it was her duty to look into it.

She had guessed, before she arrived the source of the trouble. Two veteran British nurses worked at Nebobongo – marvellous women, experienced, hard-working and warm-hearted. But John Mangadima was the assistant surgeon who operated with Herb Atkinson and the other highly qualified young American surgeons when they did their duty rota at Nebo. Who, therefore, was in charge? Who was senior? Helen did not have to be a witch doctor to smell out the root of that squabble. So many workers, teachers, nurses, helpers of all sorts in every African missionary organisation could not rid themselves of their parental outlook. The African was a child. He could not be allowed to to take responsibility.

In vain Helen reiterated that they must step out of the nineteenth century and into the twentieth. This was the century of the African in which he had inherited the right to run his own affairs.

At Nebobongo John greeted her with warmth and affection. Then he said quite simply that he and his fellow African medical workers would like to talk to her confidentially.

'Yes,' Helen agreed. 'Right away.'

John went off to collect his staff and the senior of the British nurses said that perhaps it would be better if she also attended the meeting.

'No dear,' Helen replied. 'They have asked for a private talk with me, not a general discussion, so let me have first go.'

There were half a dozen African male nurses assembled in the room with John. They were quiet, courteous, and gracious. They did not wish to condemn Helen but fourteen months previously at a medical conference held at Nebo she had been aware of their grievances and promised to try and deal with them. At the moment they were compelled to work under the overall direction of two British nurses. This was not good enough. John's capabilities and skills made this situation absurd. The atmosphere affected them all; they could not work to their maximum potential under such conditions of service. They had been patient for fourteen months waiting for Helen to change things and she had not done so.

'Are you or are you not,' asked one of the senior medical workers, 'the Head of W.E.C.'s medical service in Congo?'

Helen could not answer that, at least not in the straight clear terms she would have preferred, because whilst theoretically, in terms of the Congo Government, she was leader of the W.E.C. medical team, W.E.C. itself did not really appoint such directors. Jack Scholes was leader of the mission at Ibambi and therefore in most terms Helen's boss. This did not satisfy them. They answered: 'Dr Roseveare, if you *are* in charge will you please make changes. If you are not in charge we intend, as a group, to leave Nebobongo.'

Helen looked across at John. He had scarcely spoken. But by his face she could tell that he agreed with their sentiments.

'Please think it over,' she said.

'We have thought it over for fourteen months.'

'If John and you – this team – leave, Nebobongo as a medical centre will close down.'

'No, no, others will come and replace us.'

'No. We've built Nebo. We are Nebo. If we go, Nebo goes, and the people of the forest will have no one to help them.'

She looked at John and knew she had scored perhaps unfairly. That thought hurt him.

There was a tap on the door. It was the senior British nurse. She hated to interfere but a patient with a strangulated hernia had just hobbled in from the forest. Without an immediate operation he would die very quickly.

The middle-aged African crouched on the verandah outside was an abject figure wrapped in a cocoon of pain and bewilderment. As Helen examined him with the others standing around one of the great inspirational moments of her life occurred.

'We must operate at once,' she said.

'I thought so,' said the senior British nurse. 'I'll prepare the theatre.'

There was a moment's pause, then Helen said firmly, 'John will operate. I shall act as his assistant.' The effect on the small audience gathered around her in the breathless heat of that March morning was dumbfounding. Dr Helen Roseveare was handing over the responsibility for a highly complex major operation to an unskilled and unqualified African male nurse. The senior British nurse tried to pass it off as a joke in rather poor taste.

'Yes, Helen, but of course you'll be in charge.'

'No,' she said. 'John will be in charge. I shall be his assistant. Is that all right, John?'

John was staring at her with those intense dark eyes of his. She knew that look well, and smiled as he nodded.

Twenty minutes later, masked and gowned, they stood beside the operating table, the two senior British nurses similarly dressed ready to assist. Helen knew that whatever private feelings distressed them it would not influence their actions one iota. They would be as totally professional as ever.

It was one of the most astonishing experiences in her medical life. She believed John was brilliant. He'd worked under Dr Becker, Dr Wilkie, Dick Ulrich, Herb Atkinson, highly qualified surgeons educated in the best medical schools in the U.S.A. He had assimilated their techniques. He loved surgery, Helen hated it. Hardly out of his teens he had nagged her to do more surgery so that he could assist and learn.

Now his fingers were deft and practised, his technique amazed her. Some of the time she did not know what he was doing. At one point she said, 'But John where are we now?'

His eyes above the mask did not move from his task. 'Dr Ulrich showed me that if the bladder gets involved in one of these difficult hernias it's a good idea to evaginate the peritoneum. D'you see?'

She watched him in sheer amazement. She could see what he was doing and he did it beautifully. Everything he did was carefully thought out and performed with minute accuracy. There was no panic, no haste; there were difficult moments but he saw his way through them and overcame them. She was so thrilled she could feel herself smiling behind her mask. That John, her very first student, was capable of such a performance excited and thrilled her so that she was almost speechless.

At the end of it she thanked him politely for allowing her to assist, and he nodded and smiled, and between them was such a conspiratorial joy that neither could speak.

She went back to her old house of so many memories to have lunch with the two British nurses, the visitor and the young American pilot who had flown over the rain forest a thousand times but never really penetrated it before and was excited by the experience. The two British nurses were cool and distant. Helen had betrayed them.

Helen understood how they felt and yearned to comfort them. They were old friends, old comrades in arms, and they had toiled and laughed and suffered together for many years; the fact that now they could not let go, could not comprehend what she was trying to do saddened her immeasurably. Helen knew that John's qualifications were in a sense better than theirs for the particular job to be done; perhaps they felt an inferiority because of that; perhaps they were jealous of him and even jealous of her relationship with him. Perhaps they clung to the feeling that Nebo was really theirs, and they were frightened they might lose their positions or that people would not respect them if they worked under an African; perhaps it was because they simply could not bring themselves to believe that he could do the job properly.

Of course she had a special relationship with John. Together they had struggled for seventeen years, seen the place grow from absolutely nothing: no equipment, no drugs, no laboratories – only an endless succession of patients needing help and skill to assuage their pain. Often everything seemed against them but they supported each other; he persevered, therefore she kept on. At any time John could have found a job with the Government hospital service which would have paid him about three times what the mission gave him, but he stayed at Nebo, married and brought up his children there because he believed that God had called him to serve at Nebobongo.

So she *must* be on John's side no matter what the others thought.

Lunch ended and they went outside into the sunshine to board the Land-Rover to take them to Ibambi where they would spend the night before flying on to Wamba.

One of the orderlies brought the news. Another villager had just staggered in suffering from the same complaint as the first: a strangulated hernia with death only hours away unless an operation was performed immediately.

John Mangadima was already examining the man on the verandah when they walked across. The visitor asked. 'Is this just a coincidence or is a strangulated hernia commonplace in this area?'

'Common enough,' Helen replied, 'though I've never had two in one day before. It's something to do with their diet, but we're always operating on hernias or strangulated hernias.'

She straightened up, her plan already made. This was not coincidence or luck, it was God. He had put this final and decisive opportunity into her hands and she intended to use it.

'John,' she said. 'You can do this operation by yourself.' She glanced at the two British nurses. 'You have two very able assistants. If you need me I shall be at Ibambi which is only seven miles away. I'll come back tomorrow morning to have a look at both patients.'

As they drove along the familiar red rutted road past the rubber estate which Helen knew better than the lines on the palm of her hand, she had no fears about the outcome of her decision. The right moment had arrived to resolve the situation at Nebo and she had seized it. And she had things to say at Ibambi.

The meeting with Jack Scholes and the committee that night lasted three hours, and Helen emerged from it tired from arguing, reasoning and persuading. Next morning when they returned to Nebo she walked straight into John Mangadima's house. 'Sit down, John,' she said as he approached her. 'I've got some news.' She couldn't sit as she continued, 'It's worked out. You're officially going to be made director of the hospital with the right to do emergency operations. We shall have to clear it all with W.E.C. back in England and with Nyankunde, but we've done it, John, we've done it!'

He stared at her. Then he got up and flung his arms round her and hugged her, the tears running down his face. She wept too for all the years of waiting, praying, believing and trusting. Being Helen, a minute later she could not help giving him a little Christian homily on the future because the situation seemed to call for it. 'Hold tight to a testament of humility and graciousness,' she said. 'Every operation you do you must ask God to do it with you. The day will come when you'll have the tragedy of a death on the operating table, and it will be very hard to bear. You must understand this and be ready to meet it.'

She examined the two hernia patients with him. Both were doing well. Then she went back to the house to pick up the rest of the party for the flight to Wamba.

One of the younger mission girls said 'Oh they've been on the radio circuit from Nyankunde for you, Helen. They wanted to pass on the message that they've received an official government acknowledgement that the school is accredited. They said you'd want to know that.' She smiled sweetly and asked, 'Is it important?'

Helen, still overcome from her session with John, was in no fit state to take it in. March 20th, 1971 was a day to remember. And by an odd coincidence the people of Wamba decided to seize their opportunity.

The small party flew out of the jungle airstrip at Nebobongo and landed at Wamba some twenty minutes later. The indefatigable Daisy Kingdon met them with a Land-Rover and as they jolted towards her mission the visitor inquired, 'What are all the drums going for?'

Helen smiled. 'Talking drums, saying "Our doctor's here." '

'I think,' Daisy intervened, 'they have something arranged for after lunch.'

They drove first to the grounds of the old convent. Helen had not revisited the place since her traumatic departure in 1964. It was quiet and almost deserted. Eventually they found an African nun who took them apparently to the only priest in residence. He was a tall pale Dutch father who spoke good English. No, the nuns had not returned, and he thought it very unlikely that they would ever do so. The Mother Superior, Marie Frances and the other Belgian nuns could be found in convents in their native country; Sister Dominique and the Italians were in Northern Italy. Perhaps one day other sisters would return. He did not know. He thought it sad for it was so quiet and peaceful here.

Helen walked along the corridors and stared out over the sun-lit expanse of countryside. It seemed impossible that their terror could ever have existed.

Wamba still showed signs of war damage but its citizens had certainly recovered their resilience. In the distance they heard the drums begin to beat, the bugles and trumpets begin to shrill.

Slowly the enormous procession of school-children and adults came into sight marching in line abreast and singing. It looked as if every school in Wamba had been closed for the afternoon by order of their headmasters and were doing their party pieces in honour of 'our doctor's visit'.

They marched and counter-marched. The drums beat and the bugles sounded. The flags flew and the children smiled. They lined up in ranks outside the mission, several hundred of them, the entire population of Wamba so it seemed, and sang more songs.

Of course there was a sting in the tail. The senior headmaster stood up to make his speech of welcome apologising for its brevity because it was only three hours ago that he had heard of Helen's coming. His speech lasted half an hour and chided Helen on a number of counts. Why did she think only of the west bank of the Nepoko river where they had a huge hospital at Nebobongo? What was she doing for Wamba and the east bank where all they had was a dispensary? Why did she not open a leprosy clinic for them? Why did she consider them poor cousins? The harangue was long and searching.

Then all sang another song and Helen replied.

'It is not possible to forget you,' she said. 'After all, the National Army helped to rescue us from here in the time of the troubles, and I shall never forget the kindness and consideration of the people of Wamba during all the years I've known them. But you must remember that a new-born baby has to crawl before it walks, and walk before it runs.' There was no point in being less than direct, as they had been. She continued, 'You've just reached the crawling stage. You have a dispensary and next year we'll open a maternity ward.' Now she turned to the things *they* had to do. 'But the airstrip is not really long enough for Nyankunde's planes and you'll have to lengthen it so that your hospital can go on the rota of visiting doctors. And, remember, most of these things depend on you. You need trained medical personnel to run your dispensaries, clinics and hospitals. Therefore you must send us your sons and daughters to train as nurses and doctors. Send them to us and we'll return them ready to be of service to the community.'

They all cheered again after that, formed up with military precision and banged and blew their way back to town. Helen smiled and waved them goodbye. There was something so wonderfully self-deflating about these Congolese occasions. They turned out to greet you with flags, trumpets and bugles as a returning heroine, but seized the occasion to remind you of your continuing deficiencies.

She went back into the mission where Daisy Kingdon was preparing tea for everyone. What a great day it had been! Accreditation for Nyankunde, promotion for John Mangadima. In her heart she knew she was probably more pleased about what had happened to John than anything that had happened to her in Congo. It was an event comparable with the success of those first students – of whom John had been one – nearly twenty years ago. This promotion ushered in a new era; it marked a watershed in their affairs: an African was the medical director at Nebo. She knew that she would now go back to England in the autumn of 1973, well pleased, knowing that the medical school at Nyankunde was fully established and that others could inherit her role, and that John could cope perfectly at Nebobongo. Whether she would return to Congo, whether W.E.C. would have new pastures ready for her attention she did not know. She did not really care; the future could take care of itself.

A few months later John was officially confirmed in his appointment. There was a celebration and he was presented with a new motor bicycle. It was a beautiful machine sparkling with chrome and enamel on which he would be able to visit Nebo's wide-spread clinics with speed and regularity.

As he swung his leg across the saddle he caught Helen's eye and smiled. She smiled back. Their triumph like their love and affection, was shared. They had come a long way together, the black man from the rain forest and the white girl from England.

Index

[277]